Cri

ONE WE.

7 OCT 2008

Criminalising Social Policy
Anti-social behaviour and welfare
in a de-civilised society

John J. Rodger

WILLAN
PUBLISHING

Published by

Willan Publishing
Culmcott House
Mill Street, Uffculme
Cullompton, Devon
EX15 3AT, UK
Tel: +44(0)1884 840337
Fax: +44(0)1884 840251
e-mail: info@willanpublishing.co.uk
website: www.willanpublishing.co.uk

Published simultaneously in the USA and Canada by

Willan Publishing
c/o ISBS, 920 NE 58th Ave, Suite 300,
Portland, Oregon 97213-3786, USA
Tel: +001(0)503 287 3093
Fax: +001(0)503 280 8832
e-mail: info@isbs.com
website: www.isbs.com

© John J. Rodger 2008

First published 2008

ISBN   978-1-84392-326-8 paperback
       978-1-84392-327-5 hardback

British Library Cataloguing-in-Publication Data

A catalogue record for this book is available from the British Library

Project managed by Deer Park Productions, Tavistock, Devon
Typeset by GCS, Leighton Buzzard, Bedfordshire
Printed and bound by TJ International Ltd., Padstow, Cornwall

Contents

Acknowledgements   *ix*

Introduction   **xi**
Outline of the book   xvi

**1   Criminalising social policy:
      some general observations**   **1**
      Criminalising social policy   2
      Welfare and discipline   4
      Civil law and *natural justice*   9
      Dysfunctional families and anti-social children   16
      Concluding observations   18

2   Incivility and welfare in a de-civilised society   **20**
      The theory of the civilising process   22
      De-civilisation and welfare retrenchment   30
      Attitudes, emotions and post-emotionalism   37
      De-civilising tendencies in penal policy   43
      Concluding observations   46

**3   Disorderly behaviour and underclass culture:
      the emergence of the 'chav' and 'NEET' generation**   **48**
      The creation of the 'NEET' generation   48
      The enduring issue of the underclass   51
      The coarsening of culture   52
      Class, culture and consumption   57

Culture and instrumentalism   61
Value orientations or cultural toolkit?   65
Concluding observations   71

4   **The politics and policy of incivility**   **72**
Informalisation and crime as a normal social fact   74
The 'new politics of welfare': from social steering
    to social regulation   79
The politics of withholding benefits   86
Regulatory communities and the politics of
    social inclusion   93
Concluding observations   94

5   **Family life and anti-social behaviour**   **97**
Personal relationships in contemporary society   98
Family life and criminality   100
The de-civilising of parents   106
Family policy and anti-social behaviour
    under New Labour   115
Intensive family support: the case of the
    Dundee Family Project   118
Concluding observations: desistance from crime
    and anti-social behaviour   123

6   **Child welfare and juvenile justice**   **125**
Punishing parents and the anti-social
    behaviour strategy   128
Youth offending and juvenile justice in England   129
The Children's Hearing system in Scotland   134
Restorative practices   143
Concluding observations   146

7   **The strategy for civil renewal and
    community safety**   **149**
The 'third way' and the voluntary sector   154
Civil renewal, welfare and inauthentic politics   157
Community safety and established–outsider relations   162
Concluding observations   168

8   **Fear of the uncivil and the criminal**   **171**
Civilising security   173
Signal crimes and fear   176

Streetwise behaviour as inverted fear   188
Social policy and the problem of security   191
Concluding observations   194

9   Conclusions: criminology and social policy   195
Social policy or moral regulation?   199
Welfare and institutional anomie   201
Social policy and criminal justice: finding the balance   203

References   209

Index   227

Acknowledgements

I only have a few people to thank. I am grateful to Pierpaolo Donati of the University of Bologna and Director of the *Osservatorio Nazionale Sulla Familglia* for inviting me to present a paper in Bologna in 2005. The European Congress on families, welfare and subsidiarity which he organised created an opportunity for me to consider issues surrounding the relationship between families, welfare and personal responsibility that stimulated my thinking about anti-social behaviour in families, which I subsequently developed in this book. I must also thank Peter Squires for his encouraging and helpful comments on the first draft of the book. Brian Willan has been helpful and accessible from the submission of the initial proposal through to the delivery of the final manuscript.

John J. Rodger
Lochwinnoch, Scotland

Introduction

Criminalising Social Policy refers to the processes and policy debates that bring the worlds of welfare and criminal justice together. While it is wrong to claim that the relationship between these two major fields of state responsibility has been characterised in the past as being distant, indeed I will argue throughout this book that the normal face of the welfare state is to manage the incentives of the population to work, and pay taxes and social insurance, and to discipline those who refuse to participate in the form of institutionalised solidarity that the welfare state represents, nevertheless for most of the twentieth century the world of welfare retained some measure of detachment from the field of crime prevention. This measure of separation was maintained partly because there was an acceptance that there existed forces, both economic and social, which shaped lives and fortunes beyond the control of the individual. It was understood that the levels of poverty and social disadvantage in society did not cause deviant behaviour in a direct and mechanistic way, but there was at least recognition that criminality was a good barometer of the sense of grievance that existed in society about unfairness and injustice. The primary task of the welfare state was to address the worst excesses of disadvantage in order to bring about a more equal and just society; reductions in crime and anti-social behaviour would be a welcome and indirect consequence of enlightened social policy (see Cook 2006; Knepper 2007: 3–18). This focus on the state's responsibility to alter social and economic structures through intervention in society has changed in the past 30 years. Contemporary Western societies have concluded that matters of social justice and social inequality are best addressed through the anonymous workings of the marketplace. And state responsibility lies mainly in securing the conditions of an orderly society in which markets can flourish in an uninhibited way. In this context, social policy has shifted its gaze from problem social and economic processes to problem populations. Social policy increasingly is viewed in terms of its direct consequences for incivility and crime in terms of both inhibiting them or, in the opinion of those such as Marsland (1996) and Murray (1994), encouraging them.

This change of focus can be seen clearly in the preoccupation of most Western governments in the past 30 years with matters of incivility, crime and disorder. The recent government action on anti-social behaviour, in both its individual and familial forms, has brought the two fields of policy together in a distinctive way. The tendency to criminalise social policy can be seen in two main ways. First, it is evident in the *subordination* of social policy objectives designed to address social injustice and tackle the problems of poverty and disadvantage to those of the criminal justice system aimed at controlling and managing deviance, especially what is defined as anti-social behaviour in its many guises. The justification for policy developments in the fields of early childhood development and community regeneration is that they will tackle incivility and criminality rather than that they should be pursued because of their social justice aims. Second, it is evident in the tendency to *blur professional boundaries and paradigms* between the criminal justice system and the world of welfare in the fields of child welfare, youth justice, and community education and development. The current emphasis on joined-upness and partnership working may have unforeseen positive consequences that have not yet been fully assessed but there is some justification in thinking that welfare concerns have recently been undermined by strategies primarily aimed at emasculating the autonomy of social welfare professionals as government strives to appear to be tough on law and order violations. These are some of the issues that will be discussed in this book.

There is a general change in culture that has occurred since the late 1990s in many Western societies that is shaping both official and popular thinking about crime and incivility. This book is an attempt to capture those changes and examine their implications for the policy agenda of the world of social welfare. In a classic intervention in the American debate about welfare, family life and crime in the early 1990s, US Senator Daniel Patrick Moynihan formulated a brief but illuminating analysis of what he perceived to be a tendency to 'define deviancy down' (Moynihan 1993). Moynihan situated his analysis in the context of Durkheim's famous observation that 'crime was a normal fact of social life', and that should its level fall too low that was a sign of an unhealthy society rather than a reason for celebration. The assumption underlying Durkheim's view is that levels of crime remain fairly stable over time, perhaps oscillating up or down a little in relation to the resources and effort that a society devotes to its detection and control. The primary purpose of the police, the courts and the army of social control agents from social workers to teachers is to ensure that deviance is maintained within acceptable bounds rather than to attempt to eradicate criminality altogether. The absence of deviance entirely would, therefore, indicate a repressive society and one in which difference and unconventional thoughts and actions would not be tolerated. However, Moynihan observed a different phenomenon at work in American society in the 1980s and 1990s. He pointed to increased deviance and criminality 'beyond the levels that a community could afford to recognise'. The increased levels of deviant activity did not lead to increased levels of action designed to lower rates of behaviour deemed to be deviant. The response to the problem was instead to redefine deviance down and effectively reclassify what was once a social problem as something now to be regarded as part of the plurality and diversity of society and culture.

The policy responses to this phenomenon are illustrated by Moynihan through three examples of the redefinition of what constituted deviance in American society over a period from the 1950s to the 1990s. First, he offers the example of what he calls the *altruistic* response which led to the deinstitutionalisation movement and the view that mental patients were the product of labelling not medical pathology. Second, the *opportunistic* response, he argued, led to the reinterpretation of the changing family structure resulting from increased divorce and lone parenthood as a lifestyle choice, compatible with the desire for the individual to attain fulfilling personal relationships and not a matter for social concern. Third, and the one which is of most interest to me, was the *normalising* response to unprecedented levels of crime. Moynihan described a society in which there was a growing insensitivity to historically high levels of criminality, especially violent crimes. Lower percentages of violent acts were being reported to the police, and the media devoted less effort to report on horrific murders in the 1980s and 1990s compared with the classic crime episodes of the Prohibition era. Crime and violence had become what Garland (2001) calls 'a normal social fact'. American society in the early 1990s was losing its 'sense of outrage'.

The consequence of this saturation of society with unprecedented high levels of crime and deviance was to find other means of coping with its true levels by simply reclassifying as 'normal' what could not be easily eradicated, as in the 'war on drugs'. Crime and violence became something that the citizen had to *live with* rather than something that needed *action to change*. Certainly, the 'liberal' moment in social policy throughout the 1960s and 1970s did redefine what was problematic in a social order that was changing and was occasionally in flux: value orientations and social behaviour changed during the latter part of the twentieth century, and the concept of 'defining deviance down' captures the reassessment of social priorities and social realities during that period. Moynihan articulated a sense that somehow social standards had declined and social judgements had become overly relativist – a view that eventually was picked up by the neo-liberal movement from the 1980s onwards.

However, in British society since the late 1990s a strange but related phenomenon has been occurring. It is not the loss of outrage that can be witnessed in British society but the exaggerated outrage of a society that is 'defining deviance up' rather than down. The New Labour government's criminal justice strategy since the passing of the Crime and Disorder Act in 1998 has been to shift attention towards the everyday incivilities and petty criminality that are being described as anti-social. Noisy neighbours, intimidating neighbours and disorderly conduct of all descriptions are now to be eradicated as part of a 'respect' agenda. Increasingly, the press are finding more and more cases of anti-social behaviour worthy of reporting and comment. For example, in an article in *The Sunday Times* entitled 'The Enforcers', Gillian Bowditch (2006) reports on the Manchester schoolgirl fined £75 for leaving a wooden lolly stick on a wall, a woman in Luton fined £75 for throwing a Cheesy Wotsit from a car and a smoker in Solihull fined £350 for dropping a cigarette butt. While these cases may appear trivial, they are indicative of the changing social atmosphere in contemporary society within which general attitudes and approaches to anti-social behaviour are changing in ways that might be regarded as intolerant.

Without wishing to over extend my argument, it is worth considering the historical circumstances when there was a similar tendency to 'define deviance up'. Writing about crime and crime control in Germany in the first half of the twentieth century, Reinke (2005) describes policing strategies in Germany during the 1930s when Heinrich Himmler was the Reich's Minister of the Interior. A primary objective of the *Kriminalpolizei* at the time was to develop preventive strategies to monitor and control those people regarded as 'dangerous' to the state. This objective was accomplished by extensive surveillance of targets combined with frequent use of 'supervisory orders' to control the residence and leisure activities, including a prohibition of alcohol consumption or ownership of pets, of those considered 'dangerous'. The interesting sociological feature of this period was the extension of the police gaze from what was euphemistically considered to be 'crime fighting' to what in present-day society we would describe as anti-social behaviour. The Nazi concept of the *a-social* was used to classify and bring within the scope of the *Kriminalpolizei* a wide range of other categories of behaviour as a response to the privately acknowledged but publicly denied failure to eradicate all crime and disorder completely in a totalitarian, controlled society. Reinke (2005) observes that the criteria for preventive permanent detention were expanded by Nazi officials and senior officers of the *Kriminalpolizei*:

> A-socials were defined as people 'who demonstrate through their behaviour, which is alien to the community but not necessarily criminal, that they will not adapt themselves to the community.' The list of these a-socials also included … beggars, vagrants, prostitutes, drunkards, people with contagious diseases, particularly transmitted diseases, who evade the measures taken by the public health authorities. (Reinke 2005: 57)

Reinke goes on to identify other categories brought within the definition of the 'a-social'.

> Persons, regardless of any previous conviction, who evade the obligation to work and are dependent on the public for their maintenance (e.g. work-shy, work evaders, drunkards). (Reinke 2005: 57)

Other examples can no doubt be found throughout history. What is interesting is that whenever a society and its government appear to be under strain in maintaining social and public order, or maintaining levels of deviance and criminality within what would be considered from a Durkheimian perspective 'normal' limits, then the tendency to define deviance down, but also up, frequently occurs. The implications for the character and direction of both criminal justice and social policy in such contexts are very significant. Whenever incivility becomes a public issue requiring a public policy response, the character of support provided by the law-abiding community to those accused of deviance, invariably through their taxes and the welfare state, comes into question. It is precisely the process of 'defining deviance up' that has led to a re-evaluation of British social policy and its role in present-day society. The central questions confronting the New Labour government when it took office in 1997 was, should social policy compensate people for their structurally generated social disadvantages when they behave in an anti-social way? And, should government policy actively seek to divert those inclined to incivility and minor criminality towards community reparations by the use of civil law and by limiting their entitlement to welfare support? The answer to these questions in terms of no and yes has led to a realignment of social welfare policy to support measures targeted at incivility which has brought social policy and criminal justice policy closer together. Since the late 1990s, through a process of revising welfare entitlement, and creating a public debate about what precisely constitutes citizenship today, social policy has become preoccupied with issues of how best to manage problem populations who are socially excluded from consumer society by their own actions and attitudes. Increasingly, governments from the Left and the Right throughout Europe and North America have moved away from social causal models of explanation for deviance and towards behaviourist models in which understanding of social actions is exhausted by reference to the individual. In terms familiar to criminologists, the trend has been to seek solutions to social disorder by developing policies aimed at 'civilising' the 'kinds of people' who behave in an uncivil way. The preoccupation in policy circles is with how best to anticipate the risks posed by anti-social people and anti-social groups and manage their incivility by a combination of conditional welfare and criminal justice sanctions. It is this phenomenon that is the main focus of this book.

Outline of the book

The first chapter provides some general observations on the phenomenon at the centre of the discussion, namely, the criminalisation of social policy. There are three dominant themes at the centre of the current debate: welfare and discipline; human and civil rights, and family dysfunction. While the contemporary concern about the relationship between social policy and criminal justice policy has manifested itself in a number of policy debates, especially regarding the management of anti-social behaviour, I stress that welfare and discipline have always been closely related since the inception of the notion of social welfare. What is different today is that we live in a global world and belong to international organisations, including the European Union (EU) and the United Nations (UN), which establish legal and human rights principles that constrain policymakers irrespective of their national laws and policy predilections. Issues of human rights have always been at the centre of debate about criminal justice, and they remain important in the present and future development of social and criminal justice policies aimed at reducing incivility and deviant behaviour. The wider legal and normative principles issuing from the United Nations are that social policy should retain as its key objective the elimination of social injustice and is validated by that goal. Whether or not the policy interventions of the welfare state improve the living conditions of some social groups, and so indirectly reduce rates of criminal and anti-social offending, should not be the primary purpose of social welfare. A key issue for discussion is, of course, whether that principle is undermined by recent strategies aimed at eliminating anti-social behaviour from British society. Chapter 1 also highlights the significance of the family and parenting as a site where the two domains of social policy and criminal justice meet and where the principles about human and civil rights are being tested.

It is a key argument of this book that the current concerns about anti-social behaviour, and what should and can be done about it, are at a fundamental level about the changing nature of social solidarity in present-day society. In a sense, I share the analytic interest in the problems posed for social order by late modernity that Jock Young (2007) has recently addressed. He is critical of the fondness for what he calls binary thinking in both official discourse and social science which divides populations into the *included* and *excluded* and generally encourages everyone to engage in a process which he calls 'othering': defining oneself by marking others as being different or beyond normality. He rightly rejects 'the crisp boundaries' implied in this way of thinking because it creates 'false binaries' (stable family/single mothers; society at large/the underclass, etc.) and fails to recognise 'the abhorrence of late modernity for boundaries and separateness': it is the blurring of boundaries that characterises postmodern society and, of course, which sets in motion the processes which criminalise social policy. Problems and contradictions are generated within society and culture and in the relationships between people and social groups; they are not the product of people and intellects external to it (see

Young 2007: 6–7; 21–23). I have a preference to resolve these analytical dilemmas by grounding my thinking in the figurational sociology of Norbert Elias, someone that Young ignores. More specifically, the way people interact, and the changing patterns of interdependency between people, at social, cultural and spatial levels, frames the way social problems are defined and how causal explanations get embedded in policy responses. As the subtitle of the book suggests, I am situating my analysis in the notion of a *civilising process* which Norbert Elias (1978; 1982) developed, or more accurately I am basing my understanding of incivility and criminality in present-day society on the concept of *de-civilisation*, which Elias acknowledged but left others to embellish (see; Mennell 1990; Fletcher 1997).

De-civilisation may well be the cost that present-day Western societies must pay for their failure to attend seriously to issues of social justice and the redistribution of wealth. I will argue throughout the book that in order to understand anti-social behaviour, and the social policy response to it, we should transcend the inclination to view incivility as the product of deviant or pathological individuals. Social identities and statuses are always the effect of the material and institutional realities that shape the way people think and act. The figurational sociology of Elias guides us to examine the character of the relationships between those defined as behaving badly and those doing the defining. However, it is important to focus attention less on the labelling and name-calling that are a product of conflictual relationships and more on the strength of the bonds that connect and disconnect people. Are those relationships characterised by interdependence, reciprocity and solidarity, or dependence, social exclusion and rejection? The societal reaction to social problems is always mediated by the ways the mass media and political debate identify those whose conduct is considered to be culpable in generating disorder and, in addition, by the strategies that social policy planners formulate to manage them. If we want to understand anti-social behaviour and criminality today, our enquiry will not be exhausted by studying individuals in social isolation. The fuller theoretical statement informing my analysis is set out in Chapter 2.

In Chapter 3, the analysis turns to the cultural dimension of incivility. In a sense the discussion deals with the object of public and policy concern, the anti-social youth. In recent years there has been a succession of moral panics about youth cultures, which today are less likely to be dismissed as purely stylistic expressions. *NEET* (not in education, employment or training) is the semi-official acronym for a new classification for disengaged youth. This is frequently conflated with other terms which are more pejorative, such as 'chav' and 'ned'. It is the association of unemployed young people and their behaviour in public places that has stimulated much of the recent legislation and policy debate.

The analysis turns to the political response to incivility in Chapter 4. Having situated the political response in the context of the tension between *formalisation* and *informalisation* phases of the civilising process, which are described in Chapter 2, the chapter discusses the shift towards inauthentic modes of political governance of the anti-social behaviour issue. Insight into this can be obtained from the Parliamentary debate surrounding the private member's Bill presented by Frank Field MP in 2002 to withhold housing benefit from anti-social offenders. This helped to define the policy field, particularly the principle that the withholding of the benefits of the welfare state is justified in circumstances where individuals fail to live up to their side of the welfare contract by behaving badly. The chapter concludes by arguing that New Labour has moved away explicitly from their early concerns about social inclusion to embrace a moral underclass discourse which is informed by a focus on 'dysfunctional anti-social families'.

Chapter 5 addresses an issue that is considered by both New Labour and the Conservative Party to be pivotal for controlling anti-social behaviour in children and in society more widely, namely the family. It is also the primary site where social policy and criminal justice strategies converge. The chapter sets the policy discussion in context by identifying the issues of intimacy and divorce as being implicated in the process of changing conventions about social and moral obligation in marriage and so creating the context in which popular and policy opinion can target the failing and dysfunctional family as the 'cause' of anti-social behaviour in children. The chapter reviews the research on the relationship between family life and criminality before concluding that New Labour's family policy is contradictory and in tension with its children's policies and anti-social behaviour strategy. The chapter ends by examining the 'family sinbin' policy by referring to the original Dundee model.

The question of the balance to be struck between punishment and welfare in youth justice is the focus of Chapter 6. The discussion turns to the changing nature of parenthood, and the pressures on being an effective parent, with the increasingly strident call for parents to be punished for the deeds of their children. The focus here is on comparing the English and Scottish approaches to these issues. My main concern at the end of that chapter is one for the integrity of the Scottish system of placing the welfare of the child above the clamour for punishment. There may be standardising influences at work throughout Britain driven by the anti-social behaviour and 'respect' agendas.

If the failing family is culpable in creating anti-social children, and the youth justice system is insufficiently punitive, then community efficacy, or the capacity of a community to defend itself against social disorder, is seen as part of the solution to the problem of taming the unruly and uncivil in our midst. New Labour has developed and refurbished a strategy on civil renewal which concentrates on releasing the energy and enthusiasm of the voluntary sector to combine with community action to combat incivility and criminality. The concentration on building social capital is the primary objective, but there are dangers in that established–outsider relationships can also be a by-product of community safety partnerships and informal neighbourhood action against anti-social behaviour.

In Chapter 8, the analysis turns to the problem of fear of crime and social disorder. This leads to a discussion initially of *civil security* before turning to consider the role of the media in shaping public conceptions of fear and disorder. The issue of fear of crime is also discussed from the point of view of those said to be the perpetrators of disorder, mainly male youths occupying street-corner society. I characterise streetwise behaviour as a form of inverted fear and raise questions about what kind of social policy is required to deal with that phenomenon.

The book closes by discussing drugs policy as an exemplar of the current situation where the apparently unassailable position of criminalising strategies is being challenged by a range of policy discourses from health and social policy. The announcement in November 2007 of a Children's Plan containing a 10-year agenda to improve the lives of children and young people in England is a further example of the contemporary rebalancing of the relationship between the social and punitive aspects of children's policy. But it also tends to confirm that social policy is indeed being *criminalised.*

Chapter 1

Criminalising social policy: some general observations

The role of the welfare state in a capitalist society was always conceived of in terms of its compensatory functions. The social and economic dislocation that accompanied the inevitable social changes wrought by capitalist industrialisation required a mechanism to *steer* society towards an acceptance of the view that while inequalities would inevitably occur, and that collectively produced wealth would be appropriated privately, social order and social justice could nevertheless be achieved by institutionalising a sense of social solidarity through a benevolent state system that redistributed resources through welfare benefits and social services. Within this arrangement, social policy would compensate those who were the main losers in the rapidly changing occupational structure and support them when they were made redundant. The pursuit of full employment in the demand-side economy, which was a feature of the Keynesian welfare state, was premised on the assumption that redundancy would be a temporary feature of the ebb and flow of an industrial economy and, consequently, the period of exclusion from work and the full fruits of society that accompanied productive activity would be short. Today that assumption no longer holds, and many of those ejected from the occupational structure because of their outdated skills and absence of credentials to compete in the knowledge society have discovered that their redundancy is long term.

Today the welfare state has fundamentally changed its role and its function in response to the changing social and economic circumstances of post-industrialism. It has largely abandoned the strategy of *social steering*, aimed at encouraging people to adapt to social change by offering them fiscal and service incentives, in favour of its social control function, aimed at encouraging behaviour to change by cutting back on the benefits and services provided by the welfare state. The task is no longer to compensate the losers in the competitive market system that characterises post-industrial society (so-called because it relies on knowledge and services to create wealth rather than primary industrial manufacturing) but to make them more actively self-reliant; to equip them to compete better and more effectively in the marketplace rather than lick their wounds. The problem is that there are many in present-day society who cannot or are unwilling to accept the incentives being provided in a post-welfare society. How should this problem be addressed? Increasingly, the purpose of social policy is to align with the problems of managing problem populations. The world of welfare and the world of criminal justice, while never very far apart, are now moving increasingly together in terms of establishing modes of social discipline considered appropriate for living and working in a complex, postmodern society.

Criminalising social policy

The relationship between social policy and criminology has until recently been left unexplored at both the academic level and the level of political debate and policy design (see Knepper 2007). While criminologists have tended to treat issues surrounding the development of social policy and the welfare state as a backcloth, dealing with concerns about poverty, disadvantage and citizenship that are correlated with criminality and anti-social behaviour but not necessarily causal in a determinist way, social policy specialists have tended to ignore criminology and the working of the criminal justice system as fields which study the consequences of failed social policies. There is often an implicit relationship that can be identified in the literature of both fields of study, but recently that relationship has become more explicit, and this book is primarily concerned with the boundaries between criminal justice and social policy that have been uncovered by the very contemporary preoccupation of governments with issues such as social exclusion (treated as a central concern of social policy) and anti-social behaviour (treated as a central concern of criminologists). Increasingly, these areas of policy are being drawn together in a process that is criminalising social policy.

Students of both criminology and social policy may have noticed variations on a frequently mentioned phrase in the social science literature in recent years: a number of texts have referred to the criminalisation of social policy (Crawford 1999: 228–32; Swaaningen 2002: 273–5; Stephen 2005), the *criminalisation of incivility* (Hillyard, Sim, Tombs and Whyte 2004), the *criminalisation of everyday life* (Presdee 2000), *criminalising social policy* (Muncie 2004: 242–4), and the *penalisation of poverty* (Wacquant 2001), and students have had their attention drawn to the *convergence of social policy and criminology* (Gilling and Barton 1997; Boutellier 2001; Gilling 2001). Jonathan Simon (2007) has even advanced the argument that American society is *governed through crime* in the wake of the collapsing social consensus around the welfare state. Similar tendencies are evident in Europe too. While the development of social policy from the Poor Law tradition to the present day has always been framed by socio-moral considerations, such as the need to avoid providing benefits and services that might act as perverse incentives that encourage inactivity and indolence, this precept has become a defining feature of modern welfare systems that equate indolence and inactivity with a propensity for anti-social behaviour. Since the late 1990s, the New Labour government has signalled this change through the creation of hybrid policy units such as the Social Exclusion Unit and the Civil Renewal Unit, as well as allocating responsibility to specialised groupings working from within the Office of the Deputy Prime Minister (ODPM), reincarnated as the Department of Communities and Local Government, and the Home Office for driving forward strategies to enhance 'active citizenship' and 'community efficacy'. The coordination of a broad range of policy initiatives affecting anti-social behaviour, criminality and dysfunctional families has been shared between the ODPM and the Home Office and drawing in the Departments of Education and the Treasury, particularly relating to strategies to develop the voluntary sector as part of the civil renewal programme. The devolved authorities in Scotland, Wales and Northern Ireland have also participated in these initiatives. The effort to develop 'joined-up' policies across the field of what might be called the *politics of behaviour* has been a distinctive feature of British social policy in the early years of the twenty-first century. Social policy today appears to be founded on the principle that there is a need to connect welfare benefits with disciplined behaviour and active rather than passive citizenship. The notion that social policy and criminality are closely tied together has moved, therefore, from being merely an assumption to a phenomenon that must be named and understood more rigorously. The dominant themes in this movement can be identified briefly before they are examined in more detail in the book.

Welfare and discipline

The welfare state project has always been driven by a modernist zeal of political and policy elites to shape attitudes and manage behaviour in the name of realising a vision of a welfare society. In response to what might be described as an idealist view of the welfare state set out by Viet-Wilson (2000), who argues that only those welfare systems that provide for the needs and suffering of those at the bottom of the social hierarchy regardless of desert are justified in being called welfare states, Atherton (2002) argues that a welfare state cannot be defined by such an unattainable goal: all welfare systems have pragmatically directed a significant effort to the management of incentives to work. Atherton supports the view, therefore, that the welfare state from the twentieth century until the present has been a system primarily designed to meet the needs of the working class through employment and social insurance rather than the chronically poor, the socially excluded or the deviants. In his view it should more accurately be described as a *worker-benefit state*. While the social security system has been geared to addressing the needs of the deserving claimants who have worked and contributed to the welfare system, the principles of eligibility, together with social work services primarily designed for the management of problem populations, have also been an integral feature of the welfare state. Eligibility rules have been underpinned by criminal law for those who might seek to 'cheat' the system. What is perhaps new today is that the relationship between welfare and discipline, and between social policy and criminal justice, is changing from being an implicit feature of welfare state development to becoming a more explicit and strategic characteristic.

Without being diverted to a history of the welfare state, it is sufficient to note that the provision of social welfare has gone through a number of what Stanley Cohen (1985) called 'master shifts' in relation to penal policy but which apply equally well to changing welfare paradigms. Those 'master shifts' in welfare policy reflected, and were accompanied by, major changes in thinking about entitlement, discipline and deviance and, crucially, what constituted deserving and undeserving behaviour. As Squires (1990) has observed in his analysis of the emergence of the disciplinary state, the Poor Law tradition in social policy harmonised issues of moral worthiness and entitlement that provided the normative foundation of future attitudes to welfare. It was a system of welfare that was primarily concerned to police entitlement to benefits in a context of building a disciplinary society that would complement the needs of the growing and developing capitalist economy. Comparing the 1834 Poor Law Amendment Act with the haphazard system that had preceded it, Squires (1990) describes the new Poor Law as 'a more cohesive and calculated system of social policy which would combine the poverty and subsistence of the working class with the discipline of the capitalist economy, and in so doing, force the working class to give freely of their only possession, their labour' (p 49). The processing of those unwilling to submit to the disciplines of the new society was, therefore, from the outset the responsibility of social policy planners. The two subsequent and related 'master shifts' in welfare reform that followed the transcendence of the Poor Law tradition; the first straddling the nineteenth and twentieth centuries and culminating in the Liberal reforms prior to World War I, and the second consolidating welfare reforms after World War II that had been incubating in the interwar years, and giving birth to the modern conception of what a welfare state is, both had at their core a preoccupation with discipline and the management of problem populations. They were part of what I have called the *modernist* impulse in social welfare (Rodger 2000), which was primarily concerned with the application of scientific method and reason to socially engineer a new society. That social engineering was largely a top-down-led project of intervention and policy development that was driven by political and policy elites and consisted in augmenting the social security system by adding a range of social services primarily aimed at professionalising the social work gaze begun by the nineteenth-century philanthropists. (see Ashford 1986; De Swaan 1988: 9; Pierson 1991: 98–101). The social work and criminal justice services took responsibility for those unable or unwilling to submit to the regulation required to live in the emerging welfare state. In the 1950s, 1960s and 1970s, problem populations were understood as being a residual problem of an evolving welfare system that had to be processed by the adoption of the language of rehabilitation. The welfarist impulse in prisons and community corrections described by Garland (1985) and Cohen (1985) was merely reflecting the wider approach to building a 'modern' and socially integrated society. However, the decline in what has been described by Jessop (2002) as the Keynesian welfare state and the emergence of the Schumpeterian workfare state in the period since the mid-1970s has signalled the adoption of a more coercive vocabulary in the sphere of welfare. Social problems once regarded as residual and unthreatening to social order are today considered to require 'tougher' policy responses. Therefore, when it is suggested that social policy is being criminalised there is an assumption that there is an ongoing process of redefinition of the aims and purposes of the welfare state: an abandonment of concern for the alleviation of poverty, disadvantage and the meeting of human need as ends in themselves in favour of focusing policy on criminality and criminals in order to maintain a disciplined and orderly society. Increasingly, social policies are forced to address explicitly what historically was left implicit: the thrust of social welfare is to provide care and social support but only on the condition that citizens lead orderly lives (see Crawford 1999: 228–32).

The key to understanding the growing complementarity between social policy and criminal justice today lies in what Deacon (2004) has acknowledged is the shift towards greater conditionality in a wide range of policy areas. This movement in thinking about welfare entitlement has accompanied a shift from a concern about structural causes of social problems to a preoccupation with 'choices, lifestyle and the culture of the poor themselves'. This change is identified by Deacon as marking out New Labour's broad welfare strategy. However, more accurately, the concentration on the politics of behaviour continues an approach to social administration that began in the early years of the Thatcher government of the 1980s and which the instincts of 'New' Labour found congenial when taking power. When individualism is pre-eminently valued, and dependency on public goods and welfare is especially vilified, as it was under Thatcherism and increasingly appears to be under New Labour, it is inevitable that the focus of policy will be on behaviour rather than wider social and economic forces. By way of illustrating this perspective, we can briefly consider the case of housing management as an illustration of some of the emerging issues involved in criminalising social policy. The movement away from structural towards behaviourist diagnoses of social problems has been clearly evident in the area of housing policy.

Housing management and the anti-social tenant

The Thatcher project of rolling back the state faltered in many social policy areas but housing policy was in general terms one of the successes of her strategy. While the reduction of public expenditure remained stubbornly intractable in social security, education and health care, housing provided a rare success largely through the right to buy initiative. What made that policy a success can partly be explained by the language of 'rights' and individual choice used to sell it and which became generally accepted as the most appropriate vocabulary to describe housing and housing needs. For example, the image of municipal socialism and the large-scale urban renewal programmes of the 1950s and 1960s, which led to the creation of the vast peripheral council housing estates, were attacked in behaviourist terms precisely because they were said to go against the grain of human nature to own private space and property. The vision of a property-owning democracy which accompanied the Thatcher right to buy policy, evoking images of 'pride' in house and neighbourhood and attachment to communities, was later readily mutated into the New Labour vision of the stakeholder society. The stakeholder concept was applied to those who did not own their own property but who could nevertheless become full participants in their communities through active engagement with, and support for, their 'social landlord'. The decline of the municipal landlord, and the rise of the 'social' landlord through an expanded role for housing associations, aimed to improve the quality of life in the inner cities and peripheral housing estates by both improving the housing stock and, importantly, managing that stock more effectively. As Cowan, Pantazis and Gilroy (2001) observe, budgetary disciplines imposed on housing managers after the Housing Act 1996 transformed them from agents who rationed council housing stock to active promoters of their estates in order to avoid empty properties and financial penalties. This has meant that problem tenants who threaten neighbourhoods and communities in what are considered residualised housing areas (the poorer and more dilapidated housing stock that has not been sold and which accommodates those that cannot afford to buy) are targeted by a new, professionalised group of housing managers in what amounts to social and behavioural cleansing. It is the crime-control role that has become increasingly prominent in social housing management at the expense of the concern for meeting social need. Flint (2006b) argues:

7

> Changes in social housing governance are emblematic of a wider evolution of social and urban policy in the UK that emphasises community ownership, neighbourhood interventions, multi-agency working, self-government and a focus on moral conduct. The synergy between social housing and wider governance has resulted in social housing agencies being given an increasingly prominent role in government strategies aimed at delivering care in the community, reducing anti-social behaviour, fostering community cohesion and minimising risks arising from the housing of sex offenders. (Flint 2006b: 172)

As housing managers have become key agents entrusted with the task of overseeing the *responsibilisation strategy* introduced by the New Labour government, they have acquired a new form of professional status. For example, Brown (2004) suggests that the acquisition of 'soft-end' clients and problems in the social housing estates from the police has created a professional space within which housing managers are increasingly usurping the authority of the police in the investigation and decision-making about anti-social tenants and anti-social families. This role has been formalised by the passing of the anti-social behaviour legislation, which both imposes duties on social landlords to prepare policies on anti-social tenants and provides powers to seek Anti-social Behaviour Orders (ASBOs) through the courts. Placing the issue in the context of Cohen's analysis of 'net widening' (Cohen 1985), Brown views the growing involvement of social landlords in dealing with anti-social behaviour as 'mesh thinning' rather than 'net widening' (bringing moderately deviant people and problems within the scope of the criminal justice process rather than expanding the institutional sweep of the social control apparatus). Crucially, what she is pointing to is the blurring of boundaries between housing policy as a welfare issue about meeting social need and the social control of dysfunctional families and anti-social tenants as part of a criminal justice agenda. Describing this new role, she observes:

> Landlords attempt to reform dysfunctional families. Anti-social families are offered a support worker to help develop positive discipline and regular routine in the home, at the same time as the threat of eviction is held up to them. Community reparation orders aim to ensure that the perpetrator makes amends to 'the community' and, through this process, comes under its socialising influence. (Brown 2004: 206)

As Flint (2006b) observes, social housing governance has been leading and testing new 'rationales about the delivery of welfare services in the UK' (p 174). Beyond the specific mediating role between the world of welfare and criminal justice, the housing manager is involved in 'non-core' housing functions involving community development, neighbourhood renewal and crime prevention and community safety partnerships. Perhaps the role of the social landlord as manager of problem populations has arisen as a by-product of the spatial concentrations of poverty and disadvantage in the peripheral housing estates following in the wake of economic restructuring and welfare state retrenchment. In a context of growing *conditionality* in welfare, the role of the housing manager lies at the intersection between the imperatives of meeting social need and the administration of a moral code of public propriety. In the execution of this function by the housing manager, social policy is sometimes imperceptibly criminalised. However, recent policy developments, which have reinforced the responsibilities of social landlords in the anti-social behaviour legislation, points to a strategic intent to reconfigure the landlord role by New Labour policy designers.

Civil law and *natural justice*

The criminal law is often slow and demanding in terms of investigation and evidence gathering, while anti-social behaviour typically requires immediate situational action to release the social tensions it creates. The solution to this dilemma for government is to bring about a complex but effective 'double convergence' between social policy, criminal law and civil law. First, social policy strategies targeted at issues that may have deep-seated social causes (a child's unwillingness to attend school, a teenager's unwillingness to find employment having left school, or, as I have described above, unruly behaviour inconsistent with being a good tenant in a social housing estate) are replaced by a focus on medium-term goals primarily concerned with behaviour modification. This is accomplished in alliance with the criminal justice system through the issue of supervisory orders ranging from ASBOs, Parenting Orders, Curfew Orders and Dispersal Orders. Second, civil law is used in preference to criminal law to control sub-criminal anti-social behaviour because the standard of proof required to impose a restricting order on anti-social offenders is lower, and the remedy quicker and potentially more flexible, combining surveillance and

9

restrictions on movements as well as counselling and therapy. Third, the recourse to criminal law can be used as the ultimate threat to force conformity through the back-door mechanism of enforcing a criminal sanction against anyone found guilty of breaching a civil law order.

Legally and sociologically, there are many complexities surrounding the tendency for social policy and criminal justice to converge. While a great deal of the public debate about behaviour and incivility concentrates on the use of restrictive powers such as ASBOs, focusing on the legal principles underpinning their application, there are deeper sociological issues attaching to the exercise of social control in the context of incivility that must be addressed. The debate tends to revolve around whether or not *natural justice* is violated by the use of civil law standards of evidence, which require only that facts are established by the balance of probabilities, and can allow the admission of hearsay evidence, rather than the criminal law standard, which requires that facts be established beyond reasonable doubt, and allows confrontation of witnesses. One way in which this can be conceptualised is to think of natural justice as having two primary dimensions. First, it has a legal aspect that concerns the upholding of human rights as established by the European Convention of Human Rights (ECHR), which was incorporated into British law by the Human Rights Act 1998. The issue raised by the application of restrictive orders to secure social control objectives is that the weaker standard of evidence required of civil law means that an expedient mechanism of social control can be used to effect immediate regulation of undesirable behaviour, but in doing so the principles of natural justice for the accused may be violated. Second, natural justice has a sociological aspect which relates to the underlying collective or community voice driving policies and legislation. Each of these issues requires further consideration.

Human rights

The use of civil law as a social control mechanism explicitly targeted at anti-social behaviour is relatively recent in British law, and it coincides with the identification of incivility as a social problem. As Burney (2005) points out, the Housing Act 1996 was essentially rewritten to allow greater scope for social landlords to address the behavioural problems of some tenants. The widening scope of responsibilities falling on social landlords in recent years has included the imposition of a duty to ensure that anti-social tenants are managed and regulated by mechanisms such as 'introductory' tenancies, demotion from secure tenant status and the removal of the right to buy. These devices can have far-reaching consequences for those involved and can be visited upon unruly tenants because of their incivility rather than their unlawfulness. A controversial feature of the housing management of problem tenants has been the use of hearsay evidence to convict people of anti-social behaviour. Particularly controversial is the use of 'professional witnesses' hired to observe and report on miscreant behaviour. Anyone evicted on this basis will be regarded as being intentionally homeless. The methods which have been used in housing management have now been extended to cover a wide range of behaviour identified as anti-social by the 2003 Act. This type of action has been called 'managerial penology' by Burke and Morrill (2002) and has stimulated concern about whether the use of civil law in these contexts is violating human rights.

The use of civil law has consequences for how natural justice is commonly understood. In legal terms, the principle of natural justice relates (a) to the right to a fair hearing and to have advanced notice of the case to answer (*audi alteram partem*), and (b) to the right to be heard by impartial adjudicators (*nemo judex in causa sua*) (see de Smith 1973). In cases of anti-social behaviour where a person's movements are restricted, possibly on the admission of hearsay evidence and without being formally charged or appearing in court, it is clear that issues of natural justice will be involved. In terms of legal practice, the use of civil standards of proof will often be set aside, and courts may insist on establishing the facts of a case beyond reasonable doubt (see Ashworth 2004; Guthrie 2005: 15). Where the civil standard of proof is adopted, it could be claimed that judges actually abandon the scrutiny of evidence in favour of exercising judgement and evaluation (see Guthrie 2005). As the Anti-social Behaviour Act 2003 works through civil law, and does not allow the confrontation of witnesses while permitting the use of 'professional witnesses' and hearsay evidence, it could be argued that if people are not given advanced notice of the case that they must answer, and an opportunity to test the validity of the claims against them in front of impartial adjudicators, their right to natural justice has been undermined. In the broader field of public administration, particularly the application of natural justice principles in public inquiries, cross-examination of experts and evidence is allowed, and where this is prevented the courts have overturned ministerial decisions.[1] These principles appear to be particularly insecure where restorative justice practices are involved. The anti-social behaviour legislation has encouraged the exploration of the greater use of mechanisms to bring victims and perpetrators together. Borrowing from the antipodean tradition of family conferencing and restorative and reparative justice, recent legislation has pointed to greater community involvement in the resolution of civil cases involving anti-social behaviour and petty criminality. The replacement of adversarial forms of justice with processes based on conflict resolution and consensual participation appears positive. However, some have questioned whether the participation of perpetrators is always consensual and, significantly, whether victims take emotions and attitudes into the process that undermine claims to impartiality (see Ashworth 2004; Dignan 2005 Johnstone 2002).

An overlooked issue surrounding the use of civil law to deal with the politics of behaviour is that it appears to allow greater scope for the imposition of social interventions on offenders precisely because it does not allow imprisonment as a form of disposal. What is clear is that the use of extra-legal forms of intervention, including family therapy and social work supervision, to manage anti-social behaviour brings the worlds of social support and social control together in a way that is distinct from routine probation and aftercare work with offenders. However, a broader issue is raised here. As Johnson (2004) points out, the Human Rights Act 1998 was not intended to protect social, economic and cultural rights. While the ECHR and the Human Rights Act secure political and civil rights, which are referred to as *first-generation* rights, social and economic rights, referred to as *second-generation* rights, are left outside the scope of both. What people are entitled to with respect to their welfare and well-being is unclear, and that lack of clarity is compounded when the language of social rights is compromised by the insistence of governments that rights must be balanced by responsibilities.

Beyond the questions raised about 'rights' to welfare benefits, and whether measures to remove welfare benefits, including rights attaching to housing tenure, are against the spirit of the human rights legislation and the ECHR, there remain civil and human rights relating to the imposition of unrequested social and therapeutic intervention. Do people have the right to be left unmolested irrespective of their unconventional behavioural traits and deviant but lawful behaviour? The answer to that question is probably yes. However, matters become more ambiguous in cases involving parenting and unconventional domestic management practices that impinge on children and neighbours. On this issue Burke and Morrill (2002) observe that the ECHR has generated debate about whether the *negative obligations* provided by the ECHR (the protection of individuals from the actions of others including the state) should lead to actions involving a *positive obligation* on organisations and local authorities to take action against those deemed to be threatening communities. There is a legal view that the issuing of an ASBO, for example, is compatible with the ECHR because it is essentially preventive in its intentions and seeks positively to defend the rights of the majority to live peaceful and orderly lives. Clearly, in the case of housing management, *positive actions* have been taken in accordance with this interpretation of the ECHR. The principle driving the Anti-social Behaviour Act is that there is an obligation on public authorities or agencies acting as semi-public authorities to protect the human rights of the majority of tenants affected by an anti-social minority. However, a contrary view also exists in law. Burke and Morrill (2002) make this point through quoting Lord Goodhart:

> Human rights are not just the right to behave well ... People have a right to be bloody-minded; they have a right within reason to make a bit of a nuisance of themselves ... We want to live in a law-abiding society with a low level of crime ... and a low level of vandalism and disorder of all kinds ... but, at the same time, we do not want to live in an authoritarian state. (Burke and Morrill 2002: 11)

In developing forms of social and therapeutic intervention to support problem behaviour outside and beyond the normal reach of social work, there is an issue about whether the imposition of unrequested 'support' for people whose actions are not strictly unlawful may be an intrusion that undermines their human rights. The issue of parental responsibility is obviously the most significant issue in this context and a subject that will be returned to later.

Perhaps the biggest controversy surrounding the use of civil law to control anti-social behaviour has been the imposition of criminal punishment of up to five years in prison for breach of an order. At its simplest, it would appear that people could, in principle, find themselves incarcerated for behaviour that began as uncivil rather than unlawful. What is not allowed in law, and underpinned by the ECHR, is the relabelling of proceedings brought to a court under civil law as subsequently criminal. This is secured by what is called the antisubversion doctrine (see Ashworth 2004). However, the rules of evidence and standard of proof necessary to convict an individual of the criminal breach of a civil order would be that of criminal law (see Guthrie 2005: 15). This is clearly an area of legal process that could be said to be promoting 'net widening', particularly by criminalising behaviour that required social support rather than criminal prosecution. It is also an area where civil law could be said to be used to control criminal activity. The large question remains whether law and legal processes are being used where social policies aimed at community development, family support, and individual and community education would be more effective in both tackling the underlying causes of anti-social behaviour and halting the tendency for modern Western societies continually to 'net widen' their criminal justice systems.

Moral economy

The notion that the welfare state institutionalises social solidarity and provides support for all regardless of desert is no longer a credible principle in a society that has converted the concept of citizenship from guaranteed rights of access to benefits in times of need to guarantees of minimal support in accordance with one's contribution to work. It is the American concept of *citizenship as praxis* that has become influential in contemporary Western debates about the future of welfare (see Cook and Barrett 1992; Hill 1992). In a society in which activeness and industriousness are particularly valued, it follows that those who are passive and indolent will appear deviant and, significantly, require to be managed and to be socially controlled. Idleness and social exclusion that result from non-work can lead to what appear to be ill-disciplined lives because the rhythms of existence of the bored, unemployed youth and unsupervised congregations of children in materially impoverished communities are different from those who are engaged with mainstream activities. And when the behaviour is annoying rather than criminal, the problem of how it should be controlled is made even more difficult.

The ways and means used by communities to socialise and control their members give rise to what we can call the *moral economy* of social life. The principles shaping interaction and protocols of behaviour in a neighbourhood or community form a moral economy which people create and recreate through their exchanges and social interaction in their daily lives. The normative principles shaping routine neighbourhood life is unreflexive and taken for granted. Historically, the concepts of natural justice and moral economy were indivisible and related to common-use rights and related primarily to custom and tradition. If a community's common understandings were violated, as historically they were at the times of the enclosure movement in England when common-use rights were arbitrarily removed, then it was an affront to natural justice that was felt. The historiography of E.P. Thompson is the best scholarly source on this broader historical and theoretical argument (see Thompson 1970; 1975). There is a sense in which this phenomenon remains a concern in present-day society, especially with respect to the debate about the decline of neighbourhood solidarity and the rise of incivility. It has been expressed more recently in terms such as 'social capital' and 'community efficacy'. What is at issue, therefore, is the attack on the collective rights of community as embodied in its moral economy.

The view has been expressed that anti-social behaviour effectively undermines the community moral economy and so compromises the human rights of 'respectable', law-abiding citizens by weakening their capacity to act and live in concert with each other (see Field 2003). Legislative changes providing for community safety partnerships, restorative justice and reparations to communities and individual victims are, therefore, to be understood as an attempt to strengthen the moral economy of the community. It could be argued that natural justice is protected and met by allowing the community a voice and a right to be heard. This line of argument has led to the justification for the anti-social behaviour legislation. Other than former Prime Minster Tony Blair, Frank Field MP has been the most vocal representative of this view. His argument (Field 2003) is that legislation embodies and consolidates in law principles about social order that are the product of the moral economy of community and neighbourhood life. For example, he argues that tackling the 'yob culture' is primarily about rebuilding the social ecology of the working-class community (Field 2003: 94–109). This view considers norms of behaviour relating to a peaceful existence as historically grounded and part of an implicit contract between the citizen and the state which is readily understood by ordinary people in their routine lives. He argues that it is incumbent on governments to ensure that those principles are enshrined in law and order policies that protect the law-abiding and respectable majority from an unruly minority. The issue raised here is whether the demand for immediate solutions to what are perceived to be intolerable levels of social deviance in some communities is leading to the abandonment of social policies aimed at socially steering behaviour in positive ways by the incentives provided by state benefits and services. In their place we may be inserting short-term restrictive and punitive fixes that enable problem populations to be better controlled rather than changed. Indeed, we may ask whether the underlying social and interactive causes of anti-social behaviour are being addressed at all by the search for immediate punitive resolution of the discontent.

Dysfunctional families and anti-social children

Lying at the heart of the policy debate about anti-social behaviour is the image of the dysfunctional family. British social policy has grappled with the 'family question' since the nineteenth-century philanthropists attempted to remoralise the poor by a combination of strategies to enhance moral hygiene, thrift and work. Very little has changed and governments today continue to focus on how to manage and control the private decisions people make about marriage and child rearing in what policy planners consider is in the public interest. It is because family life is generally accepted as providing children with the social and moral foundations of what Field (2003) calls the cardinal virtues that the absence of those virtues in children today has led to the conclusion that the family is at fault for the rise in incivility. In particular, parenting practices and parental responsibilities are key issues in the politics of behaviour.

Mooney (2003) has pointed to the continuities in British politics on the subject of the dysfunctional family. While competing political analyses of the contemporary 'family question' have placed emphasis on a range of distinctive issues, Mooney is right to argue that the main political parties share a focus on the microstructures of society, particularly the family and the school: the social democratic stress on divorce and working mothers in the 1960s and 1970s; the Tory obsession with lone parents, illegitimacy and the fatherless family in the 1980s and 1990s; and New Labour's preoccupation with the anti-social family from 1997 to the present, all share the same policy dilemma of how to control deviance in family life in the public interest. While the New Labour government has acknowledged that there is a need for a broad strategy to tackle family and child poverty, and there is some evidence that it has achieved some success in reducing child poverty by a quarter and putting in place policy programmes targeted at early childhood development (see Stewart 2005), it appears more intent on being associated with policies that target anti-social behaviour in children rather than reduce their social disadvantages. The 'respect' agenda has been far more prominent than the strategy to eliminate child poverty in New Labour's third term. This indicates that there are more votes in the politics of enforcement than the politics of redistribution. It also reveals the underlying theoretical drivers of New Labour's policy thinking about anti-social behaviour: it is value orientations and not social structures that must be changed if anti-social behaviour is to be eradicated. The understanding of the broader economic and global forces shaping working-class community life and child poverty may be part of the government's broader policy agenda, but it is not being allowed to get in the way of the more populist and short-term political gains to be won through being 'tough on crime and those labelled anti-social'. It is clear that being tough on the causes of crime and incivility raised too many politically and economically contentious issues to be allowed a central place in the policy agenda for the first post-Blair general election, and there is little to indicate that either Gordon Brown or, indeed, David Cameron will change the direction of criminal justice policy in the medium to long term. This reality has led Jonathan Simon to conclude that crime and deviance control provides a template for modern governance (see Simon 2007).

The family has become a social institution that is at the intersection of a range of policy initiatives targeted at anti-social behaviour, particularly relating to early childhood development, education, and youth behaviour and employment. Indeed, the transfer of the 'Respect Unit' from the Home Office to Ed Balls' new Department for Children, Schools and Families is emblematic of this new trend in criminalising social policy. The family has also become an explicit object for policy intervention from sources of government which have typically skirted around the private sphere for fear of violating cherished liberal democratic mores about the privacy and individualism. For example, the Home Office has become involved not only in monitoring 'anti-social neighbour nuisance', which might be expected, but also in the coordination of intensive family support and parenting programmes in 50 designated action areas. Such and Walker (2005) have pointed to the tension between child welfare, family policy and the anti-social behaviour strategy. In particular, there lies a different and conflicting image of the child at the heart of these competing policy domains. The child at the centre of anti-social behaviour policies is a 'dangerous' 'tearaway', while the image of the child emanating from the children's legislation and in family policy is variously disadvantaged and socially vulnerable. I will return to these themes in Chapter 5. Similarly, the legislation affecting youth development and welfare can appear to lack a coherent approach. The creation of Youth Offending Boards in England and the debate about the form and purpose of the Scottish Children's Hearing system have highlighted the contemporary concern about the relationship between welfare and punishment. Meanwhile, at the centre of that debate, lies the notion of the 'irresponsible parent' and whether, and to what extent, parents should be punished for the deeds of their children. It sometimes appears that the debate has swung away from a focus on the errant children in our communities and on to the incompetence and selfishness of parents who fail to control and socialise their children appropriately. The Parent Order is now likely to vie with the ASBO as a defining symbol of the modern approach to criminal justice. I will return to these themes in Chapter 6.

Concluding observations

The relationship between social policy and criminal justice has always been close, but there have been boundaries between them marked out by both academic focus and, crucially, professional practice and responsibility. While the boundaries have been less marked in Scotland with the training of generic social workers, in England and Wales the separation of social work with families from activities relating to probation and aftercare signalled a clear division of labour between the world of welfare and the world of criminal justice. The mechanism used in Scotland to manage the boundary between care and control was the creation of a system of diverting *all* children up to the age of 16 years away from the criminal justice system: the Kilbrandon principles underpinning the Scottish system foregrounds issues of child welfare above those of punishment. Elsewhere in the UK, those principles have been less guided by principle and have largely been shaped by expediency in politics and policy. The tendency today is for multidiscipline work in the policy field, and that has led to a variety of professional partnerships being created, with the pre-eminent objective being to see and understand social problems in a 'joined-up way' because that has been the prevailing orthodoxy of government.

This introductory chapter has attempted to set the scene for those that come later. The weakening boundaries between social policy and criminal justice are being driven by the demands of a post-industrial society for a post-welfare settlement in which the citizen will no longer be assured of support in times of redundancy and inactivity. The *social investment state* will instead provide learning and retraining opportunities for people to re-engage with work and reconnect with the accompanying 'benefits' of membership of the consumer society. However, the strategy being adopted for those who refuse to participate in this new settlement, or create problems for others by their refusal to participate, will be social control management. Conditionality is a core principle of the welfare state today, and those that fail to meet the conditions of active citizenship by their readiness to work and be civically engaged will be subject to supervision and, in some cases, re-education. This is a strange subject to be writing about in what is a liberal democratic society. Issues of civil and human rights are being renegotiated as part of this movement into the post-welfare society. The legislation that has been passed, such as the Crime and Disorder Act 1998 and the Anti-social Behaviour Act 2003, has posed real questions for the world of welfare through its impact on housing, benefits, and family and children's welfare. These are the issues to be explored in the coming pages.

Note

1 *Nicholson* v *Secretary of State for Energy and Another*. Before Sir Douglas Frank QC sitting as a Deputy Queen's Bench judge 1977.

Chapter 2

Incivility and welfare in a de-civilised society

A feature of the criminalising tendency of contemporary social policy is that anti-social behaviour is understood and treated almost entirely as a product of individual pathology. The underlying assumption held by the architects of the Anti-social Behaviour Act is that offenders are variously under-socialised by inadequate families and parents; they have failed to acquire the appropriate value orientations to enable them to integrate and engage in orderly social intercourse with neighbours; they engage in deviant and criminal activities because they are particular 'kinds of people' who cannot empathise with the fears and concerns of others; they are selfish, uncaring and, in some cases, mentally ill. However, the word *anti-social* implies disconnection from others and the adoption of behaviours and activities that are beyond the control and influence of the local community and the immediate social audience. It is by its nature a very *social* phenomenon made visible by social reaction to events and acts and the construction of social definitions to frame those events. Despite this, the tendency in politics and policy is to see all anti-social deviants as being *in our society* but somehow *not of our society*. The social context generating social meaning is largely ignored. This leads prematurely to exhaust explanation of it as a phenomenon by recourse to the individual level rather than explore the wider social processes that connect people to each other and also destroys relationships between people.

A key issue to be considered is whether society is changing in ways which accentuate people's differences and achievements. There are a variety of factors contributing to British society becoming less integrated and less solidaristic and there may be reasons to believe that the issues surrounding social integration and social solidarity are worse in Britain than in other European countries. Intergenerational mobility, for example, appears to have fallen in Britain and the USA compared with most Western European and Nordic societies (see Blanden, Gregg and Machin 2005; Lampl 2007). A consequence of low levels of social mobility is that inequalities become consolidated in processes of social polarisation: economic differences can be reinforced by social, spatial, cultural and behavioural differences as those doing well from the economic system become increasingly better off and detached from those doing badly. The current trends in inequality in Britain may be complex, but recent research indicates that 'the gap between the lowest and highest paid workers has widened considerably since the late 1970s and continues to widen' (Sefton and Sutherland 2005: 240). Indeed, Britain's performance relative to other EU countries on measures of poverty and inequality is poor; in fact, in 1997, 'the share of children living in poor households in the UK was higher than anywhere in the EU' (see Stewart 2005: 298). The situation of the UK on this measure relative to other EU member states has only improved since 1997 because countries such as Italy, Ireland and Portugal have been performing even more badly (Stewart 2005: 297–321). There seems to be a growing consensus across the political spectrum on the emergence of growing social divisions and a widening gap between those doing well from post-industrial economies and those being left behind. For example, from the Left, a recent Fabian Society Commission on Life Chances and Child Poverty (2006) identifies a wide range of problems and policy solutions to 'narrow the gap'; from the Right, Ferdinand Mount, once a political adviser to Margaret Thatcher in the early 1980s, not only acknowledges that there is a growing gap between rich and poor but also partly accepts the blame for the creation of that gap, or at least he blames the middle classes and the paternalism of political elites who have systematically destroyed working-class institutions and communities over the years (Mount 2004). At the heart of any discussion of inequalities and social exclusion is the issue of social interdependence between the different parts and social groups in society. How those divisions are tackled gives shape and identity to a society and its social and political institutions. While poverty and inequality are being addressed today through a variety of social policies operating through the benefits system, what is more striking is the emphasis in government strategy on social control rather than social steering. The gap is being 'managed' rather than 'narrowed': it is criminal justice rather than social justice policies that are accentuated by the New Labour strategists. This appears to be indicative of a general shift of focus in many Western societies (see Simon; 1997; 2007).

What is required here is a theoretical context for understanding these developments but, more than that, we need a perspective that can connect issues relating to social solidarity and, in particular, social interdependence, to the debates about anti-social behaviour and welfare today. The theory of the *civilising process* developed by Norbert Elias is particularly well suited to illuminate these issues.

The theory of the civilising process

The central theme of Elias' theory of the civilising process is that over time there has been a transference of the control of social behaviour from being a matter of external force to being a matter of internal or self-control that becomes embedded in a *second nature*. Referring to the relationship between the two volumes of Elias' analysis of the civilising process (1978; 1982), or what is referred to as the *two halves* of his thesis, the one dealing with the history of manners and the other dealing with issues surrounding state formation, Mennell (1990) usefully encapsulates the central idea:

> The basic idea, and the link between the two halves, is that there is a connection between the long-term structural development of societies and long-term changes in people's social character or typical personality make-up .... In other words, as the structure of societies becomes more complex, manners, culture and personality also change in a particular and discernible direction, first among elite groups, then gradually more widely. (Mennell 1990: 207)

Elias developed his thesis by integrating three distinct but related levels of analysis: *state formation, sociogenesis* and *psychogenesis* (Table 2.1).

The success of the state in pacifying warring factions within a territory, and the state monopoly of the means of violence, taxation and punishment that followed from that achievement, created the conditions in which social and economic exchanges and relationships could flourish without war and conflict. Increased social interaction between people from diverse social and cultural backgrounds led to increased sensitivity to social conventions and the needs of others,

Table 2.1 The civilising process

State formation	Nation building and pacification of a national territory by a central political authority monopolising the means of violence, taxation and punishment
Sociogenesis	Growth of a complex economic division of labour, democracy and social exchanges leading to transformations in culture and etiquette, and long chains of interdependence
Psychogenesis	Transformation in aggression and predisposition to violence, internalisation of self-control, growth of empathy for others and increased sensitivity to cruelty

which is necessary for the successful lubrication of social encounters. Contrasts between social classes diminished in tastes and behaviour; mutual identification between individuals and peoples developed; there was a decline in cruelty and aggression towards others, especially children and animals; a decline in interpersonal violence as a means of resolving disputes; and a general recognition of social conventions about what was acceptable behaviour and civility. The purging of violence from everyday life also had consequences for the emotional life of individuals. In the absence of fear of attack, people developed internal restraints and exercised foresight through frequent social interaction and the need to anticipate the thoughts, actions and feelings of others. Gradually, the maintenance of social control in everyday life changed from being accomplished by the threat, or exercise, of violence against the individual to becoming internal to the individual. Self-control became automatic and like a second nature. Aggression and violence became, therefore, strictly regulated; indeed, both Weber and Durkheim describe similar processes through the rationalisation of the state bureaucracy and the development and codification of civil and restitutive law.

Others have observed similar processes at work in historical development. Bendix (1952) recognised that people try to act as they think they ought to act and that behaviour is shaped by social environments. The pattern of interactions in developing urban centres required the individual to accommodate to the complexity generated by the social environment. Similarly, Riesman (1969) describes the movements in social character as societies modernise and industrialise. He argues that the need to deal with increasingly varied social and economic conditions in the modern corporation, for example, stimulates change from the inner-directed character typical of early entrepreneurial capitalism into the other direction required of the modern corporate man (see Rodger 2000: 148–55). And, of course, Durkheim's classic analyses, *The Division of Labour in Society* (1984) and *Suicide* (1952), highlight the importance of understanding social bonding for social behaviour and societal reactions to deviance and punishment. Elias is not, therefore, alone in pointing to the significance of changing patterns of interdependence for the development of social order and social behaviour. A number of key concepts illuminate Elias' broader thesis and his unique contribution to this subject.

Functional democratisation and power

At the heart of the civilising process is a concept of power that Elias uses in a distinctive way. The notion of *functional democracy* evolves through the process of denser and longer chains of interdependence. The gradual incorporation of all social classes into markets, polity and community accompanying the development of denser networks of interdependence inexorably leads to the attenuation of status distinctions between superior and inferior social groupings. The lengthening chains of interdependence lead to more people and social categories associating with each other and influencing each other's tastes, behaviour and social mores. Or, as Mennell observes, 'more people are forced more often to pay more and more attention to more other people' (see Mennell 2006: 430). Increasing numbers of diverse groups develop their contribution to the economy, society and culture. As societies have industrialised and urbanised, the sense of interdependence has also grown. De Swaan (1988), for example, has argued that a growing sense of solidarity was stimulated by the threats of poverty and contagion experienced collectively in the rapidly growing urban centres of the nineteenth century, leading to strategies to deal with public health issues, poverty and ignorance. The growth of the welfare state, and strategies of full employment in the second half of the twentieth century, consolidated the sense of social interdependence evolving in industrial societies. The enlargement of citizenship, to include what T. H. Marshall (1965) called 'social citizenship', consolidated rights of access to a range of services and benefits, such as education, social insurance and health care, that gave populations substantive use powers to exercise the rights that they had won and achieved between the late nineteenth and mid-twentieth century. This change brought about a heightened sense of social solidarity, or as Elias describes it, *functional interdependence* indicating an equalisation of power in society between social classes that ultimately diminished the contrasts in behaviour and culture between elite and subordinate groups. The meaning of power implied in Elias' conception of functional democratisation can be distinguished from the more commonly understood meaning of power in structural functionalism.

> Wherever there is a functional interdependence between people, however great the inequality, a balance of power always exists. Power is therefore not considered in a substantive way by Elias, as a thing which some possess while others do not. This would constitute a reification of the concept of power, or even a personification. He sees power as a structural characteristic of all human relationships in which people have become dependent on one another; that is, they have a function for one another. (Fletcher 1997: 56–7)

When Elias uses the term *function*, therefore, he does not use it in the structural functional sense of meeting the needs of an abstract social system. His conceptions of functional democracy and interdependence are particularly well suited to understanding social and economic relationships as 'figurations' or patterns of interactions. And, in post-industrial circumstances where sizeable numbers of people find that their labour market skills have declining utility for a modern economy, it is clear to see how the disconnection from the rhythms of work and consumption resulting from that process can be readily understood in terms of tendencies towards a de-civilising process. Those who are functionally ejected from the economy may also find that the loss of contact and social interaction that accompanies work has consequences for their self-esteem and their sense of belonging, and can also lead to a sense of disempowerment (see Sennett 2003). However, two further concepts developed in Elias' analysis require to be described in order to understand fully the interconnections between sociogenesis and psychogenesis before turning specifically to the issue of de-civilising processes.

Formalisation and informalisation phases

Western societies appear to have gone through different phases in the control of what, in Freudian terms, we might name as repressed emotions. The repression of 'dangerous emotions', which might give vent to violent, sexual and socially unrestrained behaviour, led to the development of explicit social and legal limits strictly regulating impulses as a product of successful state formation processes. Through the civilising process, the impulse to use violence against others and the fear that one might in turn be physically assaulted gave way to feelings of repugnance at violence and the barbarity displayed at public punishments and executions (see Cohen 1985; Garland 1985). In place of unrestrained social behaviour, characteristic of societies with low levels of interdependency, the state not only pacified militaristic violence but also created the social conditions in which protocols governing etiquette could flourish and social mores for eating, defecating, and addressing and interacting with others evolved. Ever more complex social mores evolved to control manners and sexual display. The Victorian era represented the height of what Wouters (2007) calls the *formalisation process,* or the 'disciplinary phase', of the civilising process. Social pressure to reject anything that seemed deviant from dominant social mores and values was embedded in social practice and law and exported globally through colonial conquest. How people should relate to strangers, inferiors and foreigners became inextricably linked to the repression of 'dangerous emotions' (see Wouters 2007; 1990). The formalisation phase seemed to be associated with stable social stratification both within societies and in terms of colonial relationships between societies (Wouters 1990). It has been described as 'harmonious inequality'. A key feature of the formalising phase in the nineteenth century was the imposition of imperial conquest on countries considered to be inferior and literally in need of 'civilisation' in the sense of developing the social, moral and cultural practices considered by the metropolitan power to be superior to indigenous traditions. The projection of labels of inferiority on to marginal and socially excluded groups was also a mechanism for managing 'dangerous emotions' in the metropolitan society: the concomitant of strict social regulation is fear of the shame, embarrassment and ridicule that would follow from a fall from grace. Shame and embarrassment are averted by the constant reminder of one's own superiority over others and the need to avoid being like those labelled as inferior or deviant. In Freudian terms, the superego dominated the ego.

Increasing social and cultural interaction between social groups and countries in the nineteenth century built denser chains of interdependence, which eroded social, cultural and economic differences and stimulated functional democratisation. A feature of that process was, of course, that conflict and resistance were generated as an outgrowth of interdependence because power and status differences became less defensible and the position of elite groups became more unstable and less able to resist pressures for change; the 'harmonious inequality' that had been a feature of British society from the Victorian period through to the end of World War II was challenged politically from below, but the elites in turn came to acknowledge the interdependence of society and the legitimacy of claims for greater equality and social justice. This culminated in the completion of the democratisation of Western societies, and the attainment of citizenship for all within a welfare state, and this led to the informalising phase of the civilising process characterised by an emancipation of emotions and impulses in societies with established high levels of interdependence. This, in turn, influenced global processes of decolonisation, as power imbalances and deference became less of a feature of colonial relations between the First and Third World. There was a rebalancing in the power relationships between the colonists and the colonised (see Wouters 1990).

The emergence of what came to be called the 'permissive society' from the 1960s onwards signalled a clear movement into an informalising phase. Elias recognised that the new permissiveness was not a change that would undermine the civilising process but rather a further stage of development. For example, the greater levels of tolerance of nudity and exposure of the female form in fashion and art are indicative of higher levels of self-control in men than was evident in Victorian times. A process of controlled decontrolling of emotions has been taking place as new frontiers of deviance are being reclassified in the wake of changing sensibilities (see Elias and Dunning 1986: 44; Mennell 1998: 242). This is similar to what was referred to in the introduction as defining deviance down: that process can be understood as being a by-product of the informalising process. Wouters captures the process well.

When, in expanding networks of interdependency, the social and psychic dividing lines are opening up and social groups as well as psychic functions are becoming integrated, the informalising phase in civilising processes breaks through. This phase is characterised by an emancipation of emotions and

27

impulses that had hitherto been repressed, resulting in a more reflexive civilising of self-regulation ... some people, formerly excluded, come to be recognised again as fellow human beings, just as some impulses and emotions which were denied to be generally human, again come to be acknowledged as such – it is a social as well as psychical de-hierarchisation, opening up, or levelling. (Wouters 2005) www.usyd.edu.au/su/social/elias/ confpap/wouters1.html (accessed 15 June 2005)

The notion of a controlled decontrolling of emotions implies that a type of measured gradualism characterises informalisation in societies that can be described as 'at peace with themselves'. Liberation from authoritarian and disciplinary social practices and norms has, in some cases, led to a quest to find excitement and thrills in a society emerging from social hierarchy and 'stuffiness', a theme developed by Elias in his collaboration with Dunning (Elias and Dunning 1986). It might take several generations before personality structure and emotional attitudes change in response to the gradual transformation in social and cultural institutions, such as the modernist movement in art, culture and social engineering evident in interwar European and American society. This may start first among elites, such as the Bloomsbury group, who tested the boundaries of morality of interwar British society in their works and behaviour, but quickly trickles down the social hierarchy to influence a wide range of social classes and social groups. This increasing reflexivity and awareness of emancipation of emotions is what Wouters calls a *third nature*.

Unfortunately, few Western societies in the early twenty-first century can be described in such a comfortable way. The phase that many Western societies now find themselves in is one in which there is a tension between tendencies towards informalisation and contrary movements towards formalisation (see Wouters 1987a; 1987b). While Wouters (2007: 202) has observed that 'social emancipation and integration *demanded* [my emphasis] psychic emancipation and integration', in relation to crime, he has argued that the tension between formalisation and informalisation tendencies has created for many a 'psychic integration conflict' (Wouters 1999). The emancipation of emotions has led to some people becoming more aware that being free from authoritarian controls leaves open to them deviant possibilities that in earlier periods were too risky to enact: sexual emancipation in all its varieties is one area where this is manifest. However, Wouters has also argued that the rising crime rate between 1950 and 1980 can also be explained in this way.

> Particularly in the period of transition, from 1950 until early 1980s, an increasing number of people will have developed a widening gap between the pattern of self-controls that had become socially expected and the pattern that they had individually realised ... many among the socially rising will have felt more liberated from direct and authoritarian controls than burdened by the higher level of demands on self-controls. (Wouters 1999: 427)

The suggestion here is that the process of functional democratisation within the burgeoning welfare state left a residual element within society who experienced that process as a conflict of emotions and that the upsurge in criminality in the period since 1950 can be explained in terms of the conflicts which are part of the emergence of a third nature:

> The overall rise in crimes can be understood from this increase of psychic integration conflicts in developing a 'third nature' personality structure, an increase which in turn resulted from a conflict between social and psychic integration processes. (Wouters 1999: 427)

Wouters (1987) has characterised the movement of informalisation in terms of 'spirals' and 'waves'. He argues that informalisation processes do not develop in a straight line, and that following the informalisation phase of the 1960s and 1970s a countermovement has developed since the 1980s and there is evidence of the reassertion of *formalisation* tendencies. There are other analyses of this phenomenon; Garland's description of the emerging culture of control is clear (Garland 2000; 2001) but so, too, is Simon's observations on *governing through crime* and the displacement of a welfarist agenda in politics by a strategic focus on crime (see Simon 1997; 2007). Certainly, since the neo-liberal upsurge at the end of the 1970s, many Western governments have placed a greater emphasis on tradition, hierarchy and orderly behaviour. In present-day Britain, the 'respect' agenda of the New Labour government is driving social and criminal justice policies that are informed by a view that there is something of a social crisis in behaviour and attitudes; and that view and its underlying assumptions is, of course, the focus of this book. Wouters (1987a) has characterised the key changes in terms of the decline of the *commercial climate* immediately after World War II, culminating in a widespread consensus about the Keynesian welfare state. The outcome of that

29

process was the ascendancy of what he calls a *government climate* that justified state coordination of the process of functional democratisation and the consolidation of rights and social justice through the creation of the welfare state. However, that period of looking to government has now given way to a dominant commercial climate in which the emphasis is placed on social, economic and political discipline and that has led to a process of governing through crime (Simon 2007) and tendencies to criminalise social policy in the service of that objective. However, we must acknowledge, as Wouters does, that residues of past developments once established are not easily erased. Cultural, attitudinal and behavioural aspects of the informalisation phase remain in tension with those forces in society attempting to return to social relationships expressing more formality and deference. It is inconceivable that strict hierarchical relationships between men and women, parents and children, and employers and employees could return to the position they were in during the interwar years. The 'harmonious inequality' that characterised social class, gender and race relations in the 1940s and 1950s would not be tolerated in present-day society. Behaviour patterns and social attitudes developed during periods of informalisation cannot easily be quelled by strategies of coercive social control, and new claims for political recognition once won are rarely given up.

The sociological and policy issue is that today the tension between formalisation and informalisation is taking place in a context in which functional democratisation has stalled for many sections of the community. It is at this point that the conditions are prepared for the onset of a de-civilising process.

De-civilisation and the welfare retrenchment

It is possible that the longer chains of interdependency that come with the globalisation process can lead to a greater sense of freedom from social constraint and informalisation for the individual who is able to break free from what Durkheim called the repressions of 'mechanical forms of solidarity' characteristic of small, closely knit communities and 'knowing one's place'. But where those chains of interdependence are broken, and smaller communities are placed in a situation of structured social, economic and spatial isolation from the centres of economic, cultural and consumer activity, then the normative influence of the wider society and global system will also be broken. It is clear that the informalisation phase of the civilising process, viewed in the context of globalisation, appears to be having precisely this dual impact. To formulate the problem in Durkheimian language, the civilising process may be taking 'abnormal forms' unpredicted and undeveloped by Elias. The possibility of the civilising process being halted or regressing was partly acknowledged by Elias, but it has been left to others to explore the tendencies towards de-civilisation in an explicit way (see Mennell 1990; Fletcher 1995; 1997). Elias observed that the processes maintaining security and order in society can be fragile.

> The armour of civilised conduct would crumble rapidly if, through a change in society, the degree of insecurity that existed earlier were to break in upon us again, and if danger became incalculable as it once was. Corresponding fears would soon burst the limits set for them today. (Elias 2000: 531–2)

In an attempt to take Elias' insights forward and develop a theory of de-civilising processes, Fletcher (1997) has reversed the process in order to provide a provisional view of what the de-civilising process may be.

> I would like to focus on three main criteria of decivilisation which are logically implied by Elias's criteria of the civilising process: one would be a shift in the balance between constraints by others and self-restraint in favour of constraints by others; another would be the development of a social standard of behaviour and feeling which generates the emergence of a less even, all-round, stable and differentiated pattern of self-restraint; and third, we would expect a contraction in the scope of mutual identification between constituent groups and individuals. (Fletcher 1997: 83)

The issue today is one of the bifurcation of Western societies into mainstream sectors connected with work, the consumer society and the global network, and their relationship to the marginalised communities within their territories that are left outside and disconnected from the arteries that facilitate economic, cultural and interactive nourishment. As interdependence weakens between core and marginal communities, movement towards de-civilisation is facilitated. Factors contributing to this change of direction in the civilising process can be identified in a number of developments in present-day society. A key factor is the gradual removal of the social safety net support provided by a welfare system geared to protect populations from the ebb and flow of economic forces; this was the original justification for the creation of the welfare state. As inequalities resulting from structural unemployment and globalisation take spatial forms, sometimes leading to hyper-ghettoisation (see Wancquant 1997; 2001), social exclusion and underclass formation have resulted in the creation of a social stratum that is without functional utility for the economy. The restructuring of welfare systems since the 1980s has had consequences for how such problems have been tackled. There has been an explicit shift away from universalist principles in welfare and a more explicit focus on means testing and the management of incentives to work. Today, social citizenship as ascribed rights of access to benefits and services is denigrated as encouraging a 'something for nothing society' and is being replaced by a conception of citizenship more in keeping with the consumer society; that is, citizenship that is achieved by work and the acceptance of the obligations of civic activeness. In circumstances where the social state is in decline, social solidarity in society as a whole weakens.

Other developments that are implicated in the de-civilising process can be listed: decline in the social interaction between mainstream employment-based communities integrated into the consumer society and those living at the margins of society in peripheral housing estates and no-go, inner-city areas; and decline in mutual identification, increased labelling, and anticipatory reaction to people based on residence and style. Widespread use and glorification of violence as a means of maintaining economic position in criminal activities and interpersonal relationships are becoming more noticeable, and contrasts in appearance, attitudes and behaviour between integrated and marginal social groups may be increasing, as there appears to be a general rejection of social conventions regarding behaviour and civility by those labelled variously as 'the underclass', 'chavs', 'neds' and 'NEETS'. I have more to say about these identities in the following chapter.

The emergence of the hyperghetto

One of the most interesting applications of Elias' perspective in the American context can be found in the work of Loïc Wancquant (see Wancquant 1997). His broader analysis of poverty and the black ghetto also points to a particularly American slant on the notion of the criminalising of social policy, or as Wancquant prefers to name it, 'the penalisation of poverty' (see Wancquant and Wilson 1989; Wancquant 2000; 2001; 2005).

Wancquant has been drawn to Elias' work in order to explain the noticeable shift in the socio-economic character of the ghetto in the major cities forming America's declining industrial manufacturing base, the 'Rust Belt' areas, which experienced a major downturn in jobs and global market position through the 1980s and 1990s (Wancquant and Wilson 1989; Wilson 1989). The particular change identified by Wancquant was the shift from what he calls the *communal ghetto* to the *hyperghetto* on the back of industrial decline and federal and local state retrenchment. The communal ghetto was a natural outgrowth of a social and political reaction by blacks to the hostility of white society and white institutions. It represented a solidaristic resistance to the racism of early twentieth-century America by the creation of a black social world. While spatially concentrated in the main northern cities, the communal ghetto had a full complement of black social classes, a heightened racial consciousness, an extensive division of labour, and, importantly, broadly based institutions and agencies that were able to articulate the voice of the ghetto, what Habermas might have recognised as a black public sphere that enabled the formulation and presentation of black opinion (Habermas 1979). Churches, voluntary organisations and community agencies established a conduit for the recognition of common interests and common identity. While the ghetto was the home of what constituted a reserve army of labour for the industrial manufacturing sector, employment was supplemented by black enterprises that were owned by a black entrepreneurial middle class. However, the impact of industrial decline in the manufacturing sector throughout the 1980s and 1990s, which historically provided employment and economic vitality to the ghetto, led to a residualisation effect as the credentialed and skilled black middle classes moved out of the ghetto and integrated into the suburban parts of the major cities. Wancquant observed the coming together of colour segregation and 'class bifurcation': the extended division of labour characteristic of the communal ghetto withered, and in place of a social structure containing a complete set of social classes, there remained only the poor, ill-educated and unemployed. The declining community-wide institutions, such as lodges, the black press and churches, were supplanted by state bureaucracies and state institutions primarily orientated towards managing incentives to work, as the social state declined, with criminal justice surveillance for those who were unreceptive to the disciplinary message emanating from the federal government.

> For the hyperghetto serves not as a reservoir of disposable industrial labor but as the mere dumping ground for supernumerary categories for which the surrounding society has no economic or political use. And it is suffused with systemic economic, social and physical insecurity due to the mutually reinforcing erosion of the wage-labor market and state support. Thus whereas the ghetto in its classical form acted partly as a protective shield against brutal racial exclusion, the hyperghetto has lost its positive role of collective buffer, making it a deadly machinery for naked social regulation. (Wancquant 1997: 342)

The link with Elias' thesis on the civilising process is made by Wancquant through his argument that the hyperghetto is the result of three master processes that together form a progression towards de-civilisation. First, at the heart of these changes is a process of *de-pacification* of ghetto life, as violence and aggression return to the streets as the mechanism commonly used to ensure survival and personal security. There has also been evidence of a process of social de-differentiation taking place as the organisational fabric of the hyperghetto withers: the middle-class blacks have deserted the ghetto for better employment and amenities elsewhere, leaving behind a population who are uniformly dispossessed of resources and hope. Second, there is evidence of a process of *de-proletarianisation* of those residents who remain. The unemployment following large-scale de-industrialisation has led to a decline in the political, class and organisational consciousness that had been a feature of the communal ghetto and its replacement by naked survivalism in a disorganised social and built environment scarred by degraded public housing. As the financial underbelly for local businesses and services disappears, there followed the abandonment of the inner cities by commercial and civic institutions and the shrinking of social networks connecting the ghetto to the wider city. The absolute decline of a sense of social interdependence and solidarity is the ultimate consequence. The third process that has become evident is *economic informalisation*, as irregular, and often highly illegal, markets have come to dominate economic activity. The hyperghetto is home to an unregulated economy in which drugs are the currency that lubricates economic exchanges and casual employment. The drugs trade in turn generates an extensive range of illegal activities and violence to maintain its buoyancy. At the heart of this analysis is a conviction that the restructuring of the post-Fordist economy, combined with both federal and local government retrenchment, has led to a 'thinning of the ghetto's organisational ecology'. The shock waves created by massive disinvestment by both the state and capital have created the conditions for the onset of a de-civilising process.

In these circumstances, classical social disorganisation theory, originally developed by Shaw and McKay in 1920s Chicago to account for crime and delinquency, is again relevant but in ways that articulate well with Elias' focus on the importance of networks of interdependency for the maintenance of the civilising process (see Shaw and McKay 1969). Bursik and Grasmick (1993), for example, have offered an extremely suggestive analysis of social disorganisation theory that connects well with the analysis of fragmenting communities and hyperghettoisation, and updates its underlying assumptions. Shaw and McKay had assumed that poor urban areas were merely 'zones of transition' containing the struggles and deviance of immigrants to America until they had carved out the skills, motivation and value orientations to grasp whatever opportunities the 'American Dream' offered them. In this version of the theory, social disorganisation is presented as a conflictual, but merely cyclical, stage in a process that eventually allows people and social groups first to assimilate into the economic structure and then move on to better residential areas. Anti-social behaviour and criminality were caused indirectly by the weak social and organisational structures in the city, and deviance was not, therefore, treated as a product of particular 'kinds of people'. However, today, failure of the education and training system and poor labour market opportunities have led to a concentration of disadvantage and poverty in the ghetto, and in many other poor communities throughout Europe too. The social and economic dynamism provided by the symbiotic struggles between ethnically and culturally diverse groups to 'get on', described by Shaw and McKay in early twentieth-century Chicago, no longer exist in the early twenty-first century. Many of the poorest areas in our large cities today are often ethnically and culturally homogeneous and devoid of institutional structures connecting them to the wider networks of mainstream society. Residential mobility for the poorest people in both contemporary America and Europe has ceased, and the ghetto is more like a holding pound for those unable to escape from the drudgery of their poor work to the riches of the consumer society beyond its boundaries. These processes are reinforced by welfare state retrenchment. Bursik and Grasmick (1993) argue in a way that reinforces the analysis offered by Wancquant:

We feel that the greatest shortcoming of the traditional social disorganisation model has been the failure to consider the relational networks that pertain to this public sphere of control ... it is very difficult to significantly affect the nature of neighbourhood life solely through indigenous neighbourhood processes .... Therefore, we would argue that the effect of economic deprivation on crime and delinquency is, in fact, an indirect one, mediated by the capacity of a neighbourhood to solicit human and economic resources from external institutional actors. (Bursik and Grasmick 1993: 279)

Further support for this view can be found in the empirical data offered by Sampson and Groves (1989) of British communities. They suggest that the social disorganisation paradigm is relevant when combined with the insights of social-network theory. They observed, 'Our empirical analysis established that communities characterised by sparse friendship networks, unsupervised teenage peer groups, and low organisational participation had disproportionately high rates of crime and delinquency' (Sampson and Groves 1989: 799). It is the weakening connectivity between core and marginal communities that is destroying the networks of interdependency, making them shorter and sparser. It is in these circumstances that anti-social behaviour, criminality and de-civilising processes flourish.

Drawing on Elias' perspective in an analysis of welfare state retrenchment, Ferge (1999) has reached similar conclusions. She, too, points to the factors contributing to increasing poverty and relative deprivation in the affluent societies and to 'tendencies of social disintegration, marginalisation or exclusion, and sometimes the appearance of an "underclass" ' (Ferge 1999: 234). She also considers the consequences that might follow if sections of Western society are left unsupported by a welfare state. If the slum and ghetto areas of the large cities and peripheral housing estates are allowed to remain outside society, the conditions for a de-civilising process will be created. In asking the question, what if the state fades away? She answers in the following way:

The consequences of the waning away of elements of civilisation in some parts of society are easy to think through (logically, if not morally). If conditions change so as to make scarce the knife and fork, inside toilet, hot water, and then water itself ... as well as privacy, then habits tied to them have to change. All these changes, including the lowering of the level of shame and the weakening of many other self-restraints set in with tragic rapidity in the case of the homeless ... the non-poor become involved too. If the institutions of social security in general are weakening, the habits developed in relation to money, to time, to space, to self, and to others are all jeopardised. (Ferge, 1999: 235)

These observations may seem extreme but their underlying reasoning is not. People adapt to their social environment and the distribution rules that are dominant in the society in which they live. If a society fails to address social and cultural divisions and social polarisation resulting from unforgiving economic forces, Elias' perspective suggests that we must expect psychological as well as social adjustment to those social conditions. Those adjustments will have behavioural and attitudinal consequences for the wider social order. However, those changes in attitude are not made exclusively by those at the bottom of the social hierarchy.

Attitudes, emotions and post-emotionalism

The attitudes and emotional responses of the rich and comfortable to the problems of the ghetto and to the anti-social behavioural traits displayed by those outside mainstream society are a neglected feature of the theory of de-civilising processes. By understanding all forms of behavioural deviance as a product of individual pathology, whether the smallest incivility or the most uncaring form of criminality, those doing well from the system can avoid addressing redistributive and social justice issues. The relationship between the civilising process and the formation of such attitudes is crucial to understanding the contemporary reaction to incivility.

A major problem today is that attitudes supportive of the institution of the welfare state, let alone to areas of social policy related to social disadvantage and deviance, may be weakening. The assumption of interdependence, upon which any form of social solidarity depends, is now problematic. In the midst of social and economic conditions that exacerbate social polarisation and reaffirm social exclusion for increasing numbers of fellow citizens, the routine interactions between different social groups that increase mutual knowledge and stimulate mutual empathy are decreasing. It is the phenomenon of functional democratisation that has begun to weaken, leading to talk about the possibility of a de-civilising tendency in contemporary welfare societies (see Ferge 1999; Fletcher 1995; Mennell 1992). One manifestation of de-civilising tendencies can be found in the withdrawal of support by the middle classes for liberal criminal justice policies in favour of more coercive strategies. While Garland (2001) has presented this phenomenon in terms of the adjustment of the middle classes to the fact that crime is now a 'normal social fact', and the middle-class conviction that nothing works in criminal justice, I would suggest that it is also part of a broader attitudinal malaise affecting ways of thinking about caring and collective obligations in post-industrial societies. I will return to this theme in Chapter 4. A by-product of the civilising process is the detachment of ordinary people from involvement in and concern for matters that have become bureaucratised and assigned to professional experts, especially those aspects of life that come to be seen as unpleasant. Pratt (2005) has made precisely this point in relation to the civilising and privatisation of punishment: the spectacle of public humiliations, and the carnivals of punishment surrounding public executions common prior to the early nineteenth century, gradually came to be perceived as an affront to the sensitivities of the public and led to the creation of the prison system which removed punishment from the public sphere. A consequence of these developments may be that civilised emotions may, under some social conditions, mutate into *post-emotionalism*. While most people may claim to be 'sympathetic' to those who suffer, there may also be a tendency today for people to compartmentalise their emotions intellectually when an 'expert' or a designated institution is known to be coping with the problems created by that suffering. It absolves the individual of having to care. For example, public attitudes to poverty and social welfare are largely grounded in the assumption that social need is being met by a welfare system policed by a professional bureaucracy. Support for the welfare state today is no longer an altruistic commitment to fellow citizens but, more likely, is based on the principle of 'mutual assurance', in which people's attitudes to welfare amount to a pragmatic acceptance that they may require support at some time in the future. However, support extends only to those areas of welfare provision that can be justified by the principle of 'mutual assurance' such as the health service and state pensions (Rodger 2003). However, in areas of public policy where reliance on the 'experts' has broken down, or the state is perceived as being ineffective, as in the field of criminal justice, attitudes can become emptied of pragmatism, and intellectual detachment can effectively become unconcern for those deemed to be deviant. The tendency for detachment by publics creates the conditions for a post-emotional society, and that, in turn, may be the foundation for the incubation of attitudes that can reinforce tendencies toward de-civilisation. This theme requires a little further development.

I am suggesting that part of the movement back into a formalisation phase of the civilising process is evident in the adoption of more illiberal attitudes by the middle classes to anti-social behaviour and criminality. The retreat from support for collective policy solutions to social problems is consistent with the individualising effects of market society. And where it is believed that authority no longer inheres in expertise, especially in the policing and criminal justice domain, support for tougher criminal justice policies has flourished together with solutions sought in privatisation and anti-welfarism. The empathy felt by the middle classes in particular for those doing less well from the economic system has attenuated because of the shortening chains of interdependence: interaction between the affluent and poor strata of society is less frequent and is often based on shallow, emotionally detached service provision. Jock Young (2007) is correct to highlight the open spatial boundaries which are a feature of postmodern society; they allow the residents of the ghetto and the poor neighbourhoods to find service jobs in the better parts of the city and in the homes of the middle classes as cleaners, gardeners and child carers. However, when he describes these work arrangements in terms of the 'feudalisation of service work', he gets to the heart of the post-emotionalism which shapes thinking and acting in many parts of present-day society. The middle-class employers of maids and cleaners (because Young acknowledges that the males are less mobile than the female residents of the poor neighbourhoods) may retain an intellectual appreciation of the impact that poverty and disadvantage have on their workers, but that understanding is enclosed within a patronising framework of moral individualism in which the poor are to be grateful for a menial service job and chastised for their demeanour and attitudes: they are assumed to be poor because they do not work hard enough and are criminal because they are intrinsically bad people. The most apt label for this is post-emotionalism because of the combination of apparent 'niceness' and 'toughness'. Post-emotionalism represents the tendency for feelings to be intellectualised rather than sincerely felt; the tendency for social interaction in contemporary Western societies to be lubricated by a false display of 'niceness'; the tendency to be oversensitive to occasions and circumstances where this display of 'niceness' is not evident or reciprocated, especially from the servant class; and by the manipulation of 'emotions' in the creation of *synthetic traditions* for both social, cultural and political objectives. Post-emotionalism is not so much the absence of feelings as the manipulation and management of feelings:

> Post-emotionalism is a system designed to avoid emotional disorder; to prevent loose ends in emotional exchanges; to civilise 'wild' arenas of emotional life; and ... to order the emotions so that the social world hums smoothly as a well-maintained machine. What Marcuse called the happy consciousness must be maintained at all costs. Psychiatric patients are therefore given 'medications' that suppress their irksome and very emotional symptoms. Political correctness ensures that nothing unpredictable happens emotionally in a social interaction. (Mestrovic 1997: 150)

It is not a psychic state that is being described here. Post-emotionalism is the end product of a historical process in which authentic feeling has been manipulated and distorted in order to make the social solidarity of complex societies possible. Mestrovic provides an alternative interpretation of Elias' analysis of the civilising process that seems particularly germane to contemporary Western societies. He observes that beneath the orderly social relations and self-restraint characteristic of the civilising process lies an inward indifference to the feelings and pain of fellow citizens (Mestrovic 1997: 92–4):

> The cool contemplation of other people's suffering while one exhibits polished manners in a society that is deemed civil is only a shade less immoral than the direct infliction of suffering. Thus, civilisation, as it is often practiced today, is really manufactured, inauthentic civilisation. (Mestrovic 1997: 94)

It is the tendency to social polarisation and the decline of functional interdependency between some parts of the social structure in Western societies that are exacerbating this movement into the post-emotional society. It is both a cultural and structural feature of Western societies. The *Disneyisation of society* and the *MacDonaldisation of society* are just two of the terms used to describe the cultural effects of post-emotionalism, as feelings have been mechanised in a culture of false 'niceness' in many areas of social, leisure and economic activity (see Bryman 1999; Ritzer 1992). The next chapter will address the cultural dimension of this issue. Here I will concentrate on the political and structural aspects.

Perhaps inadvertently, but often deliberately, policymakers have encouraged the view that those unable to participate fully in the post-industrial economy and the consumer society do so through their own indolence and unwillingness. As a consequence, governments in all Organisation for Economic Cooperation and Development (OECD) countries have steered social attitudes and public opinion towards a negative view of the welfare state, including the past liberalism of the criminal justice system, for a variety of political and economic objectives (see Bonoli, George and Taylor-Gooby 2000). What effectively has happened is that, cumulatively, the *emotion rules* governing the way the disadvantaged and welfare dependent are perceived by those in employment have been changing. The social guidelines that direct how we want to and should feel about poverty and social need have been subjected to political and social manipulation. Hochschild's classic work on 'emotion work' and *feeling rules* can aid our understanding here (see Hochschild 1979; 1983). She describes feeling rules as embedded 'framing rules' which provide an interpretative framework to assist the social actor to make sense of a given situation. Feeling rules have rights and duties attached to them: they specify the extent, direction and duration of a feeling. How we should feel about redistributive policies, for example, has been made clear by all governments since the late 1970s: they are said to stifle enterprise and contribute to indolence. This message has, of course, been repeated persistently in political debate and in media discussion, and reinforced by international opinions articulating the verities of globalisation for the past 25 years. And, of course, how we should regard anti-social teenagers roaming the streets of our council estates and inner-city ghettos has been subject to systematic instruction from politicians and media since the passing of the Crime and Disorder Act in 1998. However, there are often conflicts surrounding emotions and feeling rules because, like all rules, they can be obeyed or violated. Feeling rules are often in conflict with lived experience. What people want to feel may conflict with what they *should* feel and what they *try* to feel. We are frequently confronted with what constitutes a contradictory consciousness because what we feel may be at odds with social convention and what political discourses are guiding us towards.

Social steering by governments works on and shapes the directional flow of this contradictory or split consciousness. It is this manipulation that is generating post-emotional attitudes. It does this by providing us with what C. Wright Mills (1967) called a 'vocabulary of motive': ideas, concepts and linguistic devices that assist the social actor to neutralise the moral bind of living with but failing to act on human suffering and social need. If poverty can be presented in terms of behavioural frailty rather than policy failure or injustices in the reward structure of society; if the imperative of economic growth over social policy goals relating to social need can be accepted unquestioningly; if the idea of freedom can be associated with markets, consumerism and choice; and, significantly, if anti-social behaviour can be portrayed as a manifestation of dysfunctional families and socio-pathological youths rather than a reaction to impoverished material circumstances, then the conditions for stimulating an amoral attitude in the public will be created and the post-emotional attachment to social problems will ensue (see Galbraith 1992).

The 'fading of the state' in the field of welfare means that institutional solidarity is also weakening. While the European welfare systems are displaying more resilience in the face of cutbacks than the American world of welfare retrenchment analysed by Wancquant, the underlying economic and social analysis is fairly clear for both sides of the Atlantic. As globalising tendencies accelerate the movement into post-Fordist and post-industrial conditions for the affluent Western societies, the expectations of collective support in times of need, which were taken for granted until the 1980s, are now receding. In the absence of a strong welfare state pursuing social and industrial policies that promote reciprocal social and economic dependence between all social classes, we may be moving into conditions in which some groups variously described as the 'underclass', or the socially excluded, are increasingly viewed as being responsible for their own plight and emotionally consigned to the periphery of conscience, undeserving of recognition because they are deemed to be a criminogenic threat in an otherwise peaceful world. In this context, pockets of violence and criminality in peripheral housing estates and inner-city ghettos may reflect a growing sense of insecurity by those exposed to the ebbs and flows of a global marketplace without the support of a welfare state or a search for access to material resources denied by an exclusionary social and economic system. However, violence and incivility can also be an expression of social and interactive habits shaped by residential immobility; that is, not having to negotiate the complexities of the world of work while living in a social environment without incentives to develop a sense of possibilities for the future; and not developing mutual empathy for people who remain remote and who are only encountered either as low-paying employers or people to rob. When behaviour and attitudes are not tempered by social conventions, the process of de-civilising is set in train. These entrenched social divisions may be contributing to a post-emotional society in which knowledge of the plight of those at the bottom of the social hierarchy is gained from a distance through the mass media rather than through routine daily interaction. Knowledge of the social conditions and social needs of the most disadvantaged in our society is, consequently, rendered abstract. Sympathy, if felt at all, is manifested intellectually rather than with sincerity or empathy. And, increasingly, understanding of social need is gained by looking through a behaviourist rather than structural lens.

De-civilising tendencies in penal policy

It is unsurprising that criminal justice policy has taken a disciplinary turn in most Western societies when the dominant political messages of our time reinforce post-emotional attitudes. In a political and cultural climate in which individuals are being encouraged to 'enterprise their lives' (see Rose 1996), and social causal models of deviance have been replaced by a 'responsibilisation strategy', punitive approaches to incivility and criminality are re-establishing themselves. Western governments appear to be expressing this attitude by the policy choices they make, specifically by favouring coercive criminal justice strategies that target behavioural excesses rather than the social arrangements framing the deviance. Public attitudes may have tired of explanations of deviance that stress social causality, but there is evidence that the pendulum has swung to the opposite extreme: in 'understanding a little less and condemning a little more', to use John Major's infamous phrase, present-day governments often appear to be led by opinion formers who have lost interest in understanding altogether.

The response to the social problems created by economic restructuring and welfare state retrenchment has been to develop policies that, in the words of Wancquant (2001), amount to the 'penalisation of poverty', as the shrinking social state has been balanced by the expansion of the penal state. As prison populations rise together with a renewed stress on coercive criminal justice policies, it would seem to confirm that there is a movement back to a formalisation phase in the civilising process. Imprisonment is now being seen as the pre-eminent means to deal with the collapse of social discipline.

While the prison population in the USA rises inexorably to near 2 million, incarcerating 1 in 10 black men (the comparable rate for white men is 1 in 128) (Wancquant 2001), the prison population in the UK is also rising relentlessly and is projected to rise for the foreseeable future. The total prison population of England and Wales in February 2008 was over 82,000 with the network as a whole capable of incarcerating only 79,900 without the extensive use of police cells and court cells, and hurriedly created prison-release policies (see Addley and Travis 2006). If the Scottish prison system is added, then, as of February 2008, an additional average daily population of 8,024 brings the prison population of the UK to 90,000. Expressed as the numbers in prison per 100,000, a comparison can be made with other countries. The USA has a rate of about 686 per 100,000 and the UK a rate of 139 per 100,000 and rising, the highest in Europe (Home Office 2003). Most north-Western European countries have rates that are in two figures, ranging from the Scandinavian countries with rates between the high 50s and 60s per 100,000 to France at 85, Germany at 96, and Italy at 95 per 100,000 (Home Office 2003). It is clear, therefore, that, while the *penalisation of poverty* is not exclusively a US phenomenon, there does appear to be a correlation between prison rates and the pursuit of particular economic and welfare strategies. This is noticeable when comparing the UK with the Scandinavian countries. The close relationship in policy ideas between the USA and the UK (see Jones and Newburn 2007), and the pursuit of market economics, have meant that in European terms the UK has a distinctly divergent profile. The influence of the US strategy for crime control with respect to 'prison works' and 'zero tolerance' has been discernibly more effective in the UK than elsewhere in Europe, although other European governments may be warming to its soporific message.

In seeking an explanation for the global expansion of US ideas on penal policy, Wancquant directs attention to the worldwide diffusion of the penal model favoured by partisan US intellectuals of the centre Right. First, in an attempt to influence opinion throughout the Western world and win a consensus on the need for tougher and more coercive responses to incivility and criminality, there has been the showcasing of prime US case studies as evidence of 'what works' to opinion formers in political and policy circles. For example, the forging of links with European think tanks has had as a primary objective to create an 'acclimation chamber' preparing the way for strong criminal justice and penal strategies in Europe that will mirror the US approach. There has been an effort to encourage academic and political receptiveness to the US warnings that only a tough penal response will work (see Bowling 1999). In the UK, the most relevant think tank involved in this project has been the Institute of Economic Affairs, and its recent incarnation, Civitas. Both organisations have been influential in sponsoring the 'prison works' and 'zero tolerance' approaches to deviance (see Bratton and Dennis 1997; Murray 1997). These policy strategies are grounded in a rejection of social causal models of poverty and deviance, and the conceptualisation of social solidarity in terms of citizen value orientations and rational choice theories of behaviour; behavioural excesses are explained as the result of a profligate welfare system, which deviants relate to strategically to avoid gainful employment and maximise their opportunities for hedonism and criminality. They advocate tough, law and order policies combined with a withdrawal of welfare benefits to force behavioural change (see Rodger 2006) despite evidence that this coercive strategy is not working particularly well. Indeed, there appear to be indications that crime reduction in New York in the 1990s, the prime example for showcasing, was due less to 'zero tolerance' approaches to policing and more to 'the combined effect of preventive work among local communities and a rejection of crack cocaine and guns by a new generation of young people' (Bowling (1999: 551). 'Zero tolerance' acted on an already falling crime rate. The failure to acknowledge this by both governments and policy designers continues to legitimise the pursuit of hard policing strategies in ghetto areas that may be contributing to the conditions for de-civilisation by marking out whole areas and communities for labelling and marginality (see Damer 1976). There was an acknowledgement by the British government that the processes of hyperghettoisation described by Wancquant may apply to many European countries Ruth Kelly, then minister with responsibility for communities in England, launched the Commission on Integration and Cohesion on 24 August 2006, and signalled that there is now a real concern within government that British society is fragmenting and that many social divisions are overlain with ethnic and cultural differences that may be creating hyperghettos in large British cities. Nevertheless, the pursuit of policies that echo the hard-line US strategy continue, with attention focusing on an expanded role of the prison system for the foreseeable future.

The de-civilisation of modern punishment

The master shifts in punishment closely parallel the civilising process as described by Elias. There has been a movement away from public and spectacular physical punishment to the bureaucratisation and institutionalising of punishment in the modern prison system. As Cohen (1985) and Garland (1985) have shown, the history of penality has been to focus less on causing physical harm to the deviant and increasingly emphasise the need to re-educate and rehabilitate. However, Vaughan (2000) rightly points to the 'the Janus-face of modern punishment'. Violence was removed from public view by the creation of the prison, but violence and barbarity were not entirely removed from the prison system. However, in recent years, the principle of 'less eligibility' appears to have returned to discussions of penal policy: there has been a widespread hostility to prison regimes that appear to reward deviance with comforts and facilities not enjoyed by the poor, law-abiding citizen paying taxes. The public more generally prefers the idea of the prison as an unpleasant place where the Victorian principles of 'hard bed, hard work and hard fare' should prevail. The clamour to imprison and incapacitate rather than rehabilitate the deviant is by far the predominant attitude today. These attitudes are affecting the policy choices of governments. For example, Pratt (1998) has pointed to changes in penal culture in recent years that are leading to the reintroduction of modes of punishment thought to have been abandoned. Together with the return of chain gangs in the USA, and the continuing popularity of 'boot camp' regimes and 'three strikes and your out' laws, the call for a renewed prison-building programme in Britain in 2008 to complement the tough, law and order policies, such as the anti-social behaviour legislation, suggests that a de-civilising process is a strong current in contemporary criminal justice strategies.

Concluding observations

This chapter has suggested that the theory of the civilising process, and in particular the theoretical strands of that theory focusing on functional democratisation and de-civilisation, are key perspectives through which to view the present-day problems of incivility and criminality. What is particularly valuable about Elias' work is its attempt to link state processes to social and psychic integration levels. I have argued that the process of informalisation that accompanied functional democratisation is consistent with a broad range of theory, from Durkheim through to the work of David Riesman and Stefan Mestrovic, that has attempted to relate issues of social solidarity to attitudes and emotions.

Key questions relate to what public opinion is reacting to and what the informalisation phases of the civilising process have created. The next chapter attempts to answer these broad questions by examining the cultural features of incivility, or what has been disparagingly referred to as either the 'underclass' or 'chav' culture.

Chapter 3

Disorderly behaviour and underclass culture: the emergence of the 'chav' and 'NEET' generation

Criminal justice policies and social policies more generally have become fixated in recent years with problem populations who are visible as much for their style and posturing as for their actions. They have been identified in a pejorative sense as 'the underclass'; in a patronising sense, as 'the socially excluded'; and, more popularly, especially when the labelling concentrates on young people, as 'chavs', 'neds' and, more generally, the 'NEET' generation (*not* in *e*ducation, *e*mployment or *t*raining). This chapter will concentrate on the social and cultural underpinnings of the lifestyles and behaviour of those groups considered to be problematic in British society today. The next chapter will examine the political and policy response to them, especially relating to their perceived deviance.

The creation of the 'NEET' generation

As with all forms of deviance management, it is important to construct the problematic identity of those being targeted for policy intervention. The acronym *NEET* derives from precisely this kind of effort. It represents the formal attempt by the Department for Education and Skills and the Scottish government (under New Labour stewardship) to identify, with some precision, the scale of a problem considered in policy terms to be worrying. Young people between the ages of 16 and 18 who have left formal education without qualifications often face difficulties in acquiring fulfilling and well-paid jobs, leaving them vulnerable to boredom and perhaps attraction to anti-social activities. This group is currently estimated to be around 200,000 in any given year, the majority being young males, and seems to be stable at around about 10 per cent of the school-leaving cohort each year. Attempts to intervene with this group to effect positive change in their employability through initiatives such as the Department of Work and Pensions Jobcentre Plus, or through Connexions Partnerships, have at best been moderate. If a wider count of this problem population is used, and those up to the age of 24 are included, it is estimated that the numbers classified as NEET rise to approximately 1.1 million and growing (Winnett 2005). A Scottish study of school leavers in 2003 found that 10 per cent of males and 9 per cent of females were classified as NEET (Biggart *et al.* 2004). However, it must be stressed that formally many young people classified as being NEET within that study were actively seeking employment and training, at least initially on leaving school. Some had reasons, such as involvement in voluntary work, caring for a disabled parent, and, in the case of some young women, caring for children, which prevented them from working. It is wrong to assume, therefore, that NEET status necessarily means involvement in criminality and anti-social behaviour, and it is wrong also to assume that the problems surrounding this category of young person are attitudinal and related to under-socialisation. However, it is clear that the two main drivers of policy aimed at NEETs are concerns about the cost to the taxpayer of maintaining unproductive people on benefits and concerns about their potential anti-social behaviour given the strong statistical correlation between NEET status and involvement in criminal behaviour. Winnett (2005), for example, provides a list of 'NEET facts', some of which point to potential social problems arising from this group: NEETs are 22 times more likely to give birth under 18; 70 per cent of NEETs have used drugs compared with 60 per cent of non-NEETs; twice as many NEETs are offenders as non-NEETS, and they are 20 times more likely to commit a crime than non-NEETs; and the estimated cost to the taxpayer of maintaining a NEET for a lifetime is about £100,000, the worst cases trebling that figure.

The most recent governmental response to the NEET issue was announced in November 2007 and is as clear an example of the criminalising tendencies in social policy as can be found. The school-leaving age is to be raised to 18 in England and Wales to address the NEET issue. The SNP First Minister, Alex Salmond, has stated that the Scottish government will not introduce a similar change in Scotland. In England, a 'carrot and stick approach' will be adopted – financial assistance to stay in education or training will be given to 16- and 17-year-olds who might otherwise drift into becoming a NEET statistic. However, young people who refuse to stay on at school, or take up a training opportunity, will be served with an 'attendance order' (the educational ASBO). A breach of an 'attendance order' will be a criminal offence leading to a £50 on-the-spot fine or a £200 fine in court.

There are complexities involved in this issue which are often overlooked by educationists and politicians. In a North American context, Stearns and Glennie (2006) found that there was great variation in the reasons why young people drop out of school, but those who were 16 or younger tended to leave school for disciplinary reasons and were, therefore, predisposed to anti-social behaviour when free from the constraints of formal education. Older students tended to drop out when employment opportunities arose, did not experience the hiatus between school pupil status and young adulthood to the same extent, and were therefore less likely to engage in behaviour considered anti-social. Drapela (2006) found that school problems were strongly associated with 'post-dropout drug use'. And research by Roche et al. (2006) indicates that young males of 19 or 20 who either were not in school or were experiencing academic and disciplinary problems in school were 'at increased risk of engaging in adolescent aggressive behaviour'. NEET is a broad classification and applying it in a clumsy and undifferentiated way to young people out of education and work may lead to unfair stigmatisation.

The social background of NEETs points to a strong correlation between disadvantage, being a school dropout and deviance. A Department for Education and Skills statistical bulletin published in May 2000 (DfES 2000) noted that living in council rented housing, having parents in manual occupations, and having neither parent in full-time work all increased the likelihood of a young person becoming a NEET. Similarly, the Scottish study by Biggart et al. (2004) points to a strong correlation between multiple disadvantages and NEET status. While there are a range of policy initiatives aimed at making school more relevant to the aspirations of non-academically oriented pupils through vocational training and local area partnerships geared to placing unqualified school leavers in training and employment (see DfES 2005), greater effort is devoted to addressing truancy and discipline through behaviour support teams. Indeed, the reality is that the key criminal justice legislation since 1998 suggests that the main policy for NEETs is to manage the potential criminality of this group, particularly through ASBOs, Dispersal and Curfew Orders,

Parenting Orders and other supervisory orders devised as part of the 'respect' and anti-social behaviour agendas. The strong tendency is to place the issue of NEETs in the context of the 'underclass' debate that seems to be stubbornly enduring since Murray (1990) first introduced the term to the policy vocabulary in the early 1990s. What this means in policy terms is that stress will be placed on the apparent failure of young people to act to help themselves, as evidenced by their withdrawal from education without qualifications. And, in a context in which the welfare system is considered to provide only perverse incentives to behave badly, the choices will be between work or subjection to social surveillance.

The enduring issue of the underclass

As observed in the introduction, Young (2007) warns against the binary thinking that shapes discussions of the underclass, and he criticises the failure to acknowledge the porous nature of boundaries in postmodern society in which the poor provide the cheap labour to the service and retail sectors of employment. This is true to an extent, but there remains an inevitable tendency in both academic thinking and popular consciousness to think in terms of hierarchical and normative categories, and the notion of an 'underclass' continues to have a seductive resonance in policy circles. Charles Murray, who remains the most persistent voice blaming the poor for their feckless and deviant lifestyle choices, has moved beyond his original focus on their welfare dependency to castigate the underclass for its cultural impact. In particular, he warns against complacency about the underclass in a context in which crime rates appear to be declining in many Western societies because of the pursuit by governments of his other cherished policy theme, high rates of incarceration as part of incapacitating penal strategies. The thrust of his argument points to the camouflage effects of high imprisonment of what he considers to be the corrosive cultural impact of the underclass in the USA and, given his continuing interest in policy transfer, Britain too. At the heart of Murray's more recent analysis of the underclass is the problem group that we have referred to as NEETs. He suggests that while the challenge posed to present-day society by 'the underclass' remains largely the same as it has been in terms of indolence, criminality and failure to show commitment to family life, in addition, he argues that it is now having a malevolent impact on modern society by the contamination of mainstream culture with its anti-social and loutish value orientations.

The coarsening of culture

Murray (1999) contends that the underlying problem of the underclass is not in its welfare dependency: the Clinton welfare legislation of 1996 more or less resolved that issue by effectively removing the security safety net from US welfare and removing many from the welfare rolls. In the same way, tough measures introduced to address welfare dependency in Britain and elsewhere in Europe are having a similar impact. The problem today, he maintains, is that in the midst of the underclass communities there is a coarsening of culture, the consequence of illegitimacy and lone female-headed households that have incubated moral codes that are antithetical to orderly and disciplined living. But more than that, the condemnation that used to be expressed at vulgarity and violence has, he argues, largely evaporated as inner-city street life provides the content for a burgeoning alternative youth culture that is permeating mainstream society. The black street culture of urban America and Britain has spilled over into mainstream society, impacting on all areas of social and cultural life. The problem of the underclass is, therefore, less about welfare and has become pre-eminently a cultural issue. There has been a 'widening expression of underclass ethics'. The key features of this deviant ethic are as follows:

> Take what you want. Respond violently to anyone who antagonises you. Despise courtesy as weakness. Take pride in cheating .... Among the many complicated explanations for this deterioration in culture, cultural spill-over from the underclass is implicated. (Murray 1999: 14)

He suggests that the converts to this imperialist underclass culture are adolescents who have not been taught any better, having been raised in households and communities where there has been for many an absence of male authority figures. The key index of this expansion of the underclass is that white illegitimacy has increased and that white, working-class neighbourhoods appear to share many of the worst features that have been associated with the black ghetto. Most of this argument, especially relating to the cultural spillover from the underclass to mainstream society, is based on what Murray himself admits is largely anecdotal evidence. However, consistent with his argument that working-class sexual codes and family breakdown are travelling in the opposite direction to the 'New Victorianism' informing middle-class lives (see Murray 1994: 36), he now observes that American society is fragmenting as a result of such social processes. The compartmentalising of social classes, neighbourhoods and cultural tastes is now more evident than it has been in recent times.

> America in the 1990s is a place where the local movie theater may play *Sense and Sensibility* next door to *Natural Born Killers*. Brian Lamb (on C-SPAN) is a few channels away from Jerry Springer. Formal balls are in vogue in some circles; mosh pits in others … the country is going in different directions.
> (Murray 1999: 15)

What are the real sources of these cultural changes? Murray has a strange understanding of the ways in which cultural influence circulates and impacts in modern Western societies; he ignores the market and institutional sources of power that commercialise fast foods, music and 'style'. The significant question is why is there so little condemnation of vulgarity and deviance? John Lea identifies the central issue:

> The lack of condemnation of vulgarity and violence could be hardly due to the poor and marginalised groups who have very little influence over the mass media or 'public discourse'. It is rather the fact that such values are generated at the core of an increasingly harsh capitalism. The poor and marginalised reproduce and innovate on the basis of the dominant values and the means of achieving them: they produce another variety of them …. The 'lawless masculinity' of rioting youth … is a culture not markedly distinct from that of the financial dealing rooms of the City of London. Indeed, it is in the expanding role of finance capital that we see some of the most blatant examples of the culture of 'lawless masculinity'. (Lea 2002: 131–2)

Barry Schwartz (1999), writing in the same journal that published Murray's observations on the coarsening of American culture, offers an explanation of the problem in line with that suggested by Lea. It is the abandonment of the capitalism of Keynes and F. D. Roosevelt in favour of the capitalism of Reagan and Thatcher, or, we might suggest, the capitalism of Bush, Blair and Brown, that has contributed most to the deterioration in the material conditions which generate social marginality for disadvantaged social groups. Rather than approach the issue of the 'underclass' in terms of the behaviour of 'kinds of people', Schwartz suggests that it is the tendency to privilege markets and privatisation over public service and collective provision that has generated a narcissistic and materialist culture. What makes this line of argument interesting is that it redresses the balance of those politically popular perspectives that concentrate on social behaviour at the individual level; it challenges the analysis that explains cultural change in terms of the deviant actions and motivations of marginalised individuals in isolation from the wider influences abroad in society.

Discussing markets and morality, Schwartz observes that 'the market contributes more to the erosion of our moral sense than any other modern social force' (Schwartz 1999: 39). He makes a number of observations in support of this view. First, the market destroys other-regarding sentiments because being able to pay the price in an anonymous transaction, which today can often mean through e-commerce, makes relationships distant and impersonal. Secondly, markets undermine social justice because they seek to maximise profit rather than charge what is fair: it is what the seller can get away with and what the market will tolerate that counts. This again tends to reinforce an inward-looking and selfish attitude to relationships and commercial dealings, deviant or legal. Thirdly, capitalist America and Britain also drive a materialist and consumer culture that is 'thing addicted'.

> Americans now suffer from what I have elsewhere called "thing-addiction", and unlike addiction to drugs, addiction to things is actively encouraged by society. School kids hear no horror stories about credit-card debt; instead they are bombarded daily with enticements to buy .... Discouraging consumption seems positively un-American. (Schwartz 1999: 41)

Of course, we can also add that encouragement to acquire debt and to consume also encourages innovative strategies to participate in the consumer society for those who lack the resources to do so legitimately, an observation that Robert Merton (1939) made many years ago and called 'anomic strain'. Fourthly, those of the centre and far Right, such as Murray and James Q. Wilson (1975), and Wilson and Hernstein (1985), often bemoan the decline in the sense of duty, obligation and commitment, sometimes referred to as 'social capital', in contemporary Western societies. However, the loss of a sense of community and interdependency is exacerbated by the constant urging to maximise the individual's right to choose everything from health-care treatment to socks. The exercise of self-interest in the guise of maximising rational preferences does little to foster a sense of social solidarity. Schwartz suggests, therefore, that it is the market more than any other force in present-day society that undermines social capital. The issue is not one of a decline in morality but rather an increase in amorality fostered by the pursuit of self-interest. In the midst of a culture of materialist consumerism, and driven by a largely unregulated market economy, it is of little surprise that the social values of self-interest so prized by the middle classes and the thrusting entrepreneurs who orchestrate the financial sector of the economy should trickle down to those at the bottom of the social hierarchy. Lack of regard for others, whether expressed by the dynamic entrepreneur maximising a return on investments or the anti-social adolescent trying to maximise rewards from criminality regardless of who gets in the way, amounts to the same thing and expresses the same selfish values: they have a common source in the moral economy of the market.

As argued in Chapter 2, a consequence of capitalist market forces can be the creation of the conditions for the onset of a de-civilising process. How this has come about was well understood by Durkheim (1964) and Polyani (1957), and it can be conceptualised as the phenomenon of 'the disembedding of the economy'. In their different ways, they argued that the sphere of economic activity in the advanced industrial societies had become so disembedded from other key institutions that it operates without any significant social and moral limitations. The institutional imbalance of power between the economic sphere and the institutions of civil society has become a defining feature of modernity. This insight has been developed by Messner and Rosenfeld (2001), leading to a refashioning of classical anomie theory. They have argued, for example, that one of the main explanations of the striking difference between the high rates of crime and incivility in the USA compared with Western Europe is the anomic ethic generated by the absence of a European-style welfare state in the USA that might mediate the impact of market forces. This observation is particularly germane to a comparison of the Scandinavian countries with the USA. Indeed, by drawing on the work of Esping-Andersen (1990), they argue that there are strong data demonstrating a correlation between the low level of de-commodification of labour in the USA and criminality. The devaluation of non-monetary goals, combined with the exaggerated stress on consumerism in the USA, has encouraged a dangerous acquisitiveness in those inside the consumer society while heightening the sense of relative deprivation and resentment of those excluded from the material benefits of our materialist culture. Similar effects are now at work in Europe as welfare retrenchment bites.

The development of this phenomenon has been exacerbated by the accommodation of all Western governments to the exigencies of global market pressures at the expense of an ethically grounded commitment to maintaining institutionalised forms of solidarity in the form of the welfare state and a national political agenda. For example, in related arguments, the impact of a disembedded economy has resulted in the suggestion that we may be witnessing the 'death of the social sphere' (Rose 1996) and the 'individualisation of the social' (Ferge 1997). Rose (1996), for example, has argued that the social domain of government, what Donzelot (1979) described as the institutional space that emerged in the nineteenth century between the state and the private sphere of the family, giving rise to *social* work and *social* services, has undergone a mutation, as the social welfare of the population is no longer regarded as pre-eminently a matter for national governments but instead has been reduced to an individual and community responsibility. Governments are more concerned about managing their nation state plc in the global marketplace than about a commitment to national welfare programmes that may 'appear' to require levels of public expenditure and taxation that might frighten off mobile capital investment. Ferge (1997) has reinforced this observation by pointing to the process of the 'individualising' of welfare obligations in which people must draw on their own skills and marketability to survive in a competitive market society. The pressures of global economic forces on governments have resulted in the off-loading of responsibility for economic performance and social policy delivery to communities and the voluntary sector. These developments amount to a 'de-socialisation of economic government' (see Rose 1996). The task of governance within this new configuration of institutional power is to manage problem populations who fail to 'enterprise their lives' and invest in themselves and their families. This 'new prudentialism' requires a combination of delayed gratification and sufficient disposable income to plan for a future and, it should be added, to deal with the demands of a consumerist society (see Taylor 1999). In the absence of normative guidance from strong institutions in civil society, including a strong sense of institutionalised solidarity in the form of the welfare state, increasing numbers of people are finding contemporary economic and financial pressures unforgiving to those who fail to cope with this dilemma. The consequence of these developments is, as Arts and Gelisson (2001) have suggested, that people adjust to the 'habituation of distribution rules': they get used to getting very little from the welfare system relative to what they think they need. The transformation in work, the increasingly crass consumerist culture, and the changing structure of social divisions have led to adjustments in behaviour among some of those losing out in the new materialist culture. And, as Simon (2007) has argued, these circumstances create the conditions in which the politicisation of crime and deviance leads to policies geared less to addressing the underlying social needs of troubled citizens than to their subjugation to the demands of a society unwilling to tolerate disorder (stylistically and behaviourally) in key areas of social and economic life.

Class, culture and consumption

In rethinking the nature of class relationships in the advanced societies, Giddens (1973) made a distinction between what he called the *mediate* and the *proximate* structuration of class relationships. What this distinction points to is the differentiation of broad structural forces shaping life chances and social mobility from localised factors. For example, it is clear that industrial and occupational change since the 1980s has had an impact on life chances through the types of work and training available to young people, especially those who leave education without formal qualifications. However, what Giddens was also pointing to in making this crucial distinction is the complex ways in which the broader structural forces shaping class relationships in advanced market societies are reinforced and mediated by the patterns of social interaction in the workplace, the spatial relationships between communities, and, of course, the generation of situational meanings in society attaching to styles and identities that mark out status differences between people and social groups. These relationships require further discussion.

The fundamental problem for Western economies since the 1980s is that, while class rigidities have been broken down by industrial restructuring, residual issues relating to social marginalisation have been created. The decline of industrial manufacturing has had the consequence of weakening the strong industrial trade unions that were embedded in them and which, together with working-class institutions and voluntary organisations, used to exert influence on politics and policy in the twentieth century until the 1970s. It has also led to the dispersal of established working-class communities that grew up around shipbuilding, mining, steel and heavy engineering and the destruction of the informal networks of social control and discipline that gave shape to established working-class communities, giving them both a foundation in society and politics and an anchor for working-class cultures that were invariably ethical even when being oppositional or, indeed, sometimes deviant (see Lea 2002). There was always a strong sense of solidarity within neighbourhoods and communities underpinned by unwritten social mores prohibiting the tormenting of, or stealing from, those from one's own neighbourhood. There was the development and consolidation of what Lea (2002: 44–50) describes as the *moral economy of place and space* which ensured that the impact of street cultures was minimised to a greater or lesser extent (see Walklate 1998 on this phenomenon, which I discuss in Chapter 8). The seismic shifts in the occupational structure of post-industrial economies since the early 1980s have resulted in the creation of residualised communities without sources of secure employment, reliant on community resources that are externally imposed rather than organically grown from local people's priorities and poor life chances. Moreover, time has eroded the memory of the primary causes of such impoverished communities and popular criticisms of the apparently work-shy attitudes of those 'puked up' by an ailing industrial sector (see Young 1999) have failed to recognise that the employment opportunities that have followed de-industrialisation are not the equivalents of those that have been lost. There has been a growth in unskilled female service jobs but a sharp decline in unskilled manual jobs. The growth in the service and retail sectors has led to the expansion of the female workforce but has created few male jobs with the security and earning potential once found in the declining industrial manufacturing sector. The emerging knowledge society requires skills that are intellectual rather than physical and has demanded credentials and educational qualifications for entry to the lowest levels of administrative and managerial jobs in shops and offices. The key issue for emphasis is that while social mobility is relatively open and fluid for those who are educated, trained and qualified, there is a high degree of social closure for those who cannot compete in the new knowledge-based society. Those who are without qualifications, and experience little demand for unskilled manual labour may also discover that they have failed to acquire the social attitudes, demeanour and behaviour desired by employers that require social skills to deal with customers and the public more generally.

Giddens' (1991: 1998) more recent observations on these social processes have characterised the change in terms of the emergence of individualisation in post-industrial and post-traditional society. There is now a greater emphasis on individual agency and reflexivity. As traditional conceptions and understandings of social class diminish in popular parlance and consciousness, it is argued that it is at the level of the individual rather than society, or indeed polity, that problems of inequality have to be addressed and overcome. Gillies (2005), for example, characterises this in terms of the 'individualisation of social class'. The language of social inclusion and social exclusion has been adopted to describe the failures of disadvantaged people to grasp their opportunities, representing poverty as poor self-management. This is particularly evident in the area of family policy, which Gillies (2005) specifically focuses on. Parenting practices in the poor working-class household are found wanting when compared with the average middle-class family. I will return to this particular issue in Chapter 5. The significant issue to be stressed is that increasingly policymakers and the public more generally appear to think about inequality and disadvantage in terms of 'subjectivities' rather than as having an underlying structural reality.

Class position is structured by broad global, economic and occupational forces but is reinforced by the creation of what Giddens (1973) labelled many years ago as 'distributive groupings', which are visible by their appearance, behaviour and consumption patterns. Issues that were considered relatively insignificant in the days when class analysis was focused on the productive process at the heart of industrial capitalism have now become very significant as sociology comes to terms with the variety of ways people relate to the sphere of consumption. Indeed, without engaging in a broad analysis of the meaning of social class today, it is sufficient to say that while the global economy builds and reinforces hierarchical social structures and opportunities, people typically relate to the consequences of those processes not by considering the unfairness in the structure of rewards generated by them but by exercising moral judgement and social evaluation of the tastes, lifestyles and patterns of consumption of those individuals doing least well. The pressure to consume is relentless with or without the resources to do so. This shift has occurred on the back of popular perceptions and political discourses proclaiming the end of the class society while the idea of a meritocracy seems to have become embedded in popular consciousness as the most appropriate way to describe contemporary Western societies (Gillies 2005). This has encouraged both the tendency to view deviations from work and behavioural norms as a product of individual pathology rather than resulting from social and economic forces largely beyond the control of any individual. As Lawler (2005) has observed:

> One particularly insidious effect of claims of classlessness is that, when class is linguistically expunged, it cannot be invoked as an explanation for inequality. As a result, people on the losing end of a classed system can increasingly be blamed ... the social-structural dimensions of class inequality are now understood as being embedded only in the subjectivities of social actors. Explanations for inequality come to inhere within the subjectivities of persons who are then marked as 'wrong' or 'right', 'deficient' or 'acceptable' .... We might see the 'gentler' version of this in discourses of 'social exclusion' and the 'harsher' version in right wing forms of 'underclass' rhetoric. (Lawler 2005: 798)

Lawler goes on to make a number of important observations. First, it is important to connect issues of style, taste and identity to the material circumstances that facilitate their expression. The fact that some groups in society are despised for their lifestyle choices and aesthetic sensibilities obscures the limited choices their disadvantage gives them in the marketplace. Referring to the concept of a 'cultural and symbolic economy', and commenting on the popular media interest in 'chavs' in the UK, Lawler (2005) argues that 'working-class people are not primarily marked as lacking and disgusting through their poverty, but through their assumed lack of *knowledge* and *taste*' (p. 800). In this context, what tends to happen is that the problems relating to inequality, social injustice and global economic forces become transformed into individual fecklessness and the problems of economy and society become the *problem of working-class people* (see Nayak 2006). This has consequences for the types of resources that they can claim and the moral case that they may have for redistributive justice in unequal societies. This is very evident in the criminal justice legislation and debate since 1997, which has focused attention on 'chavs', NEETs', 'neds' and all anti-social forms of behaviour. Despite the frequent references in government policy statements to social exclusion and tackling the 'causes of crime', legislation from the Crime and Disorder Act 1998 to the Anti-social Behaviour Acts of 2003 (Scotland 2004) has concentrated on the behavioural and stylistic elements of anti-social behaviour at the expense of seriously addressing underlying issues relating to child poverty and material disadvantage, because redistributive policies have been eschewed in favour of *at arm's-length governance* involving social partnerships. As taste, style and consumption patterns exist within a hierarchical cultural structure containing dominant and subordinate cultures, and class is no longer to be understood as relating to productive and market relationships, but is instead marked by the lifestyle choices of poor people, it follows that those having the wrong set of social values, adhering to the wrong set of community mores, and having the wrong kind of life will be marked out as the most undeserving in material and social recognition. What is being suggested is that we risk losing sight of what actually makes people poor and makes them adopt particular lifestyles.

Culture and instrumentalism

The most striking cultural and behavioural change today is the adaptation of young people to the materialist consumer society in which they live. Schwartz (1999) is surely correct to draw attention to the impact of the market on adolescent delinquency, but we should also acknowledge the impact of the consumer society on their attitudes to work. The anomic ethic generated by the disjunction between a materialist culture offering the temptations of 'things' and sought-after gadgetry to everyone and the realities of low wages and limited occupational horizons restricting the means to obtain those desirable objects for many, especially young people from disadvantaged backgrounds, is shaping the practices of contemporary youth culture.

Hall and Winlow (2005) have provided an interesting comparison between what they describe as 'socially incorporated young people in low-paid service work and socially excluded criminal young men'. Their research addresses a crucial change in the significance of work for personal identity and social integration in the transition from industrial to post-industrial conditions. The period when work defined who people are and their place within a stable community has passed. In an era of flexible and casual work contracts it is often a combination of leisure, style and consumption that shapes the individual's concept of self. Today, insecurity permeates the workplace from blue-collar shop floor to white-collar management. Attachment to commercial organisations, and employers more generally, is for most people purely a pragmatic and functional means to survive economically. These changes have taken place within modern Western economies that are increasingly geared to facilitating consumption of 'things', services and lifestyles rather than the manufacture of products. Identity and stability in social life have to be negotiated in a social and economic context in which change is relentless and social order is becoming increasingly fragmentary. It is the consequences of these changes for the way young people think and organise their lives that Hall and Winlow (2005) examine. With the loss of communal bonds associated with stable industrial communities, and the fluidity and mobility characterising contemporary working life, the question they ask is, how do young people relate to each other and how do they relate to the world of work? The answer is that they relate to each other in a utilitarian way, and they certainly relate to work with a sizeable portion of *instrumentalism*, with the job simply being a means to an end that predominantly means meeting friends and enjoying life in the burgeoning nocturnal economy they inhabit at weekends and occasionally during the working week. The mutuality and solidarism associated with working environments in the 1950s and 1960s has been replaced by shallow, post-emotional relationships of pleasantries and cooperation while at work. For many, there is little in the way of enduring mutual commitment outside work. Even the friends and relationships formed at school become tainted by instrumentalism, with many of the respondents to Hall and Winlow's research acknowledging that their knowledge of their friends is fairly partial because other than the bustle of the pub and nightclub they do not spend much time together involved in other pursuits. They tend to 'use' friends as a means to access sociable events and often have little to do with them beyond the nocturnal economy. Their attitude to work is that it is to be endured in order to acquire the money to consume conspicuously and enjoy life's pleasures in the leisure industry.

The attitudes of the sample of criminal youth interviewed by Hall and Winlow reveal similar instrumental attitudes to work, money and other people: poor pay in poor jobs is for 'mugs'. Friends and acquaintances are primarily to be used only to the extent that they are functional in lubricating a criminal transaction or assisting in a criminal activity. The negotiation of the criminal marketplace is shaped by the same instrumental and entrepreneurial values that can be found in the mainstream economy, and they will pursue material advantage in market society by 'any means possible' in a way similar to that described by Messner and Rosenfeld (2001). Hyperambition and individualism are in evidence. Perhaps one explanation for these instrumental attitudes lies in what Young (2007) has called the *chaos of reward* in the late modern economy and society. In ways reminiscent of Merton's theory of anomie, there is a general perception that there are many innovative routes to wealth that do not require conforming to the rules. Young people view with envy the randomness of wealth and celebrity. And the real motivation for youth criminality and anti-social behaviour may be less to do with making rational choices in the face of criminal opportunities and more to do with the pursuit of 'celebrity', or the style of celebrity. Indeed, ordinary people can acquire wealth and fame for no particular reason or talent other than participation in a reality television programme. But more significantly, why should a young man submit to the disciplines of work when he can earn more from illegal wheeling and dealing, and shoplifting?

Hayward and Yar (2006) offer further insight into these issues by concentrating their focus on the importance of consumption for the development and maintenance of social identity and social status. The rise of the 'chav' phenomenon is symptomatic of the broader sociological changes that Lawler (2005), Hall and Winlow (2005), and Young (2007) have pointed to: in the absence of meaningful work, and meaningful family and community relationships, it is the sphere of consumption that carries the burden of identity and conception of self, and it is in the politics of aesthetics that the cultural battle of social classification and labelling is taking place. The most marginal members of society manage their social exclusion through the over-consumption of the products of the consumer society. They mark their membership of it, not by passively accepting that poverty and disadvantage are supposed to be marked by the outward expression and style of passivity and dowdiness, but by overcompensating for their economic marginality by over-consuming the clothes and material symbols of affluent society. Albert Cohen (1955) might describe this as a reaction formation in which those excluded from the accepted means of recognition and achievement invert, and subversively distort, the social values and the style that is excluding them. The politically challenging feature of this phenomenon is that it is difficult to be absolutely certain that the apparent display of doing well is associated with a 'chav' and is not simply an expression of bad taste – hence the broad pejorative use of the term for any expression of 'bad' style. However, in a context in which style is being used 'subversively' to undermine regularity and predictability in social interaction, a great deal of effort is made by the culture industry, and indeed the security industry, to delineate those stylistic expressions most likely to be associated with the 'genuine' underclass and the 'genuine' 'chav', who are perceived as being threatening and intrinsically criminogenic. Hayward and Yar point to the irony of those who attempt to 'recreate' the style of 'celebrity chavs' when they observe:

Street level attempts to mobilise cultural capital based on overt displays of designer clothing have instead inspired a whole new raft of bizarre micro social control mechanisms, including everything from town centre pubs and nightclubs refusing entry to individuals wearing certain brands within their premises (no Timberlands or Burberry) ... to the recent zero tolerance policy imposed on 'designer hoodies' and baseball caps (Hayward and Yar 2005: 22)

The focus becomes less concentrated on the actual items of style and more clearly on those who wear and use the style. Hayward and Yar (2005) allude to the microsocial control evolving to differentiate the big and brash styles associated with 'chavs' from the subtle and understated styles that mark out the sophisticated and genuinely affluent: they observe that there has been a 're-emphasis of the visual in the politics of the street' (p. 23). There are processes of both social differentiation and security monitoring involved in the profiling and classification of social types who may be 'dangerous' and are to be despised. Nayak (2006) reinforces these observations about 'chavs'. He draws attention in particular to the contrasting masculinities accompanying youth transitions in the post-industrial North-East and how these are reflected in different expressions of style, body capital and behaviour. The distinction between Real Geordies, who have adapted to the occupational opportunities of post-industrial society by taking the service jobs in offices, restaurants and call centres, and the incomes that go with that, and 'charvers', who have rejected work for the pursuit of masculine identity in anti-social behaviour and petty criminality, manifests itself in the exclusion of the latter from the clubs and drinking circuits of 'party city' Newcastle because of their dress, demeanour and relative poverty. Class distinctions are visible and carried in the charvers' body capital (the way they hold their head, the way they arch their backs when walking, and their tendency to spit, swear and behave loutishly in public places). The tracksuits and baseball caps provide the immediate stylistic marker of young men seeking to discover their masculinity in a world where masculine work has disappeared and the opportunities to express their aggression have disappeared for those insufficiently resourced to pay for expensive leisure activities.

Today, 'chavness' is typically treated as an expression of personal taste and the outward manifestation of a person's social marginality: just as language use and accent are ways in which people carry their social class with them, now, increasingly, it is their style, their attitudes, and their general demeanour that communicate their status as members of a problem population. However, beyond the negative appraisal of style, there is the more serious issue of the stereotyping of particular groups of young people because their fashion sense is treated as signalling a 'dangerous' and anti-social category of person.

Value orientations or cultural toolkits?

The reason NEETs and 'chavs' are regarded negatively by those shaping educational and social policies is that they are deemed to be the product of an impaired socialisation process. It is assumed that they have acquired the wrong social values from their families, especially parents, but also from their associates, whom they join in a feral existence, roaming the streets. Displays of behaviour that appear to lack self-control, or are insufficiently empathetic to those who may be from outside an immediate community, neighbourhood or gang, have been understood almost entirely as conduct that requires training to force the deviants to conform. Anti-social behaviour policies, in particular, are based on the assumption that the issue is one of value orientations: those deemed to be anti-social must be coerced into accepting, and behaving in accordance with, the values of mainstream 'respectable' society. That is why Frank Field MP (2003) talks of the welfare system as 'teacher'. He argues that benefits should be available only to those who fulfil the requirements of respectable citizenship and who live disciplined and law-abiding lives. Withholding benefits, fining the deviants, and using supervisory orders have as their main objective the teaching of the anti-social person the social disciplines necessary for readmission to a consumerist and market society.

Perhaps the issue is not so much one of a failure of some families and adults to socialise their children appropriately as it is that they have been socialised into a mindset that predisposes them to make choices about behaviour and life that may be antithetical to the rules of 'respectable' society but nevertheless conform to what is expected behaviour in the locality. An alternative perspective, and one that is more in keeping with a social welfare approach to these matters, is to view culture less in ideational terms as the pursuit of appropriate social values, and more as related to the lived realities of those identified as being anti-social. Once that intellectual shift has been accepted, a different range of social policy initiatives beyond punitive supervision suggests itself.

In an illuminating enquiry into why poverty persists in rural America, Cynthia Duncan (1999) studied the local cultures and behavioural norms of communities in Appalachia (West Virginia) and the Mississippi Delta. Drawing on the work of Swidler (1986), she argues that we should understand the impact of culture on behaviour in terms of a 'toolkit' of familiar symbols, skills, rituals, stories and worldviews that people acquire as they grow up. It is the development of a conception of what it is to be 'people like us' that is crucial. For example, the poor of the Mississippi Delta could not imagine being middle class and following a professional career, because, as Duncan suggests in reference to one of the characters in her study, 'it would take a style, skills and habits, experiences and know-how that are not in his tool kit'.

Regarding deviant values, Swidler (1986) makes the important observation that there is evidence that often those refusing to engage in behaviour said to lead to economic and social advancement share, or at least acknowledge the worth of, the same values that they violate and are prevalent in the dominant society (see Liebow 1967; Valentine 1968). That is why Cohen (1955) talks about a 'reaction formation' and the 'inversion' of social values. Swidler's proposal is that instead of focusing on the values deficit of the poor, as evidenced by their anti-social behaviour, we should instead seek to understand the meaning systems, knowledge and habits which frame their routine lives; in short the *cultural toolkits* by which they live. The insight offered to us by Swidler is 'that people may share common aspirations while remaining profoundly different in the way their culture organises their overall pattern of behaviour .... Action is not determined by one's values. Rather action and values are organised to take advantage of cultural competencies' (Swidler 1986: 275). The broader thesis being advanced is that the way people behave and the kinds of actions they take reflect the 'habits, moods and sensibilities', or focal concerns, that have been shaped by material circumstances and encountered on a routine and daily basis (see Miller 1958). It is the idea of a cultural toolkit that is at play here, not dysfunctional families and people. Those people deemed to be the anti-social or 'chavs' or NEETS in the midst of our communities adopt 'strategies of action' based on what their culture, local community and economy make available to them, and the repertoire of resources is invariably limited in the socially and economically marginal spaces of our disadvantaged urban areas. People behave and act within the limits of their social and cultural competencies: they behave in accordance with the typical practices, behavioural standards and social norms of the people in their locality with whom they most closely identify. When those same people are required to act and behave outside their cultural routines, they often resist because of the difficulties of what Swidler calls the human and economic costs of 'retooling' – the costs of acquiring the social disciplines, habits, attitudes and understandings necessary for empathetic social intercourse and 'other-directedness' can be high (see Riesman 1961; Rodger 2000). Addressing the social consequences of what Taylor (1999) refers to variously as 'infantilist masculinism' and 'protest masculinism' in contemporary youth cultures and gangs requires more patience and understanding than the imposition of an ASBO allows.

The 'cultural toolkits' perspective suggested here draws on the work of Bourdieu (1977). It is an approach to the question of social and cultural identities that takes our gaze towards the ways in which material realities, family, community practices, and social class more generally, become inscribed not only on the mind, the language and therefore the behaviour of social actors, but also on their bodies and their demeanour (see Nayak 2006). The body capital of young men labelled as 'chavs' or 'charvers' has to be learned in the street and neighbourhood, and it consists of the right level of aggression and 'hardness' being signalled to others who might threaten or challenge them. Bourdieu, and before him Elias, applied the concept of habitus to describe these processes. It is the acquisition of unconscious habits, unreflexive attitudes and predispositions that they both describe. In the case of Elias, it is the development of a *second nature* through the civilising process that he conceptualises in terms of *habitus*. While Elias discusses the psychological changes that accompany the formation of ever more dense networks of interdependency, and the development of sensitivities and dispositions that are adapted to the demands of ever closer social interaction, Bourdieu points up the constraints imposed on human development and social action resulting from habitus. In ways not dissimilar to Miller's classic statement on the 'focal concerns' of the lower-class community as a generating milieu for gang delinquency (Miller 1958), Bourdieu's concept of *field*, which supports the notion of habitus, conceptualises the way in which a community, neighbourhood, family and street relationships create and demand particular modes of response from those who inhabit them. The ways of behaving, thinking and talking that are acquired are shaped by the field and lead to habituated ways of behaving that are compatible with life in a social area. Young men and women behave in ways that are unthinking and unreflexive in order to fit in with their peers and because very often they are only doing what their parents and their friends also do and say. This view of the acquisition of cultural identity jars with those who pursue an approach to problem populations that stresses personal culpability and failure to make the choices deemed to be acceptable to those shaping policy. The anti-social behaviour strategy is grounded in a view of behaviour that is grounded in a model of socialisation deficits and condition operant responses.

The idea that behaviour and actions are socially determined and structurally constrained does not, therefore, resonate with current policy thinking or indeed with popular sociological currents informing present-day social policies. The stress on 'responsibilisation' in criminal justice policies is predicated on a view of people as acting with free choice and as being able to be reflexive about the choices they make. The voluntarism of Giddens' (1991) perspective on self-reflection and identity formation is often placed in opposition to the more deterministic perspective found in Bourdieu's work. The fact that Giddens (1998) was also at one point influential in shaping New Labour thinking about a wide range of policy issues has increased his importance in the debate about identity, self-reflection and citizenship. The impact on everyone of globalism, especially the embedding of neo-liberal orthodoxies on thinking and behaviour, has increased the awareness of possibilities and choices in life. Giddens (1991) has done more than most to argue that the consequences of these global forces has been the destruction of traditionalism and the opening up of opportunities for people to select their own rather than determined life pathways: we are all capable of being self-reflexive and becoming the authors of our own biographies. Giddens' recent sociology is populated with social actors who shape social realities rather than are forced to adapt to social realities. While he acknowledges that we all inhabit a society that is stocked with 'taken for granted' knowledge which must inevitably influence the way the social actor behaves and makes choices, nevertheless, the flux and rapidity of social change enable novel choices to be made if desired and for individuals to create themselves rather than submit to the constraining forces of rigid social and class structures. This is the image of society and the individual that lies at the heart of New Labour policy and the image that appears to be antithetical to the view advanced by Bourdieu.

Culture, reflexivity and social policy

Adams (2006) has usefully brought the two strands of sociological thinking about self-reflection and identity together in order to point to a hybridised model, as he calls it. The key issue here is that Giddens' approach, and the one which is influential in policy circles, tends to exaggerate the degree of reflexivity and choice available to most people, especially those who live on the margins of consumer society. The 'chavs', the NEETs and the 'underclass' beloved of the designers of social and criminal justice policy are regarded as wilful deviants who behave in an anti-social way because they fail to take the opportunities and make the choices that would benefit them most. It would seem that the antecedents of that behaviour tend to be of little interest to those designing strategies to combat their deviant behaviour, certainly from the evidence of New Labour's respect agenda and anti-social behaviour strategies. There appears to be a view that while rapid social change dislodges the rigidities and the stultifying forces that constrain people and their choices, post-industrial society provides new horizons and new possibilities for those who can be encouraged to reflect and organise their lives to grasp emerging opportunities. The social investment state is about providing people with lifelong guarantees of access to education and training to enable them to achieve their personal goals. As alluded to above, failure in self-management to 'enterprise one's life' leads to the negative labelling associated with 'chav', NEET and 'underclass' status. The key issue is, as Adams (2006) suggests, that 'identities are formed in the ability to translate the choices which emerge from the complex interplay into meaningful realities' (p. 522). He goes on to point to the limits to reflexive habitus and the frequent inability to change one's life and transform its pathway by quoting Ian Craib:

> in our individual and social worlds, we can look around us, identify what is going on and institute changes – some of the time. Some of the time we can look around us, identify what is going on and find ourselves incapable of instituting changes .... Sometimes our capacity for reflective thought can leave us recognising but unable to do anything about our lack of freedom. (Craib 1992, cited in Adams 2006: 522)

There are reflexive winners and losers and it could be argued that the purpose of social policy intervention is to help some people convert their disadvantaged position into positive change by assisting them to reflect on their life pathway and to assist them to make more positive choices. However, there first has to be some acknowledgement that there are real material restraints on the development of reflective capacity that are a product of what Bourdieu calls field, and which, more prosaically, we can call the focal concerns of a person's social environment of street, neighbourhood and community. The classical sociology of deviance emanating from Cloward and Ohlin (1960) and Sutherland and Cressey (1966) points to a primary factor in shaping attitudes and identities: in each field there will be *differential opportunity structures* that are a product of the social structure and they will shape *differential patterns of association*, which influence thinking and behaviour because they will be frequent and intense, have a high priority, and be of long duration given the low levels of social mobility and high levels of material disadvantage in many marginal communities. Ambition is always socially relative and structurally determined; it is never simply a case of willing an achievement for it to be realised.

To return to the theme of the culture of consumer society and its impact on youth behaviour and anti-social behaviour, it is now clear that Sutherland's theory needs to be updated and that, increasingly, the influence of the differential associations taking place within intimate peer groups, which he believed to be of paramount significance, is augmented by the penetrating influence of the consumer culture and, as Schwartz (1999) has suggested, the 'thing addiction' that lies at the heart of that culture. The institutional anomie of today has generated an intense sense of relative deprivation for many people living at the margins of our consumer society, as disembedded market rationality pervades life and culture and encourages us all to pursue material consumption. The status frustration that is created by being in but also locked out of the consumer society (because the means to participate in it legitimately remain credentials, secure employment, and the social disciplines required to be successful in work environments that require social skills that NEETS do not possess) seems to be resolved by the acquisition and display of the stylistic symbols of the affluent society and participation in consumer society by any means possible. 'Chavness' may be an outward expression of a *reaction formation* (Cohen 1955) in which the symbols and styles of the celebrities and the affluent are inverted and rearranged in a subversive and sometimes threatening style. However, 'chavness' may also be conformity, not to mainstream society, culture and taste, but to the social environments that provide the cultural toolkits that must be adopted to signal compliance with a particular social group, community and subculture. It is the stylistic and behavioural manifestation of that compliance in 'chavness' that has stimulated a political and social reaction in British society and elsewhere in Europe and North America since the 1990s.

It is the origins, nature and trajectory of that political and social reaction that the next chapter describes and analyses.

Concluding observations

The focus of this chapter has been on the enduring phenomenon of the 'underclass'. Today the concept has been subjected to both academic scrutiny and policy analysis and is being understood less crudely than it was in the early 1990s, because now it is the cultural dimension of this social phenomenon that is significant. The acronym *NEET* has been used widely to reformulate the problem in terms of the strategy to promote active citizenship: young people who disengage from school and ultimately society are being tackled because of their behaviour and their stylistic expression, which is understood as threatening to social order and social discipline. In a society based on the market and consumption, those that are marginal to the primary activities of work and consumption require supervision and designation as a problem population. The ways in which this is being done has been to focus attention on the cultural and stylistic artefacts of those labelled 'chavs' or charvers'. While the policy strategies of government continue to understand the incivility of some young people in terms of *value orientations*, I have suggested we can usefully draw insight from Bourdieu, Elias and the sociology of masculine culture to understand the issues in terms of a 'toolkit'. It is the unreflexive habits, styles, and social and body capital of the ghetto and the deprived neighbourhood that we need to understand. The issues raised in this chapter are necessary for understanding the politics of behaviour which is the concern of the next chapter.

Chapter 4

The politics and policy of incivility

There is a tendency to view criminal justice policies as logically *following* changes in levels of criminality, and as merely a response to events and developments that have first been created by a combination of structural forces (economy, globalisation, unemployment, culture) and rates of behaviour (increased tendencies for people to act in ways considered to be undesirable when measured against a social norm of orderly and disciplined behaviour). Less attention is given to the ways in which social reactions and policy interventions actually define problems and determine who and what require to be controlled. As with social welfare development more broadly, *politics counts* in shaping social policies, setting agendas for action, and picking out from the complexity that constitutes postmodern societies what is problematic, dangerous and in need of political and policy intervention. Social and public policies create the parameters within which social issues and social problems are defined and solutions sought. For example, anti-social behaviour is not a new phenomenon and the ways and means that different societies and cultures have responded to actions, styles and people that are perceived as being threatening are many and varied. The history of social policy is one in which political elites and policy champions have pursued ideas, even visions, about how society can be changed by innovative policy intervention or political strategies. The New Labour government, and in particular Tony Blair, undoubtedly have interpreted their quest to establish a third way in British politics as being measured to a large extent by policies aimed at empowering local communities by eradicating incivility from their midst. The 'respect' agenda is very much a New Labour venture that brings together a concern for communitarianism, civil renewal, and disciplined and orderly family life, reduction in social exclusion, and reduction in anti-social behaviour and criminality. Together, these ingredients constitute a unique New Labour agenda which has been bringing the universes of social policy and criminal justice closer as a distinctive political project. The actual social problems and material issues being tackled in society are not new, because poverty and deviance have always existed, but the way they are to be managed and the social policies designed to support that management process are a product of deliberate political initiative.

What is of particular interest to us is the ways and means that have been adopted by governments to deal with deviance since the collapse of the liberal welfare approach to crime and punishment from the 1970s onwards. There is a brief sociological history that will be described below. What that history indicates is that criminal justice and social policy are artefacts of political opinion, expediency, and, increasingly, a rejection of approaches and understandings that are grounded in models of social causation: it is the anti-social individual who is likely to be held to be responsible for his or her actions with little attention given to the circumstances that may have led to the deviant act. It can sometimes appear that the dismissal of what Garland (1985) refers to as 'extra-legal discourses', incorporating knowledge of the psychological, sociological and emotional predispositions of deviant social actors, is taking us back to the Victorian mindset that so dominated thinking about crime and punishment in the nineteenth century. Then, the only difference between the law-abiding citizen and the criminal was deemed to be the latter's purposive decision to act dishonestly and deviantly. Today, it is more comfortable for politicians to take an equally unreflective position: there are few votes in appearing to be sympathetic to those who behave anti-socially, and that may explain why David Cameron's efforts to entreat us to 'hug a hoodie' received such derision in the press and media. The field of criminal justice has become highly politicised. It is the politician rather than the political scientist, and the psephologist rather than the psychologist, who now influence policy (see Simon 2007). The interesting question is why has this change taken place?

There are two general issues to be identified. The first concerns the ways in which politicians and the public have come to view crime and the operational effectiveness of the criminal justice system and, the second is primarily concerned with the way politicians and the public have come to view what is required in terms of social policy intervention. These issues relate to the growing *normality of crime* and

73

the public political debate about how best to manage the problem populations associated with incivility and criminality in what is fast becoming a post-welfare society.

Informalisation and crime as a normal social fact

The processes of informalisation described in Chapter 2 were said to be in tension with political and policy attempts to re-establish formalisation in social relations and social discipline. The political reaction to the issue of NEETS and anti-social behaviour has been to recast the problems of incivility as a loss of 'respect' for social institutions, authority and the norms of social obligation. It was also suggested in Chapter 2 that these processes are an integral feature of tendencies towards social polarisation and ultimately to de-civilisation. This analysis needs to be advanced a little more.

Wouters (1987a; 1987b; 2007) argues that all Western societies underwent a transformation in their social attitudes to authority and social and moral regulation in the post-war years. The informalisation phase of the civilising process created the conditions in which traditional forms of authority relations were increasingly difficult to justify in societies undergoing widespread functional democratisation in an era of decolonisation, whether they were interpersonal relationships involving gender and generation, or race and ethnicity. Wouters (1999) also made an explicit link between those social processes of informality in social relations and the increase in criminality between the 1950s and 1980s, arguing that the conditions generating informalisation also created a 'psychic integration conflict' in some people. They became aware of a range of activities, personal choices and social attitudes that had been strictly controlled in the period leading up to the 1940s but which war disrupted and changed for ever. Once the vision of new social and cultural horizons had been revealed, it was impossible thereafter to obscure them, although the struggle to inject into society more respect for tradition and authority continues as a social and political battle between the political Right and Left. Indeed, that is precisely what the politics of conduct is about: when Field (2003) chastises the behaviour of the 'neighbours from hell', and suggests that the most important issue confronting British politics is the eradication of anti-social behaviour, he is highlighting a fundamental tension between processes of formalisation and informalisation in a society that is exhibiting tendencies towards de-civilisation in some of our more socially and economically marginal communities.

While the language of informalisation draws on Elias' theory, there is a parallel sociological history of crime in the last 30 years of the twentieth century that has been written by Garland (2000; 2001) detailing the growing recognition throughout society today that crime has become a 'normal social fact'. Garland's explanation of the present concerns about criminal justice and incivility can be interpreted as a description of the reaction to the emerging processes of informalisation since the 1950s. If, as Wouters argues, increasing informalisation led to a 'psychic integration conflict' in those who experienced a sense of release from constraint and social controls, resulting in higher levels of crime, then Garland describes the reaction to that informalisation in terms of changing middle-class attitudes to crime and their consequent retreat from supporting what he calls penal welfarism. A consequence of higher levels of 'deviance' in the period between the 1950s and 1980s was the loss of crime as a politically neutral issue: criminality moved from being understood as a residual problem in an affluent society dominated by a welfare state to an issue that was perceived as being socially and economically corrosive to social order, an observation made forcefully by Jonathan Simon in his thesis on governing through crime (Simon 1997; 2007). While there were few votes in the law and order issue in the 1950s and 1960s, politicians increasingly discovered that there were many votes to be gained by appearing to be tough on criminals and by pledging commitment to hard criminal justice policies (see Simon 2007). It is inconceivable today that crime and crime rates were ever a politically neutral subject but the redefinition of criminality as an indication of fundamental social breakdown is a relatively new development, certainly in the recent political history of many Western European societies (see Estrada 2004 on these changes in Sweden).

The key changes that are documented by Garland (2001) are as follows. In the period between the 1950s and the 1980s, the support for the welfare state in general, and liberal policy developments in penology and criminal justice in particular, weakened among the educated middle classes who had benefited from higher education and jobs in the bourgeoning public sector. Middle-class status ceased to be marked by the adoption of 'civilised' attitudes to poverty, the poor and to the criminal and instead came to be defined by conspicuous success in the neo-liberal economy of the 1980s. The most obvious British manifestation of this political change was the support for Thatcherism throughout the 1980s, and its variations elsewhere in Europe and the West. There was also a growing sense of insecurity in the midst of an apparent rise in crime rates.

The public's willingness to delegate authority to 'experts' to speak about crime and criminality gave way to a sense of disquiet about arguments drawing on models of social causality, not least because the very idea of society as something above and beyond the actions and consumer choices of individuals was called into question by the neo-liberal political voices of the 1980s. There was, therefore, an increasingly politically driven rejection of 'liberal' welfare approaches to deviant behaviour. Crime became a populist issue framed by the tabloid press and policy think tanks fixated by the vision of high-crime America showing Britain its future (see Jones and Newburn 2007 on the issue of policy transfer).

Other factors contributing to the political anxiety about crime and punishment since the 1980s relate to the lifestyle changes that have developed, especially in the spheres of work and family life. Garland identifies the spread of car ownership and the opportunities for car theft, the lengthening commute to work and the opportunities for people to experience criminal encounters on the streets, and the two-career family that makes empty houses vulnerable to burglars. These changes raise questions about our sense of social and moral obligation, or our sense of social solidarity, in an increasingly individualistic and materialist culture. In the classical criminological terms of both Robert Merton (1957) and Marcus Felson (1994), growing affluence in the midst of a social order that is socially polarising is likely to increase the sense of relative deprivation and anomie experienced by those excluded from the benefits of the affluent society, especially when they encounter the trappings of wealth through the routine activities of everyday life. Whatever may be the ultimate cause of high crime rates, the public are demanding a strong political reaction to deviant behaviour at the same time that there is a popular perception in politics and society that 'nothing works' in the criminal justice system. The police are ineffective, the courts are too lenient, and the prisons are too luxurious. The loss of public confidence in the bureaucratic effectiveness of the Home Office to deal with registered sex offenders, absconding criminal asylum seekers, and absconding murderers from the prison system in 2007 is the culmination of a long process of disenchantment with government efficiency in dealing with issues of crime. The tendency to 'define deviancy down' in the 1970s and 1980s that I discussed in the introduction has led to an over reaction today that is leading to contrary forces which seek to 'define deviancy up'. In an effort to respond to this change, the role of social welfare in modern society is no longer to steer behaviour towards goals considered desirable to meet policy objectives but is instead to control the signs of social indiscipline.

Garland suggested that the middle classes came to understand crime less as an abstract issue affecting those in poor neighbourhoods and more as a 'normal social fact' considered to be a threat to the very fabric of the social structure. That view was undoubtedly shaped by the rhetoric and policy design aimed at politicising the issue of crime and incivility for electoral popularity. Research by Estrada (2004) in Sweden indicates that this change had a political dynamic that operated quite independently of the statistical trends in actual offending: crime came to be defined as a social problem by social democratic and liberal parties as much as the conservative parties for expedient and electoral advantage despite stable levels of offending. His research reinforces the work of both Garland and Simon (2007) which suggests that a new template for governing society in an age of individualism and risk has been found in managing the 'crime problem'. This was marked by the explicitly aggressive vocabulary adopted in the 1980s in Britain by Margaret Thatcher's Home Secretary, the late Willie Whitelaw, who, in addition to announcing the expansion of the prison system, advocated the use of boot-camp style, 'short, sharp shocks' for incorrigibly anti-social youths. The language changed to talk of 'justice' rather than rehabilitation (see Hudson 1996), and indeterminate sentences rather than community corrections, although that has always been a difficult thing to deliver, as the current Home Secretary is finding with a full to capacity prison system. The approach continued with John Major's observation in the early 1990s that, as a nation, the British 'ought to understand a little less and condemn a little more' and, of course, the politicisation of the crime issue has been reaffirmed through the New Labour government's 'respect' agenda.

In relation to the public debate about 'respect' and incivility, it is germane to restate an observation made in Chapter 2 relating to changing attitudes, specifically the development of what I referred to as post-emotionalism and amoral familism (see Rodger 2000: 143–63). In an early intervention into the underclass debate, J. K. Galbraith conceptualised the post-emotionalism of the middle classes in a slightly different but related way. He drew attention to a system in which the 'most agreeable' work attracted the highest pay, and the 'contentment' of those who benefited from such a system led to an attitude towards the poor in terms of their threat, both physical and fiscal, rather than feelings of empathy for their impoverished position. The widening gap between those that Galbraith (1992) called 'the contented' and those categorised as 'the underclass' or 'the socially excluded', which has undoubtedly been created by the reduction in the tax burden of the rich and the retrenchment of the welfare state, has also been partly reinforced by significant attitudinal changes that have been shaped by behaviourist rather than social assumptions about incivility and criminality in criminal justice policy. Galbraith (1992) pointed to two emerging reactions among the middle classes to the 'social normality of crime' in the early 1990s. The first reaction was to develop a 'laager mentality – the hiring of personal, neighbourhood or apartment security guards or escape to the presumptively safe suburbs' (p. 16); this has been evident with the increase in the phenomenon known as 'gated communities' for the wealthy. The second reaction, which at the time he was writing in the early 1990s he described only as a likelihood but which has now become the reality that Galbraith predicted, is that the rising criminality and incivility

> will be attributed not to the social situation but to the inferior, even criminal, dispositions of the people involved .... The obvious fact that people of comfortable circumstances live peacefully together and those afflicted by poverty do not, goes largely unnoticed. Or, if noticed, it is not discussed amid the clamour for a clampdown on what seems an intrinsically ill-behaved and violent citizenry. (Galbraith 1992: 16)

Galbraith writes eloquently about the need to address issues of state intervention and taxation as the only means of resolving the social tensions and increasing 'underclass violence' that is a product of processes of de-civilisation. He was advocating this position at a time when the global economic orthodoxy had swung inexorably away from the Keynesian model implied in his argument. In a broad sweeping critique of the neo-liberal orthodoxy that was establishing itself globally at the time he was writing in the early 1990s, he rather forlornly argued the case for a return to progressive taxation. He recognised the resistance to this view, however, and conceded that arguing 'that taxes should now be used to reduce inequality is ... clearly outside the realm of comfortable thought' (p. 16). It is precisely the rejection of taxation as a solution to social problems that has been one of the most significant factors underpinning the growth of amoral and post-emotional attitudes.

The 'new politics of welfare': from social steering to social regulation

As referred to in Chapter 1, in a debate about whether or not it is appropriate to use the term 'welfare state' to refer to all social policy regimes within the OECD countries (see Veit-Wilson 2000; Atherton 2002; Wincott 2003), Viet-Wilson (2000) argued that a more discriminating definition of a welfare state should be applied only to those states 'which ensure a minimum real income for all'. I make reference to this debate at this point only because of the narrow and perhaps outdated conception of what constitutes a welfare state revealed by Viet-Wilson. His underlying assumption that the institution of the welfare state has been and remains primarily concerned with the relief of poverty rather than the management of deviance is increasingly unsustainable in contemporary Western societies: as suggested earlier, welfare in the Western European tradition has always been worker-centric and based on the social insurance principle, and, consequently, has always been concerned about the policing of those who do not or cannot participate in this form of institutionalised solidarity. However, where Viet-Wilson may inadvertently be correct is in the need to distinguish between welfare regimes that manage the problem of incentives to work through the traditional mechanisms of social steering (action through which a social actor or social system is moved from one state to another by the intentional decisions of a political authority, mainly through the distribution or redistribution of welfare and fiscal incentives) and those that resort to social regulation (action through which a social actor or social system is moved from one state to another by the use of legal and criminal constraint). This emphasis in public policy has been largely supported by the middle classes, who have, as Garland (2001) argues, abandoned welfarism in all its many guises.

A key theme in the analysis of the changing character and function of the welfare state since the 1970s has been the movement away from what Jessop (1999) has called the change from the 'Keynesian welfare national state' to the 'Schumpeterian workfare post-national regime'. As the subtitle to Jessop's 1999 paper makes clear, the fundamental change he describes is in the 'primary functions, scale and modes of coordination' characteristic of the welfare regimes typically found in north-western Europe. The supply-side economics driving contemporary social policy, coupled with an explicit concentration on welfare activeness (the subordination of social to economic policy and the insistence that claimants access benefits through a commitment to work and learn), has as its main objective making the practices of national welfare regimes compatible with the global logic of international markets and membership of supranational trading entities. The top-down, large-scale, Fordist welfare regime, characterised by central control of the direction and pace of social policy development, has given way to what is now referred to as a 'networked paradigm'. The key feature of this new economic and political configuration is described by Jessop (1999) as involving

> a tendential shift from imperative coordination by the sovereign state to an emphasis on interdependence, divisions of knowledge, reflexive negotiations and mutual learning. In short, there is a shift from govern*ment* to govern*ance* in the narrow sense. (Jessop 1999: 355)

The imagery that is being offered here is a movement from a state that is controlled by political policymakers, who mediate the big struggle between organised labour and capital to drive and steer the welfare state forward in accordance with a national social policy agenda, to a situation where governments respond to indirect international pressures by attempting to coordinate devolved centres of control and decision-making in order to steer them towards generalised policy goals: a movement from a formation of centralised power to one of at arms-length supervision.

Governance and public policy

The key term used to describe this fundamental change in the political management of postmodern society is *governance*. Political scientists have presented this perspective in public administration as a shift from seeing government in terms of institutions and concentrated power to seeing it as a social process that is founded on diffuse centres of control and decision-making (see Jessop 2002). Jessop's distinction between the 'national' character of Keynesian welfare management and the 'post-national' character of the Schumpeterian model is significant: responsibilities are devolved downwards because economic relations and policy agendas are no longer shaped by nationally derived priorities. Inequalities are tolerated in the name of preserving devolution and local autonomy as a virtuous principle; the orthodoxy of the governance perspective is that solutions to social problems must be found by local people and be consistent with locally understood needs. However, what is characteristic of this strategy is the expedient substitution of state funding and provision for *commercial, voluntary* and *informal* sources. This is an issue that I return to in Chapter 7. The criminal justice and social policy agendas of the past decade should be understood in the light of these broad structural changes in the political economy of welfare. Perhaps a cynical, but largely accurate, explanation of this movement in the field of criminal justice and social policy is that centrally coordinated policies are acknowledged to be difficult to manage and woeful in delivering the managerialist targets now required by rigorously audited public organisations and public funds. It is the idea of community that has emerged as the key territory to be coordinated and managed. What has emerged is a strategy of community governance through 'partnerships' between policy actors and stakeholders, which are delegated responsibility to deal with crime, incivility and community development. Priorities may be established centrally but the organisation and delivery of the policy goals is very much a devolved responsibility to local government and community partnerships. Rose (1996) argues that there has been a shift from *social government* to *government through communities*. Local authorities and communities are contracted to manage and deliver policy goals through strategies that are preoccupied with networks and joined-up policies.

Governance as inauthentic politics

A key critical issue here has been the questioning of what constitutes community and who is and is not affiliated with any given community. Governance has as its object the creation of conditions and a framework in which self-organising stakeholders can take responsibility for the management of policies shaped to meet their interests rather than those of a remote coordinating source of power. The underlying theory of this strategy is a mixture of participatory democracy and panoptic surveillance through audit and managerialism. What it has little to do with is grass-roots involvement in decision-making about local issues and strategies, and therein lies its fundamental flaw. What passes as governance from a managerialist perspective is what many years ago Etzioni (1968) called *inauthentic politics*. He suggests that 'a relationship, institution or society is inauthentic if it provides the appearance of responsiveness while the underlying condition is alienating' (p. 619). This is, of course, precisely why authority and responsibility are delegated while control and coordination remain centralised: 'inauthentic structures devote a higher ratio of their efforts than alienating ones to conceal their contours and to generating the appearance of responsiveness' (Etzioni 1968: 620). Etzioni argued that inauthentic politics manipulates people rather than alienates them. The governance perspective shares this particular problem complex with Etzioni's notion of inauthentic politics, although it draws on Foucault for its intellectual credence. Governmental power is aimed at 'constructing' active citizens who can, or are likely to, make choices in accordance with government stimulation. Subjectivity is to be cultivated rather than suppressed; it is about the choices people make about their lives whether they relate to work, consumption, community management, or, crucially, lifestyle and behaviour patterns. The development of community-based crime-prevention partnerships must be understood within this framework, because it is the local communities that are being contracted to deal with their own deviants once the legislative mechanisms and community powers are put in place.

Crawford (2003) has drawn attention to the movements in governance which could be said to reinforce the tendency towards inauthentic politics. His particular focus is on the phenomenon of 'contractual governance', which now dominates language, thinking and practice in the fields of social policy and community crime prevention. Fundamentally, the use of contracts in the sphere of social welfare seeks to mimic the practices of the market and bring to public policy management the disciplines of the private sector; the language of objective setting, performance measurement and accountability is reaffirmed by commitment to a contractual relationship. However, it could be suggested that it conceals its purpose by suggesting a legal underbelly to an agreement that in many cases is actually absent. Indeed, many so-called contracts and agreements are not legally binding and would be insecure in terms of legal remedy if they were to be challenged in the courts. They are merely convenient and expedient devices that provide a vocabulary and a legalistic gloss to what may be fundamentally a political relationship aimed at enforcing market-type disciplines in non-market situations. The underlying coercive drive behind the contractual movement is obscured, therefore, by the *appearance* of reciprocity, mutual obligation and responsibility embedded in the contractual relationship, which is, instead, in place primarily to effect accountability and social regulation by the delegating authority and power. In the field of community crime prevention, for example, there are a number of concerns about the use of contracts: the delegation of responsibility to the institutions and personnel of civil society to take on control functions; the blurring of the distinction between the state and civil society; the emergence of 'civil property rights' as a basis for citizenship rather than one based on the social contract underpinned by statutory guarantees. The central character of the contract in the sphere of social welfare and criminal justice is its *inauthenticity*. As Crawford argues, it is 'the voluntary acceptance of imposed obligations that provides the essential quality of contracts' (Crawford 2003: 489). The widespread use of contractual governance in the areas dealing with anti-social behaviour and community crime prevention obscures the exercise of social control by legalistic social regulation. Contracts are being used widely in a variety of settings. In education, the use of home–school agreements is common, and behaviour contracts shape patterns of work and leisure in contexts where children and young people are being monitored. In housing management, there is an array of regulatory mechanisms available to the housing manager to regulate and punish those who violate contracts, such as control over the tenant status, behaviour agreements, and, crucially, the seeking of ASBOs not only for anti-social tenants but also to prevent their visitors from entering neighbourhoods and communities in a disorderly and promiscuous way. Crawford (2003) argues that the use of such contracts

> illustrate[s] the manner in which significant areas of social policy are becoming criminalised in that they are being governed through their security and disorder implications. They represent policing *through* housing, education, leisure and lifestyle opportunities. (Crawford 2003: 501)

Contractual governance is now the 'normal face of politics' because statism is considered to be antithetical to freedom, choice and individualism. The issue is, of course, that 'notions of consent are encircled by coercion' (Crawford 2003: 500). It only appears that the state is at arm's length when at a fundamental level governance is merely one mechanism of exercising political power; it is the pre-eminent method of inauthentic politics. The problem of how to control crime and anti-social disorder effectively through strategies of devolved community governance perhaps generates more inauthentic political activity than many other areas of public policy and often it fails. At that point alternative solutions are sought.

Joined-upness

One dominant theme in the politics of community governance has been that of 'joined-up' policy. While the relationship and intercourse between the different arms of the state have always been a problematic feature of government, the attempt to address actively issues of territoriality in the delivery of social and criminal justice policy has been a notable aspect of New Labour's strategy to address anti-social behaviour and criminality. The configuration of the professional demarcation lines, which spell out professional responsibilities and authority in policy delivery, was clear in the modernist phase of welfare state development: expertise was given its place, whether in the sphere of social work, penology, education, health or policing, and modernisation has typically entailed greater and greater differentiation of professional roles and responsibilities. However, a feature of the postmodernist era has been, of course, the de-differentiation of the structure of the state; the movement to weaken the boundaries, or, indeed, blur the boundaries, between arms of government in order to achieve greater coherence and rationality in the delivery of policy. What is entailed in this process is the concealment of the real source of authority, which is retained at the centre of government, the supposed heart for the strategic direction of policy, while the 'action' end of the policy chain is apparently delegated to agencies not classified as being part of the state. This appears to be passing powers away from the state but is actually a mechanism better to control and steer the commercial and voluntary sectors, which take the burden of policy delivery in this system through tightly audited funding arrangements and regulations. The de-differentiation process can be observed through the hollowing out of the state and the increasing transfer of responsibility to civil society, particularly the voluntary sector and commercial sector (see Lewis 1999; 2005). The increasing readiness of central government to concede powers to regions is justified in terms of ensuring greater autonomy and individual freedom, as well as a measure of self-determination at a local and regional level. However, it could be viewed instead as a process of inauthentic politics because the apparent transfer of authority, with perhaps the exception of Scotland with its distinctive legal system, conceals a process of centralised budgetary and legal control. I will return to this theme in more detail in Chapter 7, where I discuss the strategy for civil renewal.

I am suggesting here that the conception of 'joined-up' government is part of the wider problem involving the inauthenticity just outlined. The concept of joined-up policy is, perhaps, a slightly altered perspective on the notion first discussed by Cohen (1985) as 'net widening'. The concern remains the same with joined-upness as with 'net widening', in that the clarity often demanded by clients and the public of knowing exactly the professional auspices of agents and agencies they are dealing with is obscured. This anxiety is most obvious in those contexts which involve the interchange between the world of welfare and policing. For example, the debate in the 1980s about hard policing versus community policing was one case where there was a level of anxiety about what the latter meant in practice. Attempts to introduce not only more professional dialogue between police officers, teachers and social workers, but also actual shared practice through the active involvement of police officers in community development activities, led to debate about professional demarcation. The issue centred fundamentally on the possible clash between competing professional paradigms and, in particular, the fact that a police officer, whether working in a youth club or on the beat, is never off duty. Members of the public could be seduced into forgetting that the congenial assistant involved in the community may be noting and recording forensic information about them under the guise of befriending, a clear infringement of human rights and natural justice.

Perhaps a more recent example of this phenomenon will clarify the issues in the context of processes that criminalise social policy. Burnett and Appleton (2004) investigated the joined-up services designed to tackle youth crime in Oxfordshire. In the wake of the Audit Commission's call for more collaborative work between agencies concerned with youth (Audit Commission 1996), a number of projects have been started which have as a primary aim the bringing together of disparate professional groups to form youth offending teams as part of an attempt to improve youth justice. They situate their research in the debate about whether the demand for more joined-up policy is a benevolent development, aimed at accentuating the welfare element in the area of youth justice, or is, in fact, part of a conspiratorial strategy to move the youth justice system towards increased punitiveness and managerialism. The research relates to the wider movements in youth justice, particularly in America, where there is a definite shift towards a more punitive and less welfare-orientated system of youth justice or, as they phrase it, the repenalisation of youth offending. The movement towards joined-up policy can also be understood in terms of the long process of the 'de-professionalisation' of the criminal justice system that Garland (2001) has described and that I alluded to above. A key issue for investigation was the extent to which the competing professional paradigms of police officers, teachers, social workers and mental health nurses would be capable of being integrated into an effective collaborative effort. The tensions that required careful negotiation emerged between the ethics informing the corporate management of the programme and the professional values brought to the project by social workers and mental health professionals. They in turn had professional differences in their approach to clients when compared with police officers. The types of tensions reported by Burnett and Appleton (2004) were clashes over case-management approaches and those professional groups with backgrounds that were grounded in direct work with youth. The suppression of professional competencies had to be accepted as part of the negotiations to make the programmes work. The politics of joined-up policy demands a corporatist management paradigm to shape and inform effective practice. Strategic management requires pooled budgets to be used efficiently and multiagency teams to shape their bids for funding in accordance with the need to demonstrate value for money and evidence-based results. A key objective of the new public management of such projects is to replace the dominant welfare culture informing youth and social work with a paradigm drawn from the world of audit. This requires the transformation of working practices so that costs can be managed more effectively while clear targets for measuring success can be identified. The project reported by Burnett and Appleton appeared to be characterised by the resilience of the welfare paradigm, especially the social work ethic, but that will not always be the case, and the tensions identified in their research are real and persistent.

The politics of withholding benefits

Despite the effort devoted to fashioning a new strategy of contractual and community governance, there will always be limits to its effectiveness, and beyond its limits there is a point where punitive action is deemed to be required. While the use of civil law has been identified as the main mechanism for enforcing compliance with the new strategy, the use of the ASBO being well understood by everyone, less attention has been given to the changing role of welfare benefits in the evolving 'respect' strategy. The new politics of welfare has emerged as an area of 'negative' policy action which is designed to deal with the messy end of governance relationships. The new politics of welfare seeks to rebuild what Field (2003) calls the social ecology of the working-class community, with all that implies about strengthening social capital, supporting dysfunctional families and repairing fragmented and atomised communities. And lying at the centre of that strategy is a conception of a welfare contract which demands civility and good neighbourliness in exchange for welfare resources. The underlying axiom guiding social policy today is that we live in what New Labour has called the 'something for something society', and those on welfare benefits who reject this principle will be forced to reconsider their behaviour by the removal of their welfare benefits. The 'something for nothing society', associated with a rights-based conception of citizenship, is considered to be antithetical to *civic activeness*. What is new about the contemporary politics of welfare is that the modernist pretence that the welfare state is a grand humanitarian project, driven by the objectives of social justice and the elimination of poverty, is clearly in the process of being abandoned.

The 'new politics of welfare', as conceptualised by the New Labour government, is intent on converting the welfare benefits system into a lever for changing behaviour. If a defining principle of a welfare state is that it meets social and human need regardless of issues of desert, as Viet-Wilson (2000) argues, then the withholding of a major welfare benefit from households because of deviant behaviour surely indicates a change in the role and character of the welfare state. The concern which this proposal raises is that dysfunctional families on housing benefit, irrespective of their behaviour, will already be multiply deprived on measures of education, employment and income. By removing a core welfare benefit as an instrument of punishment, a threshold will be crossed de-differentiating the world of welfare from the world of criminal justice. This departure in housing policy has its origins in the private member's Housing Benefit (Withholding Payment) Bill introduced to Parliament in 2002 by Frank Field. While Field's Bill ran out of time, it was acknowledged at the time that it had established principles that future government legislation would incorporate. Parallel to the enactment of the Anti-social Behaviour Act in 2003 in England and Wales, a UK-wide consultation paper was circulated on the matter of withdrawing housing benefit. The result of that consultation is that a strong view emerged in many areas of present-day British society that welfare support should be available only on the condition that recipients behave in a civil manner. Field (2002; 2003; 2004; 2005) continues to be a strong voice on this subject. He has advanced the notion of a 'welfare contract' whereby access to welfare benefits from social assistance to programmes such as Sure Start should be on the condition that claimants behave in ways that are considerate to others. His view is that the welfare state should act as a teacher of 'the three cardinal virtues – politeness, considerateness and thoughtfulness' (2003: 126). The education system would reinforce these virtues through the teaching of citizenship as a central feature of the curriculum. Civil contracts would be signed by citizens at key stages of their encounter with the state from registering a birth to claiming benefit. And the role of the police in the community would be that of surrogate parent where deviance requires a swift reaction in the absence of a responsible parent. With respect to the role envisaged for the police, Field seems to be suggesting that the world of criminal justice should, quite explicitly, become involved in matters typically regarded as beyond the reach of policing, embracing elements of social work, community development activity and parenting. At the heart of this perspective lies advocacy for the teaching and training of those deemed to be unruly by 'social highway codes' and strict adherence to 'welfare contracts'. It is precisely the tendency to bring together issues of parenting, policing and education which fundamentally amounts to a significant movement towards criminalising social policy.

The policy problem of focusing on the sub-criminal anti-social deviant was constructed through the Parliamentary debate about Field's Bill. I am suggesting that he was a key political catalyst for developments in legislation that were subsequently enacted against anti-social behaviour. His private member's Bill facilitated the early debate on how to develop some of the principles and approaches first contained in the Crime and Disorder Act 1998. The extension of the New Labour approach to criminal justice to embrace welfare issues explicitly was significant. The *new politics of welfare* became thereafter primarily focused on the *politics of conduct.*

Why did Frank Field (2003) claim that welfare politics is moving into a new phase? The stimulus for his observation was a concern for what he considered to be the growth in uncivilised behaviour by a sizeable minority of what is referred to as 'young fiends' (Field 2002) who were terrorising 'decent pensioners' in his Birkenhead constituency. The concerns brought to his constituency surgeries by pensioners were, according to Field, markedly different from those he used to deal with in 1979 when he first became an MP. Gone were the concerns about housing, social security and employment, and in their place was a generalised plea that something be done about anti-social behaviour in local neighbourhoods and housing estates.

The pensioners quietly explained the hell in which they had been engulfed. Young lads ran across their bungalow roofs, peed through their letter boxes, jumped out of the shadows as they returned home at night and, when they were watching television, tried to break their sitting room windows. (Field 2002: 5)

When considered in isolation, each of these acts may seem to be nothing more than childish pranks, but what is problematic is that they were spatially concentrated in poor housing estates and, according to Field, had become a routine way of behaving for a minority of unemployed youths. The issues surrounding anti-social behaviour have crowded out traditional working-class concerns about incomes, employment and pensions and, in his view, require a different kind of response from governments than in the past.

The aim of the new welfare politics will be to change behaviour. Private virtues, if not naturally acquired, need to be encouraged through the welfare system and basic standards of behaviour set. Those who deliberately or constantly break the rules will lose entitlement to the money they receive from the taxes paid by decent families whose lives they terrorise. (Field 2002)

Field's project was expressed through his private member's Housing Benefit (Withholding of Payment) Bill which ran out of Parliamentary time in 2002, but it was subsequently picked up by the Labour government in the Anti-Social Behaviour Bill 2003, although subjected to revision and reformulation. The announcement in June 2006 that the New Labour government intended to bring forward legislation allowing the withholding of housing benefit from families and households repeatedly found guilty of anti-social behaviour signalled a significant change in the principles of the welfare state. It is identified as a key policy action in 2007/08.

It is not surprising that welfare benefit withdrawal as a remedy for persistent anti-social behaviour would become an issue for legislation. Its spirit and principles were already contained in a wide range of legislation, including the Crime and Disorder Act 1998 and the housing legislation north and south of the border. Indeed, there was also a manifesto commitment by the Conservative Party in the 2005 general election to withdraw housing benefit from tenants found guilty of anti-social behaviour by the courts on three occasions. What is at issue here is not, therefore, the frustrations and policy predilections of a maverick Labour MP but the broader shift in the way in which social policy is to be used by contemporary policymakers. Field merely captured the legislative mood of the time and rightly saw that there was a general interest in tackling anti-social behaviour through social policy legislation. The consequence of this legislation is the movement of government strategy from that of the social steering of populations towards desirable modes of behaviour by the distribution of welfare benefits, services and fiscal inducements, to that of overtly seeking to control and, in some cases, criminalise those variously described as the anti-social or the underclass that will not submit to the disciplines of living in a worker-centric and consumer society. This development in contemporary British social policy echoes many of the principles and approaches that were implemented in the USA through the passing of the Personal Responsibility and Work Opportunity Act of 1996. One feature of the harsh US approach to welfare deviance has been to remove the welfare safety net (see Eitzen and Zinn 2000). It is precisely this tendency to use social policy negatively and coercively that has crept into British social policy. A brief look at the Parliamentary debate surrounding the Field Bill will provide a flavour of the evolving policy perspective.

Housing Benefit (Withholding of Payment) Bill[1]

There was a clear commitment to the Field Bill by the New Labour government at the time, albeit in modified and possibly diluted form. Speaking in the Standing Committee debate on the Bill for the Labour government, Malcolm Wicks (then Parliamentary Under-Secretary of State for Work and Pensions) indicated that it was the intention of the government to table amendments to the Bill and to facilitate its passage to law. There was also a reaffirmation of the view 'that our welfare state needs to be underpinned again – as it was originally – by a proper balance of people's rights and duties', but he added that 'we have neglected to translate rhetoric about citizenship into workable legislation' (Standing Committee B 18 June). There was therefore an acknowledgement that in reality

> the Bill raises some complex and technical questions. Withdrawing or, as the Government envisage, reducing benefits involves what would otherwise be a person's legal entitlement ... we must ensure that any legislation complies with the Human Rights Act 1998 and that its provisions are both fair and proportionate. (House of Commons, Housing Benefit

(Withholding of Payment) Bill, Standing Committee B 18 June 2002)

In the opening exchanges in the Committee in June 2002, it was clear that there were two primary concerns in government about the change of emphasis for social policy signalled by Field's Bill: the issues surrounding the ECHR and whether the withdrawal of benefits violated human rights, and the concern that whatever sanctions were introduced should be proportionate to the offence. A number of arguments were advanced by members of the Committee in response to the government's caution. First there was an acknowledgement that beyond the scope of the Bill there would be a need to establish forms of supported living for 'families that are simply beyond the realm of normal living' (Vernon Coaker, MP for Gedling). George Howarth, MP for Knowsley North and Sefton East, entered the debate by sharing with the Committee his thoughts on this particular issue.

> I have given some thought to what we should do with such families. I am more and more inclined to the idea of weekend prisons for families that do not function properly, so that they can be given the opportunity every weekend to attend compulsory programmes that will help them to modify their behaviour. (George Howarth 18 June 2002, Standing Committee B, Housing Benefit [Withholding of Payment] Bill)

The Parliamentary debate at several stages clearly ran ahead of the benefits issue to embrace unconcealed zeal for punitive actions. However, what appeared to be a rather extreme position articulated by George Howarth in 2002 has since become common place; indeed, the idea of 'sin bins' for anti-social families is actual policy in many areas of the country, an issue that I will return to in the following chapter. Field, of course, reiterated that the purpose of the Bill was to establish the principle that welfare benefits should not be given unconditionally and that they 'should be earned by being good citizens and should not come without strings'. While he argued that withdrawal of benefit could be made by increments, his position was, and presumably remains, that there should be in some cases the complete withdrawal of housing benefit for up to a year as an ultimate deterrent. The government were inclined towards a range of other sanctions, including the extension of schemes involving the manipulation of different tenant statuses together with behaviour contracts and model tenancy agreements. Most of these policy ideas were subsequently introduced either in pilot schemes or embedded in the Anti-social Behaviour Act 2003 and the Housing Act 2004.

On the issue of human rights, many members of the Committee felt that the ECHR should not be accepted as a constraint on legislation to combat anti-social behaviour but rather that the legislation should act as a challenge to the Convention and, if necessary, that the principle of withholding benefits should be tested in the courts. The announcement in 2006 that the Labour government intended to press ahead with legislation enabling the withdrawal of benefits may trigger an exploration of its legality in terms of human rights legislation.

The differences between Field's private member's Bill and the government legislation which both preceded and succeeded it is a matter of fine tuning – more precision in defining anti-social behaviour and greater clarity regarding the conditions under which benefit may be arrested or reduced and the putting in place of measures to ensure that there was an underpinning hardship regime. The debate largely revolved around the issue of whether these measures would dilute the Bill. Indeed, Field's response to the Parliamentary Under-Secretary of State was to suggest that he had underestimated the 'new political territory' that was being traversed and argued that 'how we deal with the breakdown of the teaching and transference of private virtue is a question that will occupy the time of most Government Departments and of the House and its Committees when they consider legislation' (House of Commons, Standing Committee B 18 June 2002). More recently, Field (2006a; 2006b) has moved away from a focus on the relationship between benefits and anti-social behaviour and towards engaging with the ideological and moral dimension of the issue; more specifically, the relationship between the decline in civility and the decline in Christianity. However, that is a debate that should be joined elsewhere.

A climate has been created since the enactment of the anti-social behaviour legislation in which the issue of the conditionality of welfare benefits is likely to become accepted as a mechanism for disciplining those who are considered deviant as opposed to being indolent. The general tenor of the benefit system is increasingly geared towards activeness, whether that relates to supporting lone parents into work or filtering out the reluctant workers on incapacity benefit. The issues which seemed extreme during the passage of Field's private member's Bill now look increasingly mainstream and have generally been accepted.

Regulatory communities and the politics of social inclusion

The relationship between the Parliamentary debates about anti-social behaviour, governance and social policy is best understood in terms of its influence on the construction of what Carr, Cowan and Hunter (2007) have called the creation of a *regulatory community*. In the context of discussing the link between housing policy and crime control, they argue that the attempt by government to regulate private, as opposed to social, housing landlords required a strategy to make them visible as a community that could be monitored and regulated. What has typically happened is that problem populations are identified as targets for legislative action, and differentiated policy strategies are evolved, only after they have first been constructed as a problem grouping presenting a distinctive set of control challenges. The anti-social family, the anti-social tenant, and the incivility of children in the streets has to be converted from the status of being an everyday nuisance, requiring tolerance and give and take, to being seen as chronic criminality requiring more coercive forms of intervention. Communities, housing estates, and failing and dysfunctional families have been constructed as the main sites for policy intervention. Once the problem population has been configured, the technologies of control can be fashioned. The control of social housing tenants, for example, can be made effective through the power of social landlords to impose consistent rules about conduct and property maintenance and the use of the power to evict or relocate as a persuasive lever if necessary. Those evicted from the social housing sector invariably move to the private sector and therefore require to be identified as a distinctive problem population in need of regulation and policy intervention. Carr *et al.* (2007) suggest that the problem of how to control private landlords and their anti-social tenants has created a distinctive *crime-control housing crisis*. For example, private landlords who may be complicit in assisting anti-social tenants to defraud the state through housing-benefit scams can be brought to heel by the withdrawal of benefit for those convicted of anti-social behaviour or deemed to be causing neighbours a problem. Carr *et al.* (2007) also make the particular argument that the use of regulatory technologies furnished by the Housing Act 2004 enables private landlords to be licensed and more effectively monitored. In implementing these regulatory strategies, the government can also control criminality that is associated with housing and so bring the spheres of social policy and criminal justice together (see Flint 2006a).

Levitas (2005) can assist us in understanding the processes involved in constructing regulatory communities. In her enquiry into the broad issue of social inclusion and exclusion, she identifies three broad ways of thinking about social exclusion. She differentiates the *redistributive discourse* (RED) from the *social integrationist discourse* (SID) and the *moral underclass discourse* (MUD). It is clear that the new orthodoxy of New Labour has been SID, with a strong emphasis on social integration through work. Strategies to encourage activeness in finding work and training are the cornerstone of both their benefits and education and training policies. The integrative focus of their policy strategy became centred on the issue of how matters of social exclusion could be addressed without engaging with traditional old Labour concerns about redistribution and class inequality, which were always framed in terms of the differential power between labour and capital. The trick was to find an alternative foundation on which to address matters of inequality and injustice without appearing to be fighting the old class and inequality battles. Social exclusion, it was concluded, had many more dimensions than simply class inequality: it embraced cultural, geographical and familial dimensions. The discovery of the idea of community by New Labour prior to its 1997 election win succeeded in delineating the focus of its policy effort towards social inclusion as an antidote to the nearly two decades of neo-liberalism. Indeed, part of the New Labour political rhetoric of the 1990s was to draw on the European tradition, particularly the French concept of social solidarity through social integration (see Silver 1994; 1996). However, at the point where its strategy for social inclusion fails, and the limits of governance of the socially excluded are confronted, New Labour has moved ground since coming to political office and has increasingly embraced the MUD perspective by isolating anti-social behaviour as a particular problem requiring a distinctive set of joined-up social and criminal justice policies. The creation of the various hybridised government units, such as the Social Exclusion Unit and the Anti-social Behaviour Units, provides the organisational coordination of these strategies. As Levitas observes, the SID and MUD discourses have largely vied with each other for ascendancy since 1997, but, clearly, in the sphere of social policy and criminal justice, it is the MUD which has become dominant.

Concluding observations

I started this chapter by drawing attention to a contemporary development of the core theory of civilising and de-civilisng processes by suggesting that much of the political reaction to anti-social behaviour and deviance in the past 30 years can be understood in terms of the concept of informalisation. Wouters (1987a, 1987b; 2007) has described the emergence of less restrained behaviour in modern societies more generally and among those less integrated into mainstream society in particular. This observation is consistent with the theory of the civilising process and is suggestive of significant changes connected with trends towards de-civilising processes. Garland (2001) has described the middle-class reaction to that process, and the growing uneasiness in politics and society at the growing normality of crime in everyday life, by explaining why there has been a punitive and anti-welfare current in present-day society. The support for the welfare state and liberal penal policies characteristic of the Keynesian welfare state has weakened because of a perception among the middle classes that there is more car theft, more street crime, and generally more disorderly behaviour today than there was 10 and 20 years ago, and, significantly, that liberal welfare strategies do not work. The politics of behaviour, stimulated by this perceived social malaise, has led to public policy strategies that seek to address the security threat posed to what J.K. Galbraith called 'the contended' by those losing out in the affluent society.

In the context of the politics and policy of incivility, governance has been the strategic public policy mechanism used in response to these problems. The trick attempted by those controlling the central direction of the state has been to appear to delegate authority to key stakeholders in the localities in line with the dictates of the new public management for 'at arm's-length government' yet retain fundamental control over the process of administering criminal justice and social policy initiatives. This I described as inauthentic, following Etzioni (1968). Current policies are replete with terms such as 'contractual governance', 'joined-upness' and 'partnership' that seek to describe a networked system in which local stakeholders are supposed to have the authority and power to effect change. In reality, it may be inauthentic appearance because in reality the funding and strategic policy design are retained at the political centre.

A key task for those seeking to develop policies to tackle incivility and criminality has been to construct a 'regulatory community' against which disciplinary measures can be applied. At the heart of that regulatory community lie dysfunctional families and unruly children. The politics of behaviour has approached the question of what can be done to control the private decisions of anti-social families by using the benefits and services of the welfare state in a coercive way. No longer is access to social welfare to be seen as a right but as something that has responsibilities attached to it. The welfare contract that is implicit in recent welfare developments allows for the withdrawal of welfare benefits from those unwilling to behave in a disciplined and civil manner. The Crime and Disorder Act 1998 and the Anti-social Behaviour Act 2003 were particularly concerned with identifying mechanisms that would allow both greater control over families that were deemed to be failing children and ways of controlling children in the absence of functional and responsible families. The relationship between dysfunctional families, anti-social children and adult criminality is the subject of the next chapter.

Note

1 Quotations from the Parliamentary debate of the Housing Benefit (Withholding of Payment) Bill relate to the verbatim transcript of the Standing Committee B, which sat under the Chairmanship of Edward O'Hara MP on 18 June and 11 July 2002. See http://www.publications. parliament.uk

Chapter 5

Family life and anti-social behaviour

The family has always been an object of interest to policymakers. Indeed, the central policy issue for governments since the nineteenth century has been how to influence in the public interest the many private decisions that people make about relationships, sexuality and parenting without violating the sanctity of the private sphere and undermining liberal democratic sensibilities (see Rodger 1996). The normal route to resolve these issues of social steering has been for the state to engage in 'child saving' through social work intervention combined with social services but today the New Labour strategy has been far more all-encompassing and more direct. Tony Blair reminded the public of what he considered to be the primary object of social and family policy under New Labour at his monthly prime minister's press conference in February 2007. Responding to a debate about providing incentives to marriage through tax breaks, he argued that it was the dysfunctional family that had to be the focus of policy intervention and that justified a central feature of the government's strategy, early intervention in families deemed to be failing. The Conservative Party's focus on tax and benefit incentives for marriage did not, claimed Blair, address the problem population of families consisting of failing parents and out-of-control children requiring social regulation, although the subtext remained that, of course, marriage was desirable for the stable upbringing of children (see Social Policy Justice Group 2006 on Conservative policy). The ease with which the debate about family life rubbed shoulders with the debate about how to control incivility illustrated clearly the way in which this key area of family policy had been criminalised. To draw on Levitas' useful analysis, the resilience of the moral underclass discourse is evident in both New Labour's focus on anti-social and dysfunctional families and the Conservative Party's concerns about 'fractured families'.

Personal relationships in contemporary society

The 'family issue' can be divided usefully into two distinct sets of concerns, which I will call, for simplicity, *changing patterns of intimacy* and the *social impact of divorce and separation*. It is the narcissism said to be driving contemporary personal relationships that is implicated in the rise of anti-social behaviour.

Changing patterns of intimacy

In the past decade, the sociological literature has increasingly enclosed discussion of family and marriage in the framework of the *sociology of individualism* to capture the key change affecting social relationships (see Giddens 1992; Jamieson 1998; Lewis 2001; Beck and Beck-Gernsheim 2002). Giddens in particular has furnished us with a new vocabulary to describe changing patterns of intimacy that has drawn attention to the lack of commitment and sense of continuing obligation in modern relationships. *Confluent love, the pure relationship*, and the *plasticity of sexuality* are concepts that Giddens uses to explain the contemporary predilection for the superficial physicality and impermanence of emotional and sexual relations. He suggests that relationships are now formed only for their intrinsic qualities and only until something better comes along. Modern relationships are presented as liberating and full of choices compared with the mid-twentieth century.

This view of the empowered and reflective social actor is, however, overly sanguine about modern relationships and overlooks the gendered and class limitations constraining real lives when attention turns to the mundane realities of children and family existence. For example, many working-class women are left to negotiate the trials of parenthood on their own (Jamieson 1998). And those who try to maintain a stable family form in the face of poverty and bad housing in a cultural climate where family obligations are negotiable rather than fixed will do so as individuals, and not as part of an extended network of family relatives (see Lewis 2001). Rates of divorce increase as the social hierarchy is descended, and there is nothing more guaranteed to distract parents from their children than coping with uncertainty about household income, whether based on marriage or cohabitation. Meanwhile, young men without employment and skills are not good partner or marriage material, and a poor prospect for a woman seeking stability in her family life for her children. Young men without attachments to family and work typically pursue the project of realising their individualism by pursuing lifestyle choices that are at best selfish and amoral and at worst predatory and uncaring (see Anderson 1990: 112–14). This is the context that is leading the youth justice system to focus increasingly on the failures of parents to socialise their children effectively. The source of disorder and anti-social behaviour is increasingly being traced back to 'bad parents' behaving in a neglectful and selfish manner. I will return to this theme in the next chapter.

The social impact of divorce

A key feature of modern relationships appears to be a decline in the acceptance of an immutable understanding of social and personal obligation (Lewis, Clark and Morgan 1992; Lewis 2001). Eeklaar and MacLean (2004) have suggested that today there has been a change in people's sense of obligation from a set of moral rules about how one *ought* to behave to a set of social rules based on perceptions of *how the world works*. They argue that the reasons for marrying, divorcing or staying together as a couple are 'rooted in action not in values'. Typically, couples develop a sense of obligation to each other, their children and their partnership that is based less on a moral calculus and more on pragmatic factors relating to childcare and finances. However, in the absence of external forces to cement family relationships, no-fault divorce law, and no agreement about responsibilities and commitment beyond those that are situationally negotiated, it is unsurprising that the decisions taken about family relationships often appear to have little regard for the interests of children and even less for the notion of maintaining a family intact.

In a period when thinking about crime has been framed by concerns about social exclusion and social integration, which Levitas (2005) describes in terms of 'the new Durkheimian hegemony' in social policy, it is unsurprising that those social institutions regarded as the most important for socialising children are the focus of social control policies more generally and criminal justice strategies in particular. The divorce rate and the disappearing father role in contemporary family life are now regarded as key sites where social and criminal justice policy meet. In criminology, the renewed interest in the *institutional-anomie* theory points to the importance of the family–crime linkage and in particular the subordination of social institutions in civil society to a rampant and disembedded market economy (see Chamlin and Cochran 1995; Savolainen 2000; Messner and Rosenfeld 2001; Bernburg 2002; Kim and Pridemore 2005). Research using this paradigm has pointed to the failure of the institutions of civil society, including the family, to provide a protective insulation for young people living in marginal communities. The worst impact of these forces has been experienced in the peripheral housing estates and inner cities, where the dual influences of globalisation and industrial restructuring have combined with post-colonial migration to create residual populations struggling to maintain community cohesion and family stability amidst a crumbling built environment and an informal economy of drugs and illicit trading. Family structures are changing throughout contemporary society, but they are particularly vulnerable to disintegration in the marginal and ghettoised communities of the postmodern city.

Family life and criminality

Criminology's contribution to understanding these often complex modern relationships has been to undertake large-scale empirical research projects, often using longitudinal methodologies, which reduce the complexities and interdependencies of modern life to variables that can be manipulated by policymakers. The work of the Cambridge Institute of Criminology (Farrington 1995) and the Newcastle study by Kolvin and others (Kolvin, Miller, Fleeting and Kolvin 1988; Kolvin, Miller, Scott and Gatzanis 1990) represent examples of this type of research in the UK. Its primary purpose is to identify risk factors for delinquency and adult criminality and construct plausible policy strategies of risk prevention. The focus of that policy intervention has been on dysfunctional families and their domestic management practices and child-rearing competence. As an approach, it has been criticised for its empiricist stockpiling of data on delinquency and family life, which have sometimes been used in partisan ways. For example, those on the political Right, such as Murray (1994), Dennis (1993), and Dennis and Erdos (1992), have drawn selectively on the data in order to claim scientific rigour and neutrality for what amounts to a neo-liberal attack on lone parenthood. It is also research that has largely informed recent New Labour thinking about the family.

It is worth considering the nature of this work briefly because it has been influential in policy circles. Overall, this type of research has tended to generate three distinctive theoretical approaches, which are often synergetic in their explanatory power of the relationship between family life and criminality. Juby and Farrington (2001) summarise the theories in terms of those, such as *selection theories*, that seek to identify particularly significant causal variables associated with delinquency and anti-social behaviour out of the wide range of factors correlated with deviance, while *life-course theories* can be illuminating about those factors that moderate and mediate the effects of the traumatic and disruptive aspects of poor family experiences. *Trauma theories* focus our attention on the individual and the ways in which particular individual children cope with the experience of life in a disrupted family.

Sheldon and Eleanor Gleuck were the pioneers of the longitudinal method in American criminology. Their large-scale studies incorporated both comparative and longitudinal methods and, despite the criticism of the latter by luminaries of American sociology such as Edwin Sutherland in the 1930s and 1940s, again for being largely atheoretical, the influence of the longitudinal method in American criminology continues today (see Laub and Samspon 1991; Laub and Sampson 2003; Simons, Simons and Wallace 2004). In their major study *Unravelling Juvenile Delinquency* (Gleuck and Gleuck 1950), the Gleucks compared 500 delinquent boys (male reformatory inmates) with 500 non-delinquent boys over a 15-year period. Their original research and some of its key data have been reworked by Laub and Sampson (1998; 2003), and have been particularly helpful in developing our understanding of desistance from crime and its relationship to family and marriage. The key findings of the early research by the Gleucks have been corroborated by a number of pieces of research (see McCord 1979; 1991; Gove and Crutchfield 1982; Larzelere and Patterson 1990; Sampson 2003; Farrington 2007) and have become the received wisdom of the field today. What are those key findings? First, the age of the onset of childhood delinquency was found to be crucial in predicting and understanding adult criminality. Second, those who were delinquent as children had a pathway through life quite different from non-delinquent boys, especially regarding involvement in deviant activities ranging from minor offences, such as illicit drinking and promiscuous sexuality, through to illicit drug use and serious criminality. Third, their research suggested that the most important influence or determinant of juvenile delinquency and adult criminality is family environment: the three family factors identified as significant are parental supervision, disciplinary practices and child–parent attachment. Family life was identified as the pre-eminent social institution whose functioning is crucial to understand criminality. And the family remains at the centre of research and debate about anti-social behaviour and crime today.

Subsequent research has isolated those particular features of family life and family relationships that are considered to be specifically influential in shaping behaviour. We can distinguish between *social* and *individual* levels of impact for analytical purposes while also recognising that the two levels are inextricably linked. This distinction differentiates between those factors that relate to the family processes that structure relationships and connect the family system to the wider community and society (social determinants) and those factors that affect the psychological make-up of individuals in terms of their emotional and behavioural predispositions (psychological determinants). A key theoretical assumption of the analysis being offered here is, of course, that understanding of the relationship between these levels is enhanced by Elias' theory but is largely missing in the longitudinal research favoured in policy circles. I will explore that theme below.

Social determinants

The empirical findings emerging from the research by Farrington (1995; 2002; 2007) and by Kolvin *et al.* (1988), for example, used a number of indices of deprivation that relate to social relationships and social conditions, and suggest social policy responses that might be fashioned to deal with deviant family behaviour.

The key variables include the following.

- marital disruption and separation from biological parents;
- parental illness;
- poor domestic care of the child and the home;
- dependence on social services;
- overcrowding in the home;
- living in social housing in an inner-city area;
- socially disorganised communities;
- poor parental supervision and child-rearing techniques involving harsh and erratic discipline.

This research points to the positive correlation between exposure to three or more of these social disadvantages and the strong likelihood of a child's developing anti-social tendencies which will later develop into adult criminality. For example, Farrington (2007) identifies factors such as having a parent with a criminal or anti-social background, large family size, child-rearing methods based on violence rather than discourse, and, of course, child abuse and neglect as particularly important. While Kolvin *et al.* (1988) identify a number of family mechanisms to explain delinquency, drawing attention to the way parenting and the domestic sphere are organised. For example, offenders compared with non-offenders had parents that the research classified as ineffective. This could be interpreted in a number of ways, but primarily it is consistent with other research which points up the consequences for families who adopt overly harsh forms of discipline, often involving violence, when unable to cope with problems ranging from debt to unemployment to behavioural difficulties in children. A crucial association is identified between the mother's role in the socialisation and supervision process and conformist behaviour in children. This has frequently been hijacked by those intent on criticising lone parenthood (Dennis and Erdos 1992; Dennis 1993; Murray 1994), but what it actually confirms is a key finding of the Gleucks that the *quality* of parenting is more important than quantity and that caring and understanding are more important than corporal discipline (see McCord 1979; 1991; Gove and Crutchfield 1982; Larzelere and Patterson 1990).

Laub and Sampson (2003) and Sampson and Laub (1999) have reanalysed the data from the Gleucks' pioneering study and, together with their own work using life-course perspectives to illuminate understanding of desistance from crime, have highlighted the importance of attachment to family and adult institutions for bringing about desistance from crime. The value of their study lies in the insights which only longitudinal data gathered on boys from their teenage years to age 70 could yield. Contrary to the social control theories, which suggest that patterns of behaviour are largely fixed according to whether family socialisation is effective or not, Laub and Sampson show that the trajectories of life can be influenced by adult informal social control. Primarily, they argue that the social institutions which exert influence on people's transitions through life alter as they mature. Children are predominantly controlled and influenced by family, peer group and school, but young adults are embroiled in a different set of social relationships through higher education, the world of work and marriage. Adults in later life additionally take on responsibilities through parenthood and investment in community and other social activities. It is the social bonds to adult institutions of informal social control (family, education, neighbourhood and work) that influence adult criminal behaviour. Those that are drawn to and integrated by involvement in marriage, family and parenthood will inevitably drift away from anti-social behaviour and adult criminality. The key issue is that the presence or absence of networks of interdependencies supporting a person's life is a crucial determinant of that person's civility and desistance from criminality.

What tends to be lost in much of the research into family life is the relationship and interaction between the social and psychological levels determining behaviour, especially in the American work stressing the need for social control and self-control. These concepts in the hands of criminologists such as Hirschi (1969) have tended to justify rejection of social policy intervention in favour of more punitive intrusion by the criminal justice system and social work to dampen untamed urges in young people not sufficiently suppressed by strict socialisation. The stress is often on the structure of family relationships, particularly the authority structure, with less attention paid to the processes and qualitative features that make parenting effective and family relationships genuinely solidaristic.

Psychological determinants

It is clear that family life, marriage and parenting styles are implicated in the processes contributing to, or inhibiting, anti-social behaviour in children. Psychological levels of analysis have attempted to understand the impact of functioning on the cognitive and emotional dispositions of children. For example, Farrington (2007) has observed that there seems to be a correlation between particular types of behavioural problems in children, such as impulsivity, low levels of empathy and extreme aggressiveness, on which research into their psychological basis is suggestive rather than conclusive. This type of work has generated a range of findings that encourage a focus on the interaction between parenting, family relationships and the development of behaviour problems in children.

Joliffe and Farrington (2004), for example, have been engaged in developing 'a basic empathy scale'. What this research is pointing to is that some children fail to develop an understanding and appreciation of other people's feelings (cognitive empathy) and are incapable of actually experiencing other people's emotions (emotional empathy). Psychological criminology, of which the work of Farrington represents the best-known British exemplar, has observed that children who are hyperactive, impulsive and restless, and who operate with short time horizons, frequently engage in anti-social behaviour and persistent criminality. What explanation can be offered for these behaviour problems? I will begin to connect them to the broader thesis being developed in the book below, but there is work in developmental psychology that connects these behavioural problems in children to parenting styles.

Baumrind (1966; 1967; 1991), from the perspective of developmental child psychology, has generated a typology of parental styles which attempts to capture the normal variation in styles of parenting. The typology does not seek to explain anti-social behaviour or delinquency in children as such, but clearly her work points to styles of discipline that other research has positively correlated with delinquency. The typology initially distinguished between *permissive parents, authoritarian parents* and *authoritative parents*. Later variations on her scheme have added *neglectful parents* or *uninvolved parents*. What she argues is that parents vary in terms of their *responsiveness* to and the *demandingness* of their children. So parents who are low on both dimensions will be classified as neglectful and uninvolved. Another interesting distinction is drawn between authoritarian and authoritative parental styles; the former is low on responsiveness to the child but high on demandingness, and the latter tends to be high on both dimensions being responsive and demanding. The key to this distinction lies in the modes of 'psychological control' imposed on children. Baumrind argues that the mode of control that shapes the emotional development of a child is important. Indeed, because children, and people more generally in Western societies, live in open social systems with freedom to move from one social situation to another, and therefore to move from one form of external social constraint to another, it is suggested that the emotional and psychological predispositions to exercise constraint are more important than external forces. Reckless (1967) has made this observation too, and it is an observation that is close to Elias' underlying assumption about human and social development. The distinction between authoritarian and authoritative parents is marked by the fact that the former demands conformism without question while the latter allows negotiation and provides justification for the demands being made of the child. And because the latter is also based on being responsive, it will foster greater closeness and more active social interaction and engagement. Both types of parents seek to control the behaviour of their children. Authoritarian parents impose 'psychological control' on their children, which penetrates deep into their psyche, possibly instilling feelings of fear of parental reprisals for deviance. By contrast, authoritative parents inculcate what amounts to a 'second nature' in the Eliasian sense: their use of constraint is based on the development of empathy for others and an ability to understand and appreciate the feelings of others because it has evolved through close social interaction underpinned by reason and discussion. In psychological terms, the authoritative parental style generates both cognitive and emotional empathy, which is positively associated with conformist rather than deviant behaviour. Parental styles that are associated with anti-social behaviour in children typically are those that are neglectful or permissive, perhaps with extreme neglect being a particular facet of some families living in disadvantaged circumstances.

The key aspect of this type of research is that it points to a crucial difference between attitudes and feelings that are drilled into children externally and those that evolve as a result of responsive and positive social interaction. At the heart of Baumrind's conception of positive parenting is the partnership and interdependence between adult and child. In an indirect way, there is support for this research from Unnever, Cullen and Agnew (2006). They tested the rival claims of control theory and social learning theory in seeking an answer to the question of why 'bad' parenting is criminogenic. What is evident is that effective parenting controls children's behaviour through monitoring their activities and setting limits on their movements while also providing a model of positive learning through interaction that reinforces empathetic and non-aggressive behaviour traits. It is precisely these types of social processes that Elias' thesis places at its core. However, there is an absence of a sense of societal context in much of the work on families and criminality. While there may be a correlation between particular variables and deviant outcomes, we need to understand the social mechanisms better. Edwin Sutherland (Sutherland and Cressey 1966) encapsulated the problem when he argued that poverty, bad housing and poor parenting were implicated in the explanation of criminality only to the extent that they shaped the patterns of associations, relationships and interdependencies which young people have.

The de-civilising of parents

An integral feature of the civilising process is the development of greater levels of empathy with and sensitivity to the feelings and emotions of others, and this has also included greater adult awareness and understanding of children and their needs. Indeed, the civilising process has been inextricably linked to the modern view of children as *not small adults*. Historically, we can look back to stages of social development when child labour and child prostitution were considered a matter of economic expediency, and not as the cruelty they are now judged to be by contemporary standards (see Smout 1987: 162). Van Krieken (2005), drawing on Elias's analysis of parenthood (Elias 1997), identifies the key impact of the civilising process on childhood.

> The overall lines of historical development of processes of civilisation in Elias's sense have a dual impact on childhood in particular: first, the 'distance' between childhood and adulthood gradually increases as the requirements of societal membership become more demanding, so that childhood requires more time and effort in socialisation and education prior to the achievement of adult status through entry into the workforce. Second, adults' investment of time, skill, effort and emotions in children also increases, making them both more precious and demanding at the same time. (Van Krieken 2005: 42–3)

At the centre of these processes is the changing adult–child relationship, particularly inside a democratising family unit. The growing awareness of children as people with distinctive personalities, identities and voices replaces, slowly but inexorably, the view of children as occupying roles and *positions* within a household such as eldest daughter, eldest son or youngest son. In present-day society, children have acquired 'rights' and are able to claim a sense of 'citizenship' independently of their class and family background (see Churchill 2007). Accompanying these trends has been a concern about child abuse and neglect. This in turn has stimulated social policies designed to regulate what demands can and cannot be made of children. The consequences of these long-term developmental movements have been a greater sense of responsibility for children from their parents and, significantly, more self-restraint regarding how children are disciplined.

However, that is not the only aspect of the developmental process, as children create friction and anxiety for adults and adult relationships precisely because of their neediness, vulnerability and the sense of moral obligation they generate in contemporary societies. They create what Giddens (1991; 1992) has called 'inertial drag', and that, for some adults, can occasionally lead to reactions to parenthood that can best be described as flight from responsibility. Why has this occurred? This arises because, as Western societies have developed, and the dynamics of capitalist markets has penetrated all aspects of social life, the 'individualisation process' increasingly and continuously encourages adults to be free and independent of social constraints: to take actions that fulfil the self rather than others and that often means pursuing life goals and career opportunities without submitting to the disciplines of domestic responsibilities and childcare. With respect to this feature of modern living, Van Krieken points to Beck's ironic observation that the 'ultimate market society' is a 'childless society' (Van Krieken 2005: 43). The ambivalence of modern childhood lies in the conflicting pressures it imposes on adults, which in turn can lead to the de-civilising of parents.

The seeds of the de-civilising tendencies affecting parenting are contained in the conditions of living in a post-industrial and postmodern society. As suggested above, coping with low levels of material resources and job insecurity is not conducive to attentive and positive parenting. Child abuse and neglect by adults pursuing their own focal concerns, whether drink, drugs or respite from the tedium of work or unemployment can, in some circumstances, reverse the processes described by Van Krieken above. The de-civilising of parents means that little effort is invested in the child's intellectual, social and cultural development, and the parent's authority is replaced by the parent's violence; the socialisation of the child by the family is displaced by a vocabulary of motives acquired in the street, as the child disconnects from the family household and reconnects with the street gang. The interesting point to emphasise is that the failures of contemporary parenting are accentuated by the child centredness of civilised parenting and the obsession today in the media with the conflicting anxieties about protecting children from exposure to harmful influences yet providing them with a fulfilling and enriched childhood of positive experiences. Despite the clear correlation between class and material disadvantage and poor parenting, the focus of recent policy has concentrated on the coping strategies of poor parents in terms of moral and behavioural deficits rather than on the underlying socio-economic conditions framing family existence in a postmodern world (see Walters and Woodward 2007). Unnever *et al.* (2006) have argued that a great deal of effort is now involved in defining what constitutes 'bad' parenting. In confronting this issue, it is unsurprising that politicians have tended to draw on those theories that concentrate on the deficit model of parenting rather than address the large structural questions relating to redistribution and family policy, which would be costly to address in public expenditure terms. The two dominant theories in criminology, which also encapsulate the dominant thinking in family policy, are *control theories* and *social learning theories*. Unnever *et al.* summarise them and suggest that control theories contend the following:

> Children raised in unstructured environments fail to develop the ability to control their behaviour and therefore are prone to engage in risky behaviours that give them either a short-term reward or relief from monetary irritations. (Unnever *et al.* 2006: 5)

Social learning theories, in contrast, stress a different set of factors.

> Parents may also teach their children to engage in crime by modelling and reinforcing deviant behaviour ... parents model aggressive behaviour when they punish their children in an aggressive manner. And reinforce aggressive behaviour when they give the child what he or she wants because the child antagonistically demands it. (Unnever *et al.* 2006: 6)

Bad parenting is presented in such theories as something that is exhausted by reference to the relationships internal to the isolated family. The conclusion that is drawn from such theories is that youth offending should be tackled through early intervention into families at risk in order to bolster their effectiveness in dealing with child discipline and self-control. This is precisely what is contained in legislation from the Crime and Disorder Act 1998 through to the Anti-social Behaviour Act. Criminal justice strategies since the late 1990s have increasingly focused on issues of deviant and criminal behaviour at the expense of a holistic view of families in the community.

Parenting and the containment of masculine styles in poor neighbourhoods

Parental styles emerge from a complex of influences, shaped by both cultural and material circumstances. The pioneering sociological work on class and modes of social control developed by Basil Bernstein (1973) showed clearly that working-class family forms can generally be described in terms of their *positional* authority structure in which age and gender determine expectations about social roles and responsibilities. At the heart of that family structure is a tradition of patriarchal authority that used to be underpinned by a male breadwinner model of family that was reinforced by a social wage which augmented male income from manual industrial labour.

This masculinist family authority structure is declining in present-day society and is giving way to an alternative family form, one found particularly at the bottom of the social hierarchy although not exclusively, grounded in the material realities of large-scale unemployment among unskilled young males. This family form is characterised by 'at arm's-length' involvement with family responsibilities and is a common pattern for young men who remain uncommitted to parental responsibility for the children they produce. The main consequence of this pattern of behaviour is that lone-parent households have been identified as those presenting society with a series of policy problems. They are invariably female-headed households in which the care of children prevents the lone mother from working. Benefit dependency has led many to demonise young mothers (see Rodger 1996: 133–66). However, the family issue, involving parenting styles and supervision of children and youths, is often not about young women as effective mothers at all, or, indeed, about female-headed households, but is overwhelmingly about the social and cultural practices of young men surviving in marginal communities (see Anderson 1999). It is their unwillingness or incapacity to provide support to the children they father that is the key issue. The hegemonic masculinity that pervades the poorer communities in British and American society is grounded in modes of behaviour that are inextricably linked to the presentation of self and the maintenance of personal integrity in street life, an observation made in the last chapter and one which I will return to in Chapter 8. A commitment to either stable relationships or fatherhood has not been a noticeable feature of that masculine style. As Mullins (2006) discovered, the street life of the poor neighbourhood has tended to be gender segregated, and research has revealed that young men are predisposed 'to view women as objects for the fulfilment of their personal desires rather than equals' (Mullins 2006: 22). Committed parenthood is certainly not high on their life schemes. And as Young (2007: 41–58) has observed, criminality and deviance are about hedonism, release from the mundane, the search for the adrenaline rush and mimicking celebrity. The drudgery of being a committed father tends to get pushed down the life priorities of the average young, working-class male, and increasingly middle-class males too.

A key aspect of the analysis of civilising parents offered by Van Krieken (2005) is that while the contemporary interest in co-parenting and working to maintain the 'best interests of the child', even in circumstances of divorce and interpersonal hostility, is an indication of the increased sensitivity to the needs of children and child welfare that has developed as a product of the long-term changes brought about through the civilising process, that analysis is less sound for those who are the losers in contemporary society. The 'interests of the child' present a quite different set of issues and concerns in ghettos and poor neighbourhoods. It is the absolute neglect of the 'interests of the child' by many young fathers that becomes an issue in conditions created by de-civilising processes. The interests of children in society more generally are subordinated to the interpersonal politics of divorcing couples, and in conditions where young fathers have little attachment to their children in the first place, 'the interests of the child' are seldom considered by those seeking to avoid both financial and emotional responsibility. In circumstances where there is little emotional attachment, there is typically little regard for the child's feelings and needs. It is not surprising that the most common pattern of child abuse involves the violence and neglect of a non-biological partner of a child's mother. More broadly, where there is an absence of connection, biological or even emotional, empathy for the feelings and needs of the child fails to develop. This pattern is frequently underpinned by poverty, criminality and social marginality (Parton 1985).

Returning to the debate in criminology and family policy identified by Unnever *et al.* (2006) between social control and social learning theories, it is quite clear that they are not perspectives on family deviance and juvenile delinquency that are mutually exclusive. Children growing up in the most deprived of our urban neighbourhoods experience both a lack of social control by parents (frequently that means mothers who are overwhelmed by the concerns of negotiating life with a low income, poor housing and other factors contributing to their social exclusion, including limited access to affordable supermarkets and transport) *and* an impoverished social learning experience, especially for young males attempting to discover their masculinity in fatherless households. This has led some to suggest that young male children living in a female world have to discover what it is to be an adult man by seeking guidance in the street rather than the home (see Connell 1987; Walklate 2007: 83–103). This has been called 'compensatory compulsory masculinity' and involves embracing the 'hegemonic masculine style' in the deprived neighbourhood. The concept of 'compensatory compulsory masculinity' describes a process of self-discovery for the male child in the company of his peers. It often means that masculine identity is acquired by young males through rehearsing the worst aspects of adult male behaviour from the partial contact they may have with their absent fathers and their street interactions in the male gang.

Families and gender in the 'dark ghetto'

A key observation made in the work on the American ghetto by Wancquant discussed in Chapter 2 is that there is a relationship between the increasing social and economic isolation of the black ghettos and the upsurge in violence and de-civilisation in present-day American society (see Wancquant 1997 in particular). The plight of the African-American family has been well researched in recent years and provides useful insights into similar processes now becoming evident throughout Europe. What that research points to is that while family life and family relationships have been transformed in the latter part of the twentieth century for all social groups, parenting and child socialisation in extremely poor and disadvantaged communities has changed in ways that are perceived to be highly problematic because of their impact on public resources, specifically the growth in the numbers of lone-female-headed households. What is clear is that they cannot be understood in simplistic, moralistic ways.

Social exclusion for many families means exclusion not only from work, and the attitudes and self-discipline that tend to accompany regular work, but also from contact and social interaction with people beyond their immediate neighbourhood that may influence their aspirations. In some cases, the main ambition that parents living in poor communities may have for their children is that they survive to adulthood. In terms of the core argument of the de-civilising thesis, where networks of interdependence break down and routine social interaction and cultural mixing across spatial, class and ethnic groups become at best episodic, then empathy for, and appreciation of, the feelings of others from a different social location and class will weaken. Where that sense of social and economic isolation is thought to be a consequence of deliberate policy decisions, that lack of social contact will be reinforced by a sense of resentment of or indifference to people who are 'not like us' and people who appear to be on life pathways providing the luxuries of life, while others have little. The resistance to the election of Sarkozy in France in 2007 by residents of the French ghettos arose because he is associated with policy measures that are perceived as supplanting economic strategies to create authentic, post-colonial citizenship and employment for residents in the main disadvantaged communities with punitive policing and criminal justice policies.

The wider economic and cultural forces impinging on family life and parental styles are insufficiently recognised in the formulation of family policies, as Messner and Rosenfeld (2001) have argued. The gregarious traditions of working-class communities have probably always made it difficult for family life and effective parenting: children, especially male children, have always been attracted to 'street-corner society' and where there is the absence of an effective authority regime within the home – as may arise for a variety of reasons including the absence of male authority figures, adult drug and alcohol problems and physical and sexual abuse, not to mention the distraction of unemployment and poverty – children learn how to fulfil their gender roles and protect themselves in the public sphere. It is their peer associations that become more crucial in those circumstances where the family struggles to establish itself as the primary source of socialisation. For example, Elijah Anderson's research in Philadelphia differentiated between families distinguished by their 'value orientations' as 'decent families' and 'street families'. Anderson (1999) argues that the relationship between these families can be understood in terms of their relationship to work and a sense of social connectedness to the wider community. The 'street families' perceived conventional society as a social order that had humiliated them through racist practices and disadvantaged them through social and economic policies that left them isolated in communities without welfare support or opportunities for well-paid and dignified work. In those circumstances, conventional society lost its legitimacy and the 'street families' adhered to an 'outlaw culture' in which working-class values of social solidarity and unionism were replaced by a 'code of the street'. At the heart of that code is the preservation of self, both physically and by reputation. The 'code of the street' also demands the construction of a conception of masculinity and family obligation that is alien to mainstream society. In ways echoing W. B. Miller's earlier analysis of the lower-class community as a generating milieu for gang delinquency (see Miller 1958), the young men of the lower-class community adopt styles of behaviour, language and codes that embrace criminality, and sexist and abusive attitudes to non-family females, in order to preserve integrity on the streets. Mullins (2006) provides a very insightful overview of this 'particular' type of masculinism; it is a type that appears to have grown in those pockets of present-day society where unemployment has been overlain with welfare state retrenchment, post-colonial racism and behaviourist theory-led criminal justice strategies. An attendant feature of these situations is that the family is blamed for its inability to cope with the task of socialising children in such impossible conditions.

The power of the 'street culture' is also interestingly described by Ness (2004) in her enquiry into why girls fight. What is particularly striking about her ethnographic research on young African-American and Hispanic girls is that it illustrates that the gender patterns normally associated with aggression and violence are not found in these communities. She makes a number of observations. While female violence is normally understood as a deviant maladjustment to disrupted family and social situations, in Philadelphia, and, I suspect, in parts of London, Birmingham, Liverpool, Bristol and Manchester, too, female violence and fighting are a 'normative part of growing up'. Young girls, like their male counterparts, must protect themselves physically and by reputation. The key observation made by Ness (2004) is that girls are defying feminine norms by fighting but are adhering to what they had been taught by parents, mainly their mothers, from an early age. The maintenance of 'respect' in such communities requires preparedness to use violence in order to avoid being labelled as someone who can be easily exploited. Ness also points to the distinction between the 'relational aggression' of young middle-class girls and the physical violence of the ghetto girl. This particular analysis illustrates more broadly that family life adjusts to the demands of the material circumstances which enclose it. Family life in the circumstances described by Ness is characterised by resistance against attack because that is the reality confronting young people living in some marginal communities. To repeat an observation made above, for many parents survival becomes more important than ambition for their children. The behavioural styles that develop in such communities reflect the demeanour that is best adjusted to survival. People tend to be loud, aggressive, often ill-mannered and mistrustful of authority, whether that comes in the form of a social worker or a police officer, and by behaving in a manner considered by mainstream society as anti-social, they are adhering to the 'street code' of their neighbourhood. They are fitting in with their peers and those neighbours they regard as significant 'players' in the community struggle and hierarchy. However, by behaving in ways regarded as necessary to survive, they often annoy, intimidate and bully those 'decent families' not part of the 'outlaw culture of street families'. Other-regarding attitudes and sense of social solidarity are absent from many communities in the UK that are similar to those described by Mullins (2006) and Ness (2004) in the USA. How they are established or re-established is complex. The policy mood of the times suggests that the way these problems are best tackled is largely through the replacement of social policy with something more disciplinary and punitive.

Family policy and anti-social behaviour under New Labour

The argument of this chapter is that what family life requires in the poor communities and neighbourhoods of the UK are social and family policies that acknowledge the harsh realities of life and survival in marginal communities while also recognising the limits of criminal justice intervention. In recent years, it has sometimes appeared that the ASBO and Parenting Order are the only strategies being developed to deal with dysfunctional families when in fact there have been a range of policy initiatives, such as Sure Start and the Children's Fund, aimed at tackling child poverty and disadvantage, primarily contained within the paradigm of the *social investment state* (see Featherstone 2005). However, what is interesting about recent family policy measures is the gradual erosion of the boundaries between strategies aimed at anti-social families and strategies aimed at improving the conditions of all families.

One way of conceptualising the issue is to consider the competing policy discourses shaping contemporary family welfare. As illustrated in Table 5.1, the family lies at the centre of three primary policy fields: the disciplinary, the legal and the welfare. In terms of welfare, family policies that seek to support the functioning of family life and child rearing have attempted to boost family income and access to services in order to promote health and education. The succession of child abuse scandals from the 1960s onwards led eventually to the emergence of a second policy area that explicitly placed the child and children's human rights at the centre of legislation.

Since the late 1990s, the anti-social behaviour and 'respect' agendas have come to constitute a third policy field that is primarily aimed at subordinating issues of child welfare to those of a 'tougher' youth justice system. This is occurring as much in the Scottish Children's Hearing system as it is in the Anglo-Welsh system by targeting a problem complex consisting of bad parents and ineffective dysfunctional families (see Walters and Woodward 2007). I will return to this issue in the next chapter.

The policies on children's rights and family policy, in general, are grounded in the image of an autonomous and functioning family supported 'at arm's-length' by both statutory and voluntary

Table 5.1 Competing policy discourses on the family

	Disciplinary	Legal	Welfare
	Antisocial family discourse	Child policy discourse	Family policy discourse
Image of the child	Delinquent child	Threatened child	Child in need
Focal point	Dysfunctional family	Fragmenting family	Deserving family
Welfare principles	Conditionality: welfare support in exchange for civil behaviour	Human rights: protection of children's interests in contexts of abuse and divorce	Citizenship rights: support for the costs of social reproduction for those who work but are low paid
Parental rights and responsibilities	Parent–school contracts to ensure parental responsibilities are discharged; Parenting Orders for failing parents	Free education for all children as a human right; divorce laws to reflect the primary interests of the child in family breakdown	Parental right to choose 'style' of child's education; statutory right to child benefit and Working Families Tax Credits
Mode of intervention	Intensive family supervision: 'family sin bins' for antisocial families; removal of welfare benefits and tenancy rights in social housing	Social work intervention: interests of the child placed above those of the family in social work practice	Welfare contract: *active citizenship* rewarded with welfare support in times of need in the 'something for something' society
Instruments used for statutory regulation	Supervisory orders	Laws governing the removal of children from the family	Welfare benefits

welfare services. Devolved authority and responsibility to the family, children and parents is, supposedly, ensured by an enabling state providing benefits and child protection. By contrast, the policies geared to what are deemed to be anti-social families convey an image of the family in a state of deterioration, with children who are uncontrolled and who require surrogate parenting to be provided by the state. We have a situation today where anti-social behaviour strategies, children's policies and family policies are not harmonised or pursuing the same goals by the same principles. If we consider the image of the child that sits at the centre of each discourse, as do Such and Walker (2005), we discover that the vulnerable child of the children's legislation and the child in need at the heart of family policy are quickly being transformed into an unruly deviant who can only be controlled by the many supervisory orders generated by the Anti-social Behaviour Act. At a fundamental level, there lies a very basic contradiction between the competing discourses because each is predicated on a different causal theory of social need. The welfare discourse ultimately remains connected to a view that the social reproductive costs of raising a family, and protecting it from the vagaries of the market, are structurally generated beyond the control of individuals. The child protection discourse represents a movement towards a behavioural model in that harm to children can be caused by adult neglect and cruelty, but there remains recognition in social work practice and human rights law that the state retains a responsibility for ensuring the protection and safety of children from wider socio-economic forces. The anti-social behaviour discourse is almost entirely grounded in a view of individuals as the carriers of wilful and purposively deviant attitudes and value orientations.

A further contradiction has emerged from the 'respect' agenda (launched by former Prime Minister Blair on 12 May 2005) related to how families are expected to discharge their responsibility to care for and monitor their children's behaviour. Family policy and the benefits agency are geared to ensuring that mothers with children will work whenever possible, especially lone parents with children at primary school. That policy principle tends to undermine the concern about failing parents and incompetent parenting that the 'respect' agenda has stimulated. Why has this apparent contradiction arisen? Featherstone (2006) has observed that the model of the social investment state is supplanting the welfare state and has transformed the way we think about children, families and social policy. Indeed, everything from Sure Start, the Children's Fund and the National

Childcare Strategy is pursuing the goal of employable parents as a means of securing children's futures. And the point has been made in many places that those who fail to be engaged actively in finding work and making their lives enterprising are subject to supervision and management as a problem population (Rose 1996). The place of children in this policy configuration is that they are treated as future wealth whose education and training require investment to enable them to contribute to society at a later stage. What is missing, an observation which Featherstone accentuates, is that sometimes the immediate needs of children and families, and their circumstances in the here and now, are sacrificed on the altar of training for future opportunities. Child poverty is a problem now, and the social conditions that generate anti-social behaviour have an immediate impact that requires social policy designed to alleviate the misery of the present as much as prepare for the benefits of the future. What is eroding the boundaries between the 'respect' agenda and other areas of family policy is the disciplinary aspect that accompanies the social investment state.

The strategy being adopted by the New Labour government has been one that is supposedly twin tracked: punitive and disciplinary measures are required to protect vulnerable communities from the anti-social minority through the ASBO, the parenting order, the dispersal order and other disciplinary measures employed, but those measures are to be balanced by intensive family support for the most dysfunctional families. The fields of family policy and criminal justice are presented as complementary strategies. The best example of the strategy is the Dundee Family Project, which has now been rolled out across the UK and presented as a model of the way forward. The 'family sin bin' seems to be an example of the growing closeness of family and criminal justice policy and it uncovers the contradictory currents in present-day family welfare strategies.

Intensive family support: the case of the Dundee Family Project

The idea of isolating and subjecting dysfunctional families to intensive scrutiny and supervision is not entirely a new idea. Van Wel, for example, points to its widespread use in the history of Dutch family policy and social work.

In the aftermath of World War II, there was broad general support for the idea that Dutch society needed to launch a 'fight against anti-social behaviour', and many 'anti-social' families were relocated to residential 'living schools'. This strategy of segregating families with problems continued until the mid-1960s and was relatively unique to the Netherlands. In Great Britain and the United States during the same period, the practice of sending individual social workers to families in their original dwellings predominated. (Van Wel 1992: 147)

The particular feature of the Dutch experience was that the character of those family projects varied in accordance with prevailing social work theories, political expediency and welfare resources, very much as the current policies in the UK do. The current interest in this strategy is attributed to the apparent success of the Dundee Family Project, which was established in 1998 with Urban Programme funding. The project was run by NCH Action for Children Scotland in partnership with Dundee Council Housing and Social Work Departments. The primary objectives of the project were to target those families deemed to be extremely anti-social and at risk of eviction, and take steps that would allow the families to avoid eviction and be restored to satisfactory tenancy arrangements. The project contained a slightly broader approach than a singular focus on supervised living. There were three main ways to access the service and three distinct levels of supervision, with each level constituting a staged way back to normalcy. For example, initially, a small group of about four or five families were housed in what became the *core block* and were subject to close scrutiny of their living practices and childcare competence. Other families were part of the project through *dispersed tenancies* that were run by the project and which housed families on the road to recovery from their deviant practices. The third level of the project was the engagement in an *outreach service* for families in their own homes who were at risk of eviction. Clearly, families could be moved up and down this tenancy infrastructure as their behaviour either improved or deteriorated. The project had a full complement of staff drawn from the fields of housing management and social work and was aimed not at tackling behaviour that was serious enough to involve the criminal justice system but at those behavioural difficulties that caused problems for neighbours and schools. A brief list of the activities and tutelage provided by the workers will provide a sense of its purpose (see Dillane, Hill, Bannister and Scott 2001).

- after school groups;
- young persons group;
- cookery group;
- parenting group;
- parenting skills group;
- craft group;
- anger-management group;
- residents support group;
- tenancy workshops.

The project had an admissions process and selected families for inclusion by referrals from the housing and social work departments. While the primary focus of the project was on families 'that impinged on others outside the family', there is evidence reported by Dillane *et al.* (2001) that the social work department occasionally attempted to broaden the admissions criteria and direct families into the project because of childcare rather than anti-social behaviour concerns. Families who did not undertake to work cooperatively with the project were also likely to be rejected, but there seemed to be few of those due to the adoption of an approach which Dillane *et al.* (2001) refer to as a combination of 'persuasion and coercion': threatening families with care orders and demoted tenancies was the most commonly used device to ensure compliance. The range of sanctions available as a lever to compel some families to participate in 'sin-bin' schemes will be augmented by a measure announced in May 2007 by Home Office Minister Vernon Coaker. In England, a new power will be given to the police by the Criminal Justice legislation planned for 2008 to effect an 'immediate' eviction of an anti-social family by denying them access to their dwelling by boarding up the house. This measure is only to be used in extreme circumstances but it will be an additional mechanism forcing some families into the 'sin-bin' accommodation, probably under supervision in a core block if one is available.

In April 2007, the New Labour government and the so-called 'respect tsar', Louise Casey signalled the adoption of the Dundee model more widely and announced that a £15m scheme would roll out the *intensive family support model* across England. This was in addition to a decision by the Scottish Executive in 2006 to announce a similar expansion in Scotland, where the model had been pioneered. The English scheme was based on a number of pilot projects that had been operating intensive family support. Miles Platting in Manchester was the first area where this approach had been adopted. The numbers of families involved had been 572, but the expansion of the scheme will bring in about 1500 with the possibility that the numbers of families included in the project would rise further. The use of a core block has not been adopted by all schemes but is generally a key feature of the model. An evaluation by Nixon *et al.* (2006) of the English pilot schemes involving 256 families (consisting of 370 adults and 743 children) was undertaken and a number of interesting observations made. Disproportionately, the families brought within the programmes were white, British families relying almost entirely on welfare benefits for their income, including housing benefit. They tended to be large families with 62 per cent within the project having three or more children and 20 per cent, or 31 of the participating families having five or more children. They were also predominantly, but not exclusively, headed by a lone female: over the period of the review single-female-headed households comprised 78 per cent of the families (78 families) in the scheme in 2003, and that dropped to 68 per cent (107 families) by 2005. Many families had health issues ranging from mental health and addiction problems in adults to severe physical illness, such as asthma in some children. The picture is one of families struggling with what the report calls 'high multiple support needs'. Indeed, 59 per cent of the adults in the scheme were or had been suffering from depression and related mental health problems.

Both the reports by Dillane *et al.* (2001) and by Nixon *et al.* (2006) describe schemes that are considered to be effective and are therefore endorsed for wider implementation. Scott (2006) similarly points to a project that is cost-effective in that it reduces many of the escalating costs that might otherwise fall on local authorities and communities in the absence of supportive intervention, especially by reducing the numbers of evictions. The expansion of the intensive family support model is partly the result of those positive assessments. However, there are general issues that should be highlighted for consideration. Garrett (2007), for example, offers a range of critical comments on the evaluations, both methodological and substantive. In reference to the English evaluation, he criticises the limited nature of the feedback from those who had actually experienced the core block: 'some members of only six families who had spent time in the "core accommodation" were interviewed' (p. 220). A particular criticism made by Garrett is that there is little evidence in the assessment of the English pilot projects, beyond the comments by the authors of the report, that those families who had experience of the 'sharp end' of the core block felt positively about their encounter with the scheme. It is this silence that concerns him when assessing whether the project has attained its optimal utility. It must be acknowledged that the authors of the two reports make a robust response to this and other criticisms of their research and underline that despite the extension of the 'sin-bin' model their work contains many critical observations of its functioning.

I hesitate to engage further in that debate and wish only to draw on an observation made by Garrett relating to the potential impact of the core block process on adult behaviour (see Bannister, Hill and Scott 2007; Garrett 2007; Nixon 2007 for the academic exchange). A key concern about the Dundee model has been the use of the core block because of the intensive supervision of families that were placed in it. Under the guise of social welfare support, many marginal and fairly dysfunctional families were effectively threatened into the schemes and into the intensive supervision of their lives through the restrictions imposed on their movements and autonomy while they lived in the core accommodation. There is undoubtedly a view that such practices, which some may describe as 'tough love', are necessary in those extreme circumstances where family life has fallen into chaos and possibly dangerous and violent disorganisation. However, Garrett raises legitimate concerns about the mechanisms adopted to manage the boundary between care and control, and he brings out what must be a negative potential in all such schemes.

> All the projects examined were committed to promoting a 'positive lifestyle', 'social inclusion' and well-being' .... However, the dominant approach, within the 'core accommodation' seems to be one of infantilising the adults ... much of the emphasis, as in the DFP [Dundee Family Project], would seem to be placed on containment and surveillance of families ... the focus of project staff in the 'core accommodation' is placed on schooling families to accept new temporal frameworks and staff monitoring. (Garrett 2007: 221–2)

It is precisely the combination of family support and civil law threat that creates an uneasy relationship between social policy and criminal justice. The dominant mode of thinking here is operant conditioning: the appropriate value orientations must be inculcated in the family before they can be released back into 'normal' society. And there did seem to be evidence that if the measure of success was the absence of complaints from neighbours, then the project seemed to have worked with many families. What we need to understand more thoroughly is how sustainable the conformism is that was trained into the families.

Concluding observations: desistance from crime and anti-social behaviour

The relationship between changing family structures, anti-social behaviour in children, deteriorating communities and adult criminality is well documented in the social science and criminology literature, and this chapter has reviewed that relationship. The focus of policy today is on the value orientations and parental skills required by adults to provide an effective family life for their children. However, what I have also drawn attention to are the wider socio-economic forces that have created a loss of function and purpose for many communities on the back of the processes of de-industrialisation. The question in many deprived neighbourhoods is not one of having the right value orientations but of surviving the violence and social chaos that are a feature of many marginal communities. People living in such communities develop styles, body capital and, in short, a 'cultural toolkit' to adapt to the demands of their community. Often it is that adaptation that is marked out as signifying anti-social behaviour. The habitus of those communities is partly structured by forces beyond the control of the people who live in them. The work of Messner and Rosenfeld (2001) points to the damage being done to contemporary Western societies by a disembedded global economic system which subordinates the moral economy of community and neighbourhood to the needs of a consumer society and 'thing addiction'. There is very little that the institutions of civil society can do to fight back unless they are supported by the state and a welfare system that addresses the loss of dignity which is the consequence of the processes I have described. What is needed is, perhaps, the strengthening of the institutions of civil society. In addressing this issue, recent policy in the area of anti-social behaviour has attempted to bring communities and victims into the process of juvenile justice by introducing mechanisms of restorative justice but, perhaps, at the expense of the welfare orientation of the juvenile justice system. I will discuss this subject in the next chapter. Another area which seeks to address this issue has been the focus on civil renewal, which has been developed to bolster the institutions of civil society through efforts to enhance community efficacy and community development activities involving the voluntary and commercial sectors. I will discuss this issue in Chapter 7.

The Dundee project, and other schemes based on its basic principles being introduced throughout the UK are attempting to compensate for years of policy neglect and decades of welfare state retrenchment in the socially marginal communities. In order to understand the wider processes aimed at desistance from anti-social behaviour and criminality, we need to consider the issue of youth justice and children's welfare in more detail. That is the subject of the next chapter.

Chapter 6

Child welfare and juvenile justice

At the heart of the theory of the civilising process is the role of *shame* as a mechanism for both creating and reinforcing the social control and self-control that make social order possible, a theme Elias took from Freud's analysis in *Civilisation and Its Discontents* (1994). Repressed shame was understood by Elias as a mechanism for checking reality; that is, aligning the individual's actions with the potential reaction from the social audience. Parents are deemed to be charged with the prime responsibility of accomplishing this process of discipline in children. In a sense, shame represents the voice of 'respectable' society inside the individual and should be acquired through the process of childhood socialisation in which children develop their 'people skills', their ability to interact with others while developing foresight and empathy for the feelings of those with whom they relate. If this process is accomplished effectively, those with a stake in mainstream society will want to avoid doing anything that might exclude them from full membership of the social group and the culture with which they identify. However, Elias recognised that modern men and women are finely balanced between conformity and giving in to their 'affective impulses', which might lead to short-term gratification but longer-term shame. This anxiety is grounded in people's confrontation internally with their own thresholds of shame and *humiliation* and the 'fear' that an indiscretion, or giving in to an impulse, might project them out of 'respectable' society to face humiliation for an anti-social act. However, for those who are marginalised as a by-product of the processes of social and economic change, and exist outside so-called 'respectable' society, a different sense of propriety may develop. We should expect their thresholds of *shame* to alter in relation to their changing perception of connectedness, their sense of what is important, and their sense of what counts as humiliation. In the ghetto and in the poor neighbourhoods, shame and humiliation will mean different things compared with suburbia. The theory of the de-civilising processes suggests that the 'affective impulses' of those who have excluded 'respectable society' from their psychology, because it has excluded them from its benefits and rewards, will be unrestrained by conventional standards of shame. Elias' theory, while inspired by Freud, remains thoroughly sociological by directing our attention to the mechanisms that interfere with the creation and reinforcement of social interdependence. However, in policy and politics today, this is not regarded as a structural issue; it is a failure of effective parenting. Responsibility for the failure to socialise poor children with the appropriate value orientations, and with appropriate levels of restraint in their behaviour, is being placed at the door of the dysfunctional family. The debate about juvenile delinquency and its control has focused attention as much on punishing parents as on punishing their offspring. This is particularly interesting in a British context because the youth justice and child-welfare system in Scotland differs from the rest of the UK in that it explicitly rejects a parent-blaming approach to youth justice.

In this chapter, I will develop the analysis begun in Chapter 5 on family life and parenting by examining the issue of child welfare, youth offending, and, in particular, the policy differences and similarities between the Anglo-Welsh system of juvenile justice and the Scottish Children's Hearing system. Most texts on British social and criminal justice policy tend to neglect the system that has developed in Scotland; they are content to acknowledge its existence by brief references and footnotes but unwilling to discuss it substantively. However, the welfare principles underlying the Scottish Children's Panels, and which have given the Scottish system its distinctive global reputation as a welfare-oriented system, are under pressure today as the climate of public opinion favours a tough approach to children's offending and is suspicious of the welfare principles that emanated from the Kilbrandon Report and were embedded in the Scottish system. An appreciation of the Scottish Children's Hearings brings into sharp relief many of the concerns about the relationship between social policy and criminal justice and can contribute to a fuller understanding of juvenile justice in the UK as a whole.

The policy debate today about the relationship between child welfare and juvenile justice revolves around the effectiveness of parenting and the capacity of some families to cope with their undisciplined children. The perception that seems to be generally held in British society is that children are indulged when they should be punished; at least, that is a strong impression gained from an examination of the policy debate surrounding the enactment of legislation such as the Crime and Disorder Act 1998, the Youth Justice and Criminal Evidence Act 1999, and the Anti-social Behaviour Acts of 2003 and 2004 (see Field 2003; 2004; 2005). These Acts sit uncomfortably with other relatively recent legislation which seeks to safeguard the interests of children and mark out their welfare needs and human rights, such as the Children Act 1989 and the Children Act (Scotland) 1995, which draw their principles from the wider children's welfare milieu sponsored by the United Nations Convention on the Rights of the Child (UNCR). The UNCR contains a number of specific guidelines which are not binding in law but which present a strong moral view of how the welfare and human rights interests of children can be, and should be, protected in the juvenile offending laws in a particular nation state. For example, the United Nations Standard Minimum Rules for the Administration of Juvenile Justice 1985 (the Beijing Rules) and the United Nations Guidelines for the Prevention of Juvenile Delinquency 1990 (the Riyadh Guidelines) point to two very broad principles that should shape juvenile justice. First, the state should ensure a productive life for young people and protect them from influences that might encourage engagement in criminal behaviour through the development of educational and social policies; second, juvenile justice policies should avoid criminalising and penalising a child for behaviour that does not cause serious harm, so effectively distinguishing behaviour that is anti-social from that which may be criminal (see Arthur 2005). These standards are useful measures against which UK legislation and policy can be judged, and I will return to them at the end of this chapter.

What is clear today is that families deemed to be dysfunctional, parents deemed to be ineffective, and children deemed to be unruly and out of control are increasingly being identified as the key targets for hybridised social and criminal justice policies. While parental responsibility has always been a key ingredient in the design and management of juvenile delinquency – indeed, punishing parents for their children's misdeeds dates back to the middle of the nineteenth century (see Arthur 2005) – today, the connection between parental responsibility and the deviance of the children has become a more explicit part of the youth justice strategy of New Labour in England and Wales. An equally prominent theme in the contemporary debate about juvenile justice is the extent to which the welfare interests of children should be subordinated to the dictates of a 'tougher' criminal justice system (see Smith 2005). It is, therefore, impossible to consider the contemporary debate about juvenile delinquency without also considering the place of child welfare and the role and influence of parental responsibility in policy solutions.

Punishing parents and the anti-social behaviour strategy

The problem of controlling feral young males in some communities has tended to focus on the question of parental failure rather than on rethinking youth policy. A distinctive theme that has emerged in the juvenile justice debate, both in Scotland and England, is whether or not it is appropriate to punish parents for failing to control their children. This is not a new development as such. Arthur (2005) draws attention to the White Paper *Crime, Justice and Protecting the Public* which was published in February 1990, and proposed making it a criminal offence for parents to fail to prevent their children from committing an offence. The subsequent debate raised concerns about criminalising already fragile and impoverished families, but the enactment of the Criminal Justice Act 1991 introduced direct parental responsibility for the children's offences (see Arthur 2005: 235). The Crime and Disorder Act 1998 and the subsequent refinement of its headline provisions, such as parenting orders, child safety orders, acceptable behaviour contracts, fixed penalty notices and anti-social behaviour orders, built on a climate of opinion that had already taken its punitive turn and which largely blamed 'bad parenting' rather than material disadvantage as the prime reason for the apparent increase in disorder and lawlessness in some neighbourhoods (see Walters and Woodward 2007).

Neighbourhood security strategies that are underpinned by a view that parents in poor communities are deficient in the discharging of their responsibilities have inevitably led to a strong measure of threat behind the use of welfare intervention, particularly relating to the use of the Parenting Order (see Goldson and Jamieson 2002; Arthur 2005; Walters and Woodward 2007). The 'responsibilisation strategy' that informs the current approach to juvenile crime and justice concludes, therefore, that it is not only the errant children who must be punished but also the failing parents. Indeed, a key point of distinction between the Anglo-Welsh system and the Scottish system of juvenile justice is the explicit point of principle recognised by the Scottish system at its inception that parents should not be punished for the misdeeds of their children. These points will be discussed below.

Youth offending and juvenile justice in England

The key operational principle of the Anglo-Welsh system has been on 'joined-upness', with the accent being placed on partnership working between key agencies in the juvenile justice field, such as social work, education, community mental health and policing (see Smith 2005). This in particular has created a new professional space bringing disparate policy professionals together and raising questions about the professional goals and paradigms of each in the new partnerships. The process of criminalising social policy involves both issues of *boundary blurring*, as joint working between agencies from different fields of policy leads to the adoption of principles of operation different from those practised in the past by any one particular agency, and *displacement of goals*, as the priorities and objectives of the new joined-up multiagency team lead to models of functioning which are set by criteria drawn from sources outside professional paradigms (see Burnett and Appleton 2004). However, underlying these broad institutional processes is the enduring tension between welfare and punishment in the field of juvenile justice (see Smith 2005). That tension is the same wherever the control and punishment of children is concerned and whatever system of children's justice is being considered. What distinguishes the Anglo-Welsh system from the Scottish Children's Hearing system, as we will see, is not that one is less welfare-oriented than the other as such (in Scotland, the system only deals with children until they are 16 and then passes them on to the adult system, so that it is only welfare-oriented for the younger child) but that the balance between the broad principles shaping the systems is tilted differently. One key factor influencing the tilt is the way each system deals with social pathology: the English system largely excludes it, focusing instead on matters of culpability and punishment, while the Scottish system incorporates it as its primary focus because it is concerned pre-eminently with a child's welfare, not criminality. The Anglo-Welsh system has moved through a succession of transformations that historically appear to be a movement away from *welfarism* towards *corporatism* and finally to a system that attempts to incorporate a number of competing approaches cemented by a type of *communitarianism*. The reality is that all three broad approaches are contained in the present Anglo-Welsh system to some extent.

129

Tracing the movement from welfare to corporatism, Pratt (1989) focuses our attention on the key transition in the 1970s from a welfare-oriented system to one that became known as the 'justice model', which served the purpose of changing the basic premises of the juvenile justice system and paved the way for a 'corporatist model'. Since the 1920s, the English juvenile justice system had progressively taken into account arguments favouring a welfare approach to juvenile offenders, absorbing the spirit of reform in the post-1945 welfare state. The system became more inclined to take seriously the needs of juvenile offenders in a broad way, including their social pathologies. This in turn led to an emphasis on 'assessment' and 'treatment' rather than simply punishment. The growth of social work professionalism in the post-1945 period led to greater value being placed on the supervised rehabilitation and social integration of young offenders combined with intervention in families in need of support (see Pitts 2001: 131–59). Indeed, Pratt, writing about this period, suggests that the welfare model 'came to be taken for granted' (Pratt 1989: 236).

However, in the 1980s, the youth justice system fell prey to what Roger Smith (2003) refers to as 'populist gimmickry'. The obsession with 'prison works' led to a 'decade characterised by a spirit of prejudice, ignorance and hostility towards the young' (Smith 2003: 3) and the rising popularity of the 'justice model'. A key principle of the 'justice model' is drawn from classical penology and, as Pratt (1989) observes, imposes 'a moral obligation to inflict punishment and the right to receive it' (p. 238). In other words, offenders and prisoners should be left unmolested by the social intervention of those seeking to ensure their welfare. Social enquiry reports written by social workers on the background conditions experienced by a young offender were portrayed as subjective and unscientific. The model also argued for a decline in the personal autonomy of the judiciary and social workers by introducing tariffs and strict criteria about referrals to services and sentencing of offenders. However, despite its resonance with public sensibilities throughout the 1970s and 1980s, the 'justice model' did not develop in a way that would warrant describing it as an established model. Pratt's (1989) argument is that many of its features actually evolved into a 'corporatist model' characterised by diversity in sentencing, centralisation of authority and coordination, and growing involvement of non-juridical agencies.

The new 'corporatist model' was, and remains in its newer forms, primarily concerned with behaviour control, the containment of problem populations, and surveillance rather than punishment and naked retribution, although elements of that survive today. A feature of the post-1997 system is that the juvenile justice system has had to adapt to a new language and new managerial imperatives that drive the system towards meeting 'targets', 'meeting performance indicators', and, as Pitts (2001) observes, concern with service users rather than the public. This requires clarification because the idea of service users includes a critical local public who seek competence and protection from a system deemed to be missing targets for efficiency, measured by the number of offenders incapacitated in one way or another. It is the local public audience of disgruntled local voters and communities that has demanded change, or rather has been led to demand change by the policy agenda established by New Labour in the post-1997 period. A number of commentators have suggested that the youth justice system has become focused on risk assessment rather than on the causes of crime and disorder (see Pitts 2001; Muncie and Hughes 2002). The system supposedly concentrates on 'what works', and that is largely measured by the climate of comfort or discomfort detected in local communities but also in terms of the quantitative targets relating to the numbers of offenders processed by the system.

The developments in the Anglo-Welsh system since the late 1990s have, therefore, been characterised by the incorporation of communitarian principles into the prevailing model. The new public managerialism still predominates, and the pursuit of 'joined-upness' remains an overriding feature, but the interests of communities and victims have been brought in under the heading of restorative justice. There has not been a return to welfarism in an explicit way, although it could be argued that the movement to restorative justice practices has an element of concern for the offender that would be absent from a purely punitive system if it were actually to implement what Braithwaite (1989) has labelled 'integrative shaming'. There are features of the system that have been borrowed from other more welfare-oriented systems, particularly the antipodean tradition of 'family conferencing' and restorative justice, and the Scottish system of Children's Hearings, which has been transmuted into referral orders and lay involvement in restorative justice practices coordinated by the Youth Offending Teams (YOT). It should be noted, however, that the features that have been borrowed by the Anglo-Welsh system have been 'cherry-picked' and have been replanted into a quite different context from their origins. Ball (2000) rightly observes that whereas the New Zealand and Scottish systems pursue their objectives by seeking cooperation between parties and consensus about facts and decisions, the Anglo-Welsh system largely relies on coercion because it is part of a system that is primarily concerned with punishment: the youth justice system in England retains strong elements of a system that is geared to the progressive processing of young offenders from the first offence to custodial disposals. Roger Smith (2003) remarks that 'an array of custodial sentences ... form the apex of the penal structure', and it is those custodial sentences 'that set the tone for all other aspects of the justice system' (pp. 64–5). The Anglo-Welsh system of juvenile justice is constituted in such a way that issues of welfare have to be added to or forced into a system that has quite a different purpose: it is a system primarily geared to progressive punishment in a way that mirrors the adult system.

The Youth Justice and Criminal Evidence Act 1999 introduced the concept of mandatory 'referral orders', which replaced cautions for young offenders pleading guilty to a first offence. Where a custodial sentence is considered to be inappropriate, the court will pass responsibility for the young offender to a YOT, which in turn will form a Youth Offender Panel (YOP) to establish a programme of behaviour that the young offender will engage in under supervision. The range of activities which are used in such programmes reflect the emphasis on reparations to the local community disrupted and disturbed by a particular deviant event. The types of reparations that can be ordered include financial reparations to a victim, attendance at mediation sessions, performance of unpaid work for the community, adherence to curfew restrictions and attendance at an educational establishment if truancy has been a particular problem, participation in drug treatment programmes if relevant, and prohibition of consorting with specified peers. The referral order is the only supervisory device that can be used for a first offence, and so the imposition of ASBOs and Parenting Orders would not normally run alongside involvement with a YOT. However, the parents are very much regarded as being responsible for their child's deviance, and there is evidence that the system at every stage of the punishment process from referral order to Detention and Training Order (DTO) will draw in parents of offending juveniles to underline and reinforce their responsibility (see Smith 2003).

It is clear that the Anglo-Welsh system differentiates between young people who are offenders and young people who are, in some way or another, offended against, whether that is through their experience of poverty or as victims of violence and abuse. Those who have not offended in terms that the system defines must be dealt with either by social services or education, or by some other means external and separate from the youth justice system. This is quite different from the Scottish system, as we will see. The Anglo-Welsh system does not recognise the social causation driving young people's anti-social behaviour and criminality beyond an implicit background assumption and, in a sense, eschews the very notion of social causality in favour of a correctional posture that assumes the offender's wilful and purposive deviance which the system is constituted to punish. In terms of Matza's seminal analysis of the processes of 'becoming deviant', the system makes little attempt to appreciate the underlying complexities and social meanings involved in youth offending, or at least is not geared to addressing those complexities (see Matza 1969). In that sense, the Anglo-Welsh system cannot easily acknowledge the welfare dimension of youth justice, which David Smith (2005) might argue should be an essential accompaniment to any system of punishment because of its stigmatising and damaging impact on those it processes. The focus on restorative justice takes the gaze away from the 'needs' to the 'deeds' of the offender because those 'needs' are deemed to be subordinate to the rights of the victim, the community and the youth justice system itself.

The system as a whole contains elements of a 'tough' response to youth offending through mechanisms such as the Intensive Supervision and Surveillance Programme (ISSP) introduced to deal with young offenders at risk of receiving a custodial sentence and the DTO for those who have a more committed pattern of offending behaviour. In the circumstances where an ISSP has been established or a DTO served, the YOT will be charged with managing offenders throughout the period of their punishment, and liaising with parents and community. The surveillance and intrusion into the lives of the young offender and his parents are, again, significant.

The social policy infrastructure which supports this system has been designed explicitly to address problem populations and generalised criminality in those communities designated as marginal: this is taken to be communities where there are high levels of social exclusion as measured by such factors as unemployment, benefit dependency, high rates of child truancy, and high rates of anti-social behaviour. It is precisely the explicit linking of activities related to the management of social exclusion and the management of problem populations that has reinforced the tendency to criminalise social policy. While programmes such as Sure Start, Connexions, and the Learning and Pupil Support Schemes have a broad policy utility, their actual purpose, indeed their measure of success, is and will remain the extent to which they can reduce the number of young people subject to ASBOs and processing by the youth justice system over the medium term. It is very much a case of social policies being used in the service of the criminal justice system rather than being designed for their universal application.

The Children's Hearing system in Scotland

The Scottish system starts from quite different assumptions about the nature of children, their problems and their welfare. In many respects, the relationship between the criminal justice system and the domain of social welfare in Scotland is partly mediated through the Children's Hearing system. The process of criminalising social policy in the Scottish context is a question of whether or not the integrity, and fundamental principles embedded in the Children's Hearing system, can withstand attempts to undermine them by ideas and influences drawn from the populist criminal justice agenda which seeks a more punitive approach to youth offending and anti-social behaviour in the UK as a whole.

The Kilbrandon Committee acknowledged that one of the main deficiencies of the juvenile courts, as they operated in Scotland until the late 1960s, was the difficulty of combining a system that was constituted to make legal judgements and sanction punishments while simultaneously seeking to make those judgements address the needs of children for treatment, preventative actions and education (see Martin and Murray 1976; Watson 1976). This was a clash of fundamental principles regarded as being largely irreconcilable. A youth justice system had to decide how to admit non-legal factors in making judgements. In resolving this issue, Kilbrandon concluded that an offence has significance only as a pointer to the need for intervention (welfare or other forms of action). The fact that a child commits an act of criminal deviance does not in itself justify punishment, at least not until the full circumstances of the child's life are known, and then it may be social intervention that is called for rather than punishment. This does not necessarily mean that the child's deviance escapes lightly because a disposal is described in terms of treatment rather than punishment. Watson (1976) rightly points up a neglected aspect of the Children's Hearing system when he observes that the Kilbrandon Report conceives of punishment narrowly in the *retributivist* sense and calls everything else, such as counselling and home supervision, treatment. Today such forms of intervention can be interpreted in a broad Foucauldian, or panoptic, sense and we can recognise that surveillance can be intrusive and can amount to a form of intimidatory punishment. Whatever interpretation is placed on the Kilbrandon Report's view of 'treatment', it concluded that the welfare interests of the child require that decisions should not be intentionally punitive. As with all forms of welfare intervention, there is an assumption that it is in the 'interests of the child' that the child should be subjected to 'treatment', whether that is superficial and short term or penetrative and more extensive.

The creation of the Scottish Children's Hearing system in 1971 moved young people's deviance out of the criminal justice system to be administered by education. That change was significant and remains intact today. The system is overseen by the Department of Education within the Scottish Executive (now to be known as the Scottish government). The Minister for Children and Early Years is responsible for the Children's Hearing System and sits alongside the Minister for Education and Lifelong Learning and the Minister for Schools and Skills in the current Scottish National Party government. The Youth Justice and the Children's Hearing Division is part of a larger focused Children, Young People and Social Care Group within Education and is treated as being an integral component of a unified education and welfare approach to meeting the complex needs of those under 16. The separate Justice Department deals with criminality in those over 16 and has responsibility for policing, punishment, the court system and, interestingly, community safety with a minister responsible for overseeing those aspects of criminal justice policy concerned with ASBOs. The Anti-social Behaviour (Scotland) Act 2004 extended ASBO provisions to cover 12–15-year-olds. This is the point of tension between welfare and punishment in Scotland and potential threat to the integrity of the Scottish approach. I will return to this theme below.

The local community focus of the hearings also justified the involvement of trained lay members to make the decisions about disposals rather than lawyers or social workers: Children's Panels are tribunals, and not courts, and the main decision-makers are the three lay members of the panel while the Reporter is present to advise on matters of law and manage a system that is nationally coordinated but locally delivered. And, of course, the key principle which gives the system its distinctive character is that it is constituted to make decisions based on meeting the welfare needs of a child, not to find guilt or to punish. The cases referred to the Children's Panel are those where it is considered that supervision of a child, either at home or elsewhere, might be appropriate. The decision to refer a child to a Children's Panel can come from a variety of sources including education, social work and the police service. The process is consensual and requires all parties to agree about the facts of a case. Disputed facts are not discussed in the panel forum but are instead referred up to the Sheriff's Court where cases involving more serous criminality are considered.

Children over the age of 16 are transferred to the adult system and are not dealt with by a Children's Panel, and therein lies one of the Scottish system's limitations. The recent attempt to bridge the gap between the Children's Hearing system and the adult system, by introducing youth courts for persistent offenders aged 16 and 17 as part of piloted schemes in Hamilton and Airdrie, was found to be lacking in dedicated resources. The research by Piacentini and Walters (2006) into the pilot schemes describes a court system in which those operating it could not report a clear distinction between the youth court and the adult courts normally used to process offenders aged 16 and 17. The schemes have, for now, been discontinued, but they were testimony to a policy agenda being driven from New Labour's English base rather than Scotland (see McAra 2006).

On the matter of parental responsibility, Kilbrandon had a distinctive position. Having considered the view that parental influence on children is universally recognised, and that direct sanctions against parents, such as supervision, fines and restitution, were frequently advocated, as they are today, he nevertheless concluded as follows:

> Direct supervision on the parents implies a degree of direct personal responsibility as between parent and child which could seldom be established. Any proposal to make parents vicariously liable for their children's actions seeks to apply what are virtually criminal sanctions in situations falling far short of any recognised standard of neglect. Such proposals seem, moreover, to be incompatible with any idea of educational process. We are unable to accept the view that in matters so closely affecting their children, the co-operation and support of parents as adult persons can be enlisted by compulsive sanctions; a process of social education on the other hand implies working on a basis of persuasion which seeks to strengthen, support and further those natural familial instincts which are in whatever degree present in all parents. (Kilbrandon Report 1995: 77)

Clearly, the Kilbrandon view on this issue goes against the range of measures introduced in the Anti-social Behaviour Act targeted at parental responsibilities and competence, and, it should be added, the presumption contained in English law about the parental role in relation to child supervision. Perhaps a point of distinction can be made here about what Kilbrandon had in mind and what the recent legislation intends. Kilbrandon used the language of persuasion and social education when discussing parents because he wanted family life and parenting to be supported by welfare resources where appropriate, and parental competence to be encouraged by engagement with an active learning process based on trust and cooperation between parents and professional experts such as health visitors and social workers. The Kilbrandon Committee would not have objected to parenting classes and counselling activities that had helping parents to cope with difficult-to-control children as their primary aim. However, what the Kilbrandon Committee would undoubtedly reject today is the proposition that parents should be compelled by civil law backed by criminal sanctions to attend counselling classes to have their behaviour corrected and their competence as parents certified as acceptable. Such measures as parenting orders, parental contracts and behaviour contracts tied to effective supervision of children, would not, in my view, be dismissed out of hand, but the underlying legal compulsion attached to such measures would. I am certain they would be considered as quite antithetical to the principles embedded by Kilbrandon in the Children's Hearing system.

Perhaps the principle that distinguishes the Scottish system from most other youth justice systems is the conclusion by Kilbrandon that children who offend and those who are offended against have common disadvantages and therefore should be considered in a system that can address matters of deviance and social disadvantage holistically within a single forum. The conclusion in the report on this matter clarifies this view succinctly.

In terms of treatment measures to be applied, the children appearing before the courts, whatever precise circumstances in which they do so, show a basic similarity of underlying situation. The distinguishing factor is their common need for special measures of education and training, the normal upbringing processes for whatever reasons having failed or fallen short. (Kilbrandon Report 1995: 77)

This principle in many ways distinguishes the Scottish Children's Hearing from other juvenile justice processes, especially when contrasted with the Anglo-Welsh system, but it also raises one of the main areas of contention and public debate about the system. Both

137

the Scottish public and the Scottish government have raised doubts about this particular feature of the system in the context of a broader anxiety about levels of youth anti-social behaviour, violence and criminality (see McDiarmid 2005). For example, Scottish Labour, and the then First Minister Jack McConnell, expressed concerns that the Children's Hearing system was not dealing effectively with persistent offenders and set up a series of Fast Track Children's Hearings pilot schemes (Dundee City, Borders and East Lothian and Ayrshire) (see Whyte 2003; Hill 2005 *et al.*). A particularly controversial feature of the concept of fast-track hearings is that it breaches the Kilbrandon view of treating all children in a similar way, first, by treating persistent offenders differently from other forms of referral and, second, by insisting that there should be in all cases a compulsory programme of behaviour change imposed: concern is obviously raised about whether that deals sufficiently with the welfare interests of a child referred under the fast-track scheme (see Hill *et al.* 2007). Whyte (2003) also considers the growing popularity of electronic tagging and community service associated with conventional punitive approaches to youth justice and suggests that they may further undermine the welfare principles underlying Scottish youth justice.

The Scottish government also commissioned a review of the Children's Hearing system, *Getting It Right for Every Child*, which reported in 2004 (see Scottish Executive 2004). In assessing the continuing effectiveness of the system, a number of key debates have emerged revolving around its place in a society in which the social and economic conditions today are quite different from the early 1970s when the Social Work (Scotland) Act 1968 created the system. The key areas for discussion can be identified by posing a series of questions:

- To what extent does the integration of the system remain justified: should children referred to the Children's Panel on non-offender grounds be processed in a system that also deals with children referred on offender grounds?
- Is the use of compulsory supervision appropriate and used only when it is necessary to meet the welfare needs of a child?
- To what extent are Children's Panels able to access supporting services from social work, education and housing authorities to make key panel decisions effective?
- How effectively does the system articulate with the new battery of anti-social behaviour provisions, including parenting orders, and restorative justice practices that have been enacted since 2003?

'Mixing the deprived and the depraved'

From the outset the Children's Hearing system operated on the assumption that children in need of care and protection and those who had committed offences should be dealt with in the same place. In the Anglo-Welsh system, the problems of these two groups are treated quite separately and the juvenile justice system is maintained to punish juvenile deviance rather than address its underlying causes. That task is dispersed to education, social work, the health service and, increasingly, the voluntary sector of care. Indeed, the focus on 'partnership working', 'joined-upness' and 'corporatist approaches' to juvenile offending is partly a recognition that the system of rigid separation of functions in the past has led to problems that are only now being addressed. The answer in England has been to retain a punitive emphasis in the youth justice system but 'add-on' features from other systems underpinned by social policies geared to targeting the early signs of anti-social behaviour in dysfunctional families. The popular and political climate of today, demanding 'tough' measures against anti-social behaviour and youth offending, is forcing specialists working within the juvenile justice sphere, north and south of the border, to recalibrate the balance between welfare and punishment.

In Scotland, the debate is centred on how best to retain the Children's Hearing system while incorporating new measures designed to address persistent offending. A major piece of research undertaken by Lorraine Waterhouse and colleagues (see Whyte, Loucks, Kay and Stewart 2000; Waterhouse and McGhee 2002; Waterhouse, McGhee and Loucks 2004) has examined the social backgrounds and referral pathways of 1,155 children referred to the Children's Panel in the first two weeks of February 1995. It provides data that are generally supportive of the Kilbrandon principles. The research addresses the contention made by Kilbrandon that there were more similarities than differences in the lives of children referred to the Children's Panel, and that justifies treating them within the same forum. The particular aspect of the research that is important for the issues being discussed here was that, overwhelmingly, the children came from socially disadvantaged backgrounds and that the grounds on which children were referred frequently changed over time. Children first referred on care and protection grounds were also referred subsequently on offending grounds. Indeed, some children were referred on both grounds over relatively short periods (see Waterhouse and McGhee 2002). Half the children's families were lone-parent households, 83 per cent of which were headed by a lone mother. State benefit was the main source of income for over half the children's families. Of the 600 fathers studied for which information was available about employment, only 210 were classified as being employed, 390 being either unemployed or classified as disabled or sick. Of the 920 mothers for whom information was available, only 230 were classified as being employed and 690 were classified as unemployed, a small number being designated as disabled or sick (see Waterhouse and McGhee 2002: 284–6). The vast majority of families and children lived in local authority housing (see Waterhouse *et al.* 2004: 168). The material disadvantage for children growing up in such households was clear.

The research attempted to divide the children in the study into 'victims' referred on care and protection grounds and 'villains' referred on offending grounds, but the authors concluded that this division was difficult to maintain.

> The longer a child is involved in the hearings system the more potential there is for them to be referred on multiple grounds .... It cannot be claimed that villains and victims exist, only that some children have been formally recorded in the children's hearings system as such. (Waterhouse *et al.* 2004: 172)

The interesting difference which the study highlights is that offenders were more likely than care and protection children to be living in two-parent households. Consistent with much of the research discussed in Chapter 5, the research observes that family functioning combined with material disadvantages leads to delinquency. Simply to concentrate a juvenile justice system on punishing those who are trapped in those disadvantaged conditions is unlikely to be able to address the underlying causes of the deviance.

Compulsion and disadvantage

A separate theme in the research addresses an issue for wider public debate in Scotland about the relationship between the Children's Hearing system and the social resources available to support its decisions. The system is constituted to consider whether compulsory supervision is required for the children referred to it. That supervision can be in the home or in another setting such as secure accommodation. However, the Children's Panel can decide that children need social support and additional resources without also concluding that they require supervision. It was an assumption of the Kilbrandon Committee that the decisions of the Children's Panel were binding with respect to resources that would be made available by social work departments, housing authorities and education authorities to support the children and their families who came into the Children's Hearing system. Indeed, the imposition of supervision was considered to be a measure that was imposed only when absolutely necessary.

The concern raised by the research undertaken by Waterhouse and her colleagues is that compulsory supervision may be used not because it is essential for the welfare and interests of a child but because it is a mechanism to secure scarce welfare resources that would otherwise not be available. What was found was that children under supervision appeared to have higher levels of disadvantage than those referred to the system but not receiving a compulsory supervision order. The research rightly observes that 'compulsory measures of supervision constitute formal state intervention in the lives of the children and their families, ultimately representing the use of force to achieve objectives in the best interests of the child' (Waterhouse and McGhee 2002: 289). A supervision order should be made because it is in the 'best interests of the child', and not because a it is the only way family support, whether social work, housing or educational, will be provided. The Children's Hearing system appears to be promising more than it can deliver.

Children's hearings and anti-social behaviour control

The big debate in Scotland is whether or not the child welfare system can cope with the changed climate of public opinion and legislative activity targeting anti-social behaviour in children, which is part of the retreat from welfare internationally (see Whyte 2003; McDiarmid 2005; Piacentini and Walters 2006). In the Scottish context, a number of initiatives appear to have undermined the Scottish system, or at least signalled the potential for a criminal justice agenda constructed in England to influence youth policy in a devolved Scotland. First, the pilot project establishing a Youth Court in Hamilton and Airdrie for 16–17-year-olds raised questions about its wider applications but, more significantly, revealed a level of hostility to the welfarist approach embedded in the Scottish Children's Hearing system (see Piacentini and Walters 2006). There is, perhaps, a more populist view in Scotland that a system of youth courts similar to those in England would be more effective in tackling those young people exhibiting more committed criminality (see McDiarmid 2005).

The Anti-social Behaviour (Scotland) Act 2004 extended ASBOs to cover 12–15-year-olds, although it specified that while a breach remains a criminal offence, it cannot be punished by imprisonment. ASBOs are not issued by Children's Panels. In the Scottish context, anti-social behaviour has been dealt with holistically through the Children's Hearing system, but since the Crime and Disorder Act 1998 there are mechanisms in place that may bypass the system and place a child on a punitive pathway not examined by a Children's Panel or subject to its scrutiny. Typically, 12–15-year-olds who are reported for anti-social behaviour are reviewed and supervised by multiagency teams (police and social work), although only a small proportion lead to formal under-16 ASBO applications. While the issuing of ASBOs in Scotland was slow prior to the 2004 Act (only 9 ASBOs and 14 Dispersal Orders issued), the period up to the end of 2006 has seen a significant increase in their use (by the end of 2005 there were 547 ASBOs in operation in 28 of Scotland's 32 local authorities). This level of activity will inevitably mean that the Children's Hearing system will become involved in a moral economy alien to its original operating principles. The issuing of Parenting Orders through the Children's Panel Reporter, which is a policy idea that has been incubating since England introduced the provision, is planned (see Walters and Woodward 2007). And the power of a Reporter to decide to refer a child to restorative justice services rather than the Children's Hearing system also raises questions about how precisely the Scottish system will articulate with this battery of new punitive provisions (see McIvor 2004).

These developments are changing the moral ambience of child welfare and youth justice in Scotland. Research in Edinburgh on youth transitions and crime (see McAra and McVie 2007) has been critical of the New Labour Executive in Scotland for overseeing a punitive turn in the Scottish system and undermining its holistic approach. Lesley McAra, co-director of the project, commenting on this in a newspaper report, observed that 'they uncoupled the idea of the offender and family as part of a community. So you get an "offender" instead of a "troubled child". The offender's parents are seen as a problem and the child is seen as separate from the suffering victim' (Donald 2007). It remains to be seen whether the change of party in Edinburgh will halt the convergence with England. The Minister for Community Safety is reviewing the way anti-social behaviour is tackled. It is unclear whether a distinctive Scottish approach to welfare and youth justice will prevail over the populist demand for more punitive measures to be used against the 'neds', especially in the light of recently published statistics suggesting that anti-social behaviour and gang delinquency are a particular problem in the major urban centres of Aberdeen, Edinburgh and Glasgow (see Macaskill 2008).

'Joined-upness' and corporatism in Scottish youth justice

A final issue affecting the Scottish system is the directive issued by the Department of Education and Young People in March 2007 regarding the increase in the number of children being referred to the Children's Hearing system – 53,883 in 2005/06, representing a 6.6 per cent increase on the previous year with 40,941 being referred on care and protection grounds, representing a 9 per cent increase on the previous year. The problem with the current system is highlighted by the fact that of those referred to the system only 6,255 children were deemed to be in need of supervision. The *Getting It Right for Every Child* report seeks to tackle this issue by introducing to the Scottish system a heavy dose of interagency cooperation similar to that operating in England. The stated intention of the changes is to introduce 'personalised services' for *all* children by encouraging greater integration between the main agencies involved in children's lives. The report provides a template for interagency cooperation between the police, social work, education and health and sets out how cooperative working can act as a filtering mechanism to make better decisions about what services are most appropriate for a particular child and to determine whether compulsory supervision and a referral to a Children's Panel is called for The Children's Hearing system will be drawn into this network in a more clearly articulated way. The Children Services (Scotland) Bill was drafted by the outgoing Labour administration in 2007, and it remains to be seen at the time of writing where this legislative initiative will go.

Restorative practices

The similarities between the Anglo-Welsh and Scottish juvenile justice systems exist at the level of strategic approach: both systems are being redesigned to allow for a greater element of community responsiveness in their practices. This is occurring through the development of restorative justice. In the case of England, this is an integrated feature of the post-2000 changes based on YOPs and YOTs. In Scotland, restorative justice processes exist in parallel with the Children's Hearing system and in some respects may draw some of their power and authority away from Children's Panels (McIvor 2004). The significant change in criminal justice strategy since the late 1990s has been to redirect juvenile justice processes away from preoccupation with the offender and towards a clearer and more explicit recognition of the victims of crime and the communities affected by crime and anti-social behaviour. That is why the strategy can be described as consisting of a combination of corporatist and communitarian elements. The community safety and crime prevention partnerships, which have grown in number since the legislation of the late 1990s, aim to bring the key community stakeholders together to form a basic unit of resource and authority in the field of local security and to work with the new interagency professionals to manage the offenders in their midst. Restorative justice is a key activity in this process.

The Crime and Disorder Act 1998 introduced the notion of restorative justice into English youth justice and suggested that the changes being signalled heralded a paradigm shift in youth policy. That is not what the current system represents. As I have argued above, the system, as it has developed in England since the late 1990s, remains largely focused on the punishment of offenders, but now, in addition as part of the 'responsibilisation strategy', it also includes the process of reparations for the damage and inconvenience that offenders cause. Responsibility, restoration and reintegration are the key elements of the restorative justice process. As I have suggested above, the concern for the reintegration of offenders into the society that they have offended against does have the potential to be genuinely welfare-oriented with an element of social care and concern for those who offend. However, the tone of the Anglo-Welsh system remains punitive. The question arises as to whether or not that punitive system can realistically incorporate restorative practices into its routine operation without doing damage to the principles that are core to restorative justice. Dignan (1999; 2005) identifies the key principles relevant to the analysis here:

- Justice is about relations between the offender and the victim, not the offender, the law and the state.
- Restorative justice treats punitive segregation as morally inappropriate and should focus on reintegrative shaming (see Braithwaite 1989).
- The community has a legitimate right to be involved in the justice process.

- Formal legal processes should be minimised in favour of informal but authentic interaction between offender, victim and community.
- Restorative justice should be based on the consensus of all parties and the absence of coercion.

There are many more detailed and nuanced aspects of the process, but those listed identify the key issues. The notion that crime is fundamentally a violation of people and communities, and therefore state and formal legal procedures should remain outside the key interactions is unsustainable in a modern complex society (see Sullivan, Tifft and Cordella 1998; Zehr and Mika 1998). The relationship between criminals and their victims requires structure to coordinate effectively, and meanwhile, the problem of vigilantism must always be minimised in any system that brings victims and offenders together in a community context. Central to the theory of the civilising process is that the state retains authority and control over the processes of law and punishment. Law and order are maintained in such a way that people in a community can feel secure and consequently relate to each other without fear. However, restorative justice must negotiate a path between an informal and unregulated set of encounters between annoyed communities, victims and offenders and a state-controlled process that is little more than a tokenistic mechanism for delivering insincere offender apologies to victims and reparations that mean little because they are perceived by all as symbolic rather than real. The distinction between shame (a collectively generated judgement of repulsion) and *guilt* (an internal self-judgement that may lead to reparative action) do not seem to be clearly differentiated in this initiative.

Pratt (2002) connects these concerns to the broader theory informing this analysis when he raises concerns about vigilantism and restorative justice practices. The dividing line between restorative justice and vigilantism can be difficult to maintain without formal procedures. The call for more community information and more community justice has been raised in the context of sex offenders but has also been influential in driving the strategy against anti-social behaviour more generally. In circumstances where dissatisfaction with the criminal justice system is combined with a lack of empathy for the offender, the call for more direct forms of justice has been difficult to resist in an era when the issue of 'respect' has become highly politicised. Restorative justice is partly a response to this perceived discontent among ordinary people. It is also largely presented in an inauthentic way (see Etzioni 1968) because it is presented as being informal and largely free of legal and political interference. It would be alarming if that was the case. Discussing restorative justice and vigilantism, Pratt (2002) observes the following:

> When state power is removed or weakened – the prerequisite for the emergence of these more emotive, public participatory forms of justice – it is just possible that new social movements based on the rule of the mob will emerge, alongside some humane form of community or restorative justice. Indeed, it is not the case that restorative justice acts as an alternative to such possibilities; these possibilities are the price that has to be paid for its own emergence, and whatever its effectivity. (Pratt 2002: 189)

Concluding observations

I started this chapter by observing that UNCR has established criteria against which national juvenile justice systems can be measured. The Beijing Rules and the Riyadh Guidelines together identify two principles of importance. First, they entreat governments to ensure that educational and social policies are appropriately directed to the task of diverting young people away from delinquency. The Anglo-Welsh system fails to fulfil this principle, while the Scottish system largely meets it, but only up to the age of 16 and then not for all those under 16. The system in England is primarily about punishing young people who commit acts of criminality and deviance. The task of diverting them from anti-social behaviour is left to practices and policy activities external to the youth justice system. By contrast, the Scottish system has rightly been praised for diverting young people away from the criminal justice system completely, except for those in the transition years to adulthood and those whose deviance is so serious that the Children's Hearing system cannot deal appropriately with them. A system that has as its primary objective to address the social welfare interests of the child must be regarded as better than most other systems globally that concentrate singularly on punishment. However, these matters are not clear-cut. In England, there is in process an effort to address the welfare of children broadly, including their deviance, by developing further the integrated character of children's services through the Children Act 2004 and the integration of local education and social services. A central feature of the emerging system will be locally generated children's plans for integrated services, including greater articulation between social services, education and Youth Justice Boards. It remains to be seen whether in time this delivers a more effective and compassionate system for those children deemed to be anti-social and potentially criminal (see Churchill 2007).

Second, on the issue of whether the British youth justice system avoids criminalising young people, there must be concern that, with the passing of the Anti-social Behaviour Act 2003 (2004 in Scotland), both systems, judged by the Riyadh guidelines, are found wanting. The Scottish system again is better in terms of not distinguishing between what may be called 'victims' and 'villains', because it deals with all children up to the age of 16 irrespective of whether they are referred on care and protection grounds or for offending. The Anglo-Welsh system, from final warnings through to YOPs and YOTs through to DTOs, mops up the anti-social and criminal largely in one system of progression. However, the recent anti-social behaviour legislation affects the Scottish system as much as the English: parenting orders, restorative justice and pilot projects experimenting with youth courts are just some of the recent developments in Scotland that point to possible movements towards convergence in this area of policy, an observation shared with McAra (2006).

In evaluating the issue of the effectiveness of the juvenile justice system in the UK, both south and north of the border, David Smith (2005) comes to an interesting conclusion. Fundamentally, he argues that the very notion of effectiveness is a contested one and that there are many measures that can be adopted to assess whether a system has delivered its key target of changing the future behaviour of juvenile offenders. Punitive and interventionist strategies are no better than passive and lenient systems, and by that we can assume that welfarist approaches are not intrinsically any more flawed than those that are actively disciplinarian. What works is unclear, and as both strategies appear to have equal effectiveness or ineffectiveness, there is no justification for extending the juvenile justice system and increasing its punitive and 'net-widening' capacity. His conclusion is worth noting. He observes that condemnation, retribution and victim satisfaction will always be a part of juvenile justice systems, and that should be recognised by those who argue a progressive and reforming case, but such strategies do not justify the claim to be effective. There is also a symbolic and welfare purpose to juvenile justice that is necessary, simply because the system by its nature 'damages' young offenders and is required partially to repair that damage. The measure of what counts as being effective in youth justice is finely balanced, especially if the Anglo-Welsh system is compared with the Scottish system, but the balance can easily be tipped in response to both the forces of political expediency and populist sentiment.

However, perhaps the most significant development in this area, and the one that links the concerns of this chapter to the subject of the next chapter on civil renewal, is the decision by Prime Minister Gordon Brown to signal a new and more substantive effort to tackle the issue of youth justice by bringing it together with policies for families and education. The appointment of Ed Balls as the Minister for the Department for Children, Schools and Families in June 2007, which also sees the transfer of the Respect Unit from the Home Office, means that youth justice and youth policy are fused for the first time. Such a development underlines the general movement in all areas of government to bring issues of social welfare, criminal justice, and family and community policy into a new strategic alignment (see Margo 2007).

Chapter 7

The strategy for civil renewal and community safety

This chapter attempts to bring together two areas of discussion informing contemporary public policy: one relating to the continuing interest in using the voluntary, or third, sector to assist the political process of devolving authority and policy delivery from the state to civil society, and the other relating to the continuing emphasis on community efficacy and community crime-prevention strategies as a means to combat anti-social behaviour and criminality.

The new strategic alignment of community development and criminal justice, alluded to at the end of the last chapter, is a policy that has been forming since New Labour took office in 1997. The new premiership of Gordon Brown looks set to develop that strategy in ways that may be more explicit and theatrical than even Tony Blair. The prime minister's speech to the National Council for Voluntary Organisations on 3 September 2007 introduced the concept of 'citizen juries' and 'standing commissions', whose purpose will be to deliberate on policy and practice about a range of social issues, including crime and anti-social behaviour. This initiative is part of a wider focus on what Prime Minister Brown called 'new government', which is aimed at extending areas of public participation in the policy process and facilitating opportunities for the *civic activeness* that he was instrumental in developing in the early years of the New Labour government. Devolved responsibility for social welfare and community safety – known as the 'responsibilisation strategy' – became an integral part of New Labour's vision of a post-welfare society. This notion of a society of 'responsible and active citizens' signalled the adoption of a model of government–society relations that had been incubating under previous Conservative administrations but in the period immediately following Labour's second general election victory in 2001 developed a 'public service' gloss. The three dominant voices in the New Labour strategy in the early years of the initiative were Anthony Giddens (1999), Gordon Brown (2000) and David Blunkett (2003), who reinforced this vision in a series of public lectures to the voluntary sector. Brown in particular emerged as not only a prudent chancellor but also a great champion of public services, often considered to be mutually exclusive. In his Arnold Goodman Charity Lecture on 'Civic Society in Modern Britain' (Brown 2000), he argued strongly in favour of nurturing voluntary action as part of a broader strategy of 'civic renewal'. His use of the word 'civic' instead of the Home Office preference for 'civil' revealed an interesting division of labour between the two main arms of government – the Treasury has tended to focus on the economic dimension, concentrating on issues of taxation and funding in relation to community governance. The aim has been to build public confidence in voluntary organisations by ensuring that they were financially and managerially sound and capable of fulfilling an enhanced role in the mixed economy of welfare. It is understood also in terms of 'capacity building'. For example, the Treasury has been a prime mover in revising both the way charities and voluntary organisations are funded and the accountancy rules which shape their financial constraints (H.M. Treasury 2002). It created the Futurebuilders Investment Fund to assist the voluntary sector to obtain funding for the modernisation and professionalisation of its management structures. Longer contracts are on offer to enable voluntary organisations and charities to plan better, and the front-loading of grants can be made available to facilitate greater levels of exploratory work in areas of provision that may be new and untested. The method of control used by the New Labour government is to require voluntary organisations seeking strategic financial support to apply for funding from the Futurebuilders Investment Fund in order that they meet the government's development and modernisation criteria. This will inevitably create a division between the big players in the voluntary sector, who will effectively supplant the state in key areas of policy delivery and the smaller organisations with, relatively speaking, amateurish profiles largely consigned to working with hard-to-reach client groups with a more insecure funding base.

In contrast, the Home Office has concentrated its effort on the *social* dimension, focusing on issues relating to the strengthening of communities, tackling anti-social behaviour, and encouraging a reinvigorated civil society at community level. The Departments of Health and Education and the Office of the Deputy Prime Minister (ODPM), later to mutate into the Department of Communities and Local Government, focused on the *individual*, primarily by focusing on issues of volunteering and civic participation. Cross-cutting these initiatives is the notion of 'active citizenship': active involvement of people in all aspects of their lives, moving from government to governance and re-engaging people in decision-making that affects their lives. It is an approach that contrasts with the emphasis on citizens as consumers that was dominant throughout the Conservative years of the 1980s and 1990s.

Speaking as Chancellor of the Exchequer in July 2000, Gordon Brown outlined the New Labour government's stance towards community organisations and the voluntary sector, and signalled the beginning of a process of critical reflection on the concept of what constitutes a welfare state in the early twenty-first century. Brown said:

> It is my belief, after a century in which to tackle social injustice the state has had to take power to ensure social progress, that to tackle the social injustices that still remain the state will have to give power away, not just devolving power to empower local communities, but also enabling community and voluntary organisations to do more. (Brown 2000: 5)

On becoming prime minister in June 2007, Brown returned to the theme of 'responsible citizenship' and signalled, by the transfer of the 'Respect Unit' from the Home Office to the newly created Department for Children, Schools and Families, that the policy fields of education, family support and youth policy were to articulate with those of youth justice in a more integrated way. Brown's enduring interest in *active citizenship*, and the education of people for citizenship through community activity, was clearly underlined.

At the heart of the Brown vision is the rebirth of civil society. This evolving conception of a new welfare settlement has implications for community safety and community development. Following the 2001 general election victory, New Labour refreshed a disparate number of policy initiatives aimed at creating safer cities, urban regeneration, and dealing with crime and disorder by connecting them to efforts to strengthen the contribution of the voluntary sector to the mixed economy of welfare more generally, and tackling social exclusion in fragmented peripheral communities in particular. The policy initiatives that emerged were consistent with an approach to governance found in all contemporary European welfare systems, in which responsibility for a broad range of welfare activities is being transferred from the state to civil society, including the management of crime and anti-social behaviour. Initiatives to address community safety and community crime prevention have evolved out of this wider policy movement, and the traditional conceptions of community education and community development have become inextricably linked to strategies to combat anti-social behaviour and crime prevention since the late 1990s. Inevitably, these decisions have engineered a closer relationship between the fields of social policy and criminal justice activities, moving them closer together and placing crime prevention and the control of incivility in the vanguard of a civil renewal strategy.

A number of key speeches by the then Home Secretary David Blunkett in 2003 (2003a; 2003b) and policy documents issuing from the Home Office (see Home Office 2003b) signalled the launch of the organising theme for the new policy strategy in 2002 as civil renewal: this amounted to assigning importance to the voluntary sector, community action and individual responsibility for a range of policies in the fields of health, family life, social care and community safety. This strategy was somewhat displaced by Blair's stress on the 'respect agenda' following Labour's third general election victory, but it is returning in the Brown years, albeit in slightly different guise. This emerging strategy of 'new government' is, perhaps, the belated recognition of a key distinction that William Robson identified several years ago, and which I alluded to in Chapter 1, between a *welfare state* and a *welfare society*.

> The welfare state is what Parliament has decreed and the Government does. The welfare society is what people do, feel and think about matters which bear on the general welfare. Failure to understand the difference is the cause of much conflict, friction and frustration, for there is often a yawning gulf between public policy and social attitudes. Unless people generally reflect the policies and assumptions of the welfare state in their attitudes and actions, it is impossible to fulfil the objectives of the welfare state. (Robson 1976: 7)

What Robson is identifying here is the crucial relationship between the state and civil society and, in particular, the very important role that civil society and civic participation should play in the mixed economy of welfare that has been evolving since the 1970s. In many European countries with strong Christian Democratic traditions and political parties, that relationship has been conceptualised by the term *subsidiarity*: the principle that power and decision-making should be exercised at the lowest possible level of governance to enable the performance of a function. However, in the British context, the notion that power should be devolved to civil society, rather than simply the market, is a relatively recent development and not one that was widely accepted at the time in the mid-1970s when Robson originally wrote his book or subsequently under the Conservative governments of Thatcher and Major. State welfare, as well as, we should add, criminal justice policy, in Britain has been and remains fairly centralised since its inception in the mid-twentieth century. Indeed, Harris (1992) has described it as 'one of the most uniform, centralised and bureaucratic of public welfare systems in Europe, and indeed the world' (Harris 1992: 116). Nevertheless, while the term *subsidiarity* remains little used in the British policy debate, the notion of civil renewal has emerged as an important organising principle that has embedded the underlying values of subsidiarity in a broad range of social and criminal justice policies since 1997. The changes brought about by the New Labour approach to social policy reform has been described by Clegg (2005) as the 'Christian Democratisation of social democracy', with the relationship between government and the voluntary sector in particular undergoing a metamorphosis in the past five years. There is now widespread acceptance that government must provide funding and resources for devolved forms of policy delivery at local levels and that informal and voluntary action is crucial for the success of such a strategy. This is the era of what theorists such as Jessop (1999; 2002) and Braithwaite (2000) would call the 'new regulatory state' or 'at arm's-length' government.

These changes in the modes of governance may also be characterised in terms of the growing Europeanisation of British public policy thinking, particularly the theory of subsidiarity, as is evident in the growing commitment to the voluntary sector by New Labour. Following its second general election victory in 2001, the Home Office and the Treasury devised a number of initiatives to address the communitarian and active citizenship themes prefigured in early New Labour policy documents when in opposition and the legislation enacted in its first term in office, especially the Crime and Disorder Act 1998 (see Crawford 1999: 14–62). Six years on, those themes remained prominent in New Labour policy thinking. If there is to be a significant difference between Gordon Brown's premiership and that of Tony Blair, it will be evident in the development of the civil renewal strategy through the further enhancement of public service, public participation and a civic ethos pervading public policy: that policy drive will be grounded in civil society rather than the state. It is not surprising that Brown has echoed these themes in early speeches since becoming prime minister. The emphasis on communities doing more for themselves with state support will be a continuing theme, but it is likely to be framed in terms of building a 'civically active citizenry' imbued with public service values.

While the strategy for civil renewal has emerged as a political framework for augmenting a wide range of policies and initiatives established to address problems of social exclusion, it is overwhelmingly focused on how greater levels of community efficacy can be constructed in order to combat anti-social behaviour and juvenile criminality in marginal communities. A key component of the strategy for community and neighbourhood renewal has been the attempt to create a policy culture that treats the voluntary sector as of equal worth to government and the commercial sector in delivering policy. It has tried to achieve this, as alluded to above, by introducing a supportive funding structure that will promote the enhanced role envisaged for voluntary organisations by government, and volunteerism more generally, and working towards the institutionalising of a 'partnership culture', particularly in hard-to-reach areas of social disadvantage. The language and thinking about how social problems are addressed has been gradually changing under the momentum of this initiative.

The 'third way' and the voluntary sector

It is now widely accepted that the political vocabulary describing welfare politics in the UK has changed since 1997. The 18 years of Conservatism (1979–97) led to the common use of terms such as the purchaser–provider split, the contract culture, and the 'new public management' of the public and non-profit sectors of welfare. This has been evident in the fields of juvenile justice and community crime prevention as well as the more mainstream areas of social policy, such as community care and health care. The commercial sector of provision was seen as the main alternative provider of social services from the state. While the emergence of neo-liberalism in the 1980s has been presented as a necessary historical corrective to the corporatist labourism that was a feature of the old Labour governments of the

1960s and 1970s, New Labour developed the posture that public service and civil society had to be valued more positively. For example, the 'third way' that has been fashioned by New Labour since 1997 has attempted to be more positive than simply taking a diluted middle way: the policies emerging for the voluntary sector and community participation in particular have, therefore, been inserted into the framework created by the project for 'civil renewal'. The approach has been informed by the grandiose project of revitalising social democracy begun by New Labour theorist Anthony Giddens, who, speaking in 1999, established the parameters of the issue:

> Very few people ... any longer think that you can run the world as though it were a gigantic market place .... We don't want to go back to a 'top-down', bureaucratic, government-knows-best type of socialism. On the other hand, the electorate is saying we don't want to be left unprotected in the face of the global market place. We need the hand of active government to provide protection, to provide protection from the buffetings and fluctuations of living in a globalised market economy.
> (Giddens 1999)

The key task facing the architects of the 'third way' in British politics was how to fashion a less governed but not under-governed society (Giddens 1998). The central political and policy question has become, how can civil society, and particularly the idea of community, be articulated with a commitment to provide state social welfare in a broad sense while empowering people to act locally to address issues such as situational crime prevention? A key part of the broad conception of welfare at the heart of the civil renewal project is, of course, how a sense of security can be built in communities where there has been fear and high levels of crime and incivility. This is an issue I that will discuss in the next chapter.

In answering the more fundamental aspect of the question, the New Labour approach has been to accept the principles of 'at arms'-length' government established by the Conservatives in the 1980s and 1990s but in the social domain to concentrate policy on the voluntary sector and active citizenship. This approach is predicated on the view that strong communities can resist incivility and crime. For example, the idea of voluntarism and community has enlivened the interest in social enterprise. In the UK, social enterprises embrace a wide range of activities involving mutualism (community banks, community grocery and fresh vegetable collectives), voluntary action, ethical trading, community businesses, credit and housing management through the creation of housing associations (see Spear 2001). Until recently, such activities have not received much beyond declaratory statements of support from government. However, where social enterprises and voluntary action articulate with strategies to combat anti-social behaviour, and are therefore inextricably linked to the provision and delivery of social services for which the state has responsibility, social enterprises and voluntary organisations have come to be seen as an essential ingredient in public policy (see Spear 2001). The area of community safety has stimulated a great deal of effort in the field of voluntary action, and there is a wide range of voluntary support schemes aimed at marginal communities that have as their main goal the insulation of young people from engagement in criminality and anti-social behaviour. The intensive family support schemes discussed in Chapter 5 and Sure Start are just two of a wide range of schemes specifically aimed at families and children. More particularly in the area of crime prevention and crime reduction, schemes such as the Neighbourhood Policing Programme (see www.neighbourhoodpolicing.co.uk/), community mentoring schemes (see Shiner, Young, Newburn, and Groben, 2004), and the various community partnerships described in the recent Home Office report *Cutting Crime: A New Partnership 2008–2011* (Home Office 2007) provide a clear indication of the importance attached to civic activism by the government.

The compact between the government and the voluntary sector

As alluded to above, this policy departure has its origins in the theory of the 'third way' fashioned by Giddens (1998). It influenced the New Labour approach to the voluntary sector in its first term of office. While previous Conservative administrations had treated the voluntary sector as merely a non-state alternative to the public sector, often fulfilling statutory obligations to meet social needs more cheaply through the process of contracting out, New Labour has adopted a more positive approach through the creation of a *compact*: an agreement between the state and the voluntary sector acknowledging its independence and replacing what had become known as a 'contract culture' with a 'partnership culture' (see Home Office 1998; Scottish Executive 2002). The idea of a compact rests on the concept of a 'partnership' in which policy goals are agreed through negotiation and discussion between government and the National Council for Voluntary Organisations' representatives who meet at regular intervals. The process is premised on the notion of a partnership in which the two sides agree a division of responsibility: basically the principle of value added has been recognised as being important, resulting in the voluntary sector dealing primarily with hard-to-reach client groups beyond the effective intervention of the statutory services, such as those who have drug and alcohol addiction problems, rough sleepers, and, significantly, various client groups identified in the field of anti-social behaviour management. However, the voluntary sector is also a key partner in major government-sponsored programmes such as Sure Start. The system is, supposedly, one of working together towards an agreed programme of action and funding rather than the previous system of tendering in which a bidding war was encouraged, awarding contracts to the cheapest bidder – such a process led to what became known in the Thatcher government years as the contract culture. Fundamentally, the pressures to make the non-profit sector more efficient and better managed, begun under Conservative governments in the late 1980s and 1990s, have continued but with better financial and service support and improved contracts containing better conditions and terms. By enclosing the plan for improving the voluntary sector in a broader strategy for tackling a range of social problems under the heading of civil renewal, the centrality of the non-profit sector in the emerging social and welfare vision has become more pronounced.

In New Labour's second term, there was an effort to develop 'joined-up' policy on the compact more explicitly, involving the Treasury, the Home Office, the ODPM and the Department for Education and Skills. The Scottish government (Executive) has developed its own approach to the voluntary sector, albeit highly influenced by the Westminster Government (Haylon, Gray and Stirling 2005). It appears, therefore, that the culture of partnership has been given a sound underpinning with new funding and organisational procedures geared to integrating the voluntary sector into the mixed economy of welfare and so making the process of civil renewal a reality. However, the degree of change required to bring about the modern civic society envisaged by Gordon Brown may be more challenging and require more robust measures than has been contained in the civil renewal strategy.

Civil renewal, welfare and inauthentic politics

Comparing the relative success of the UK in pushing through welfare reform compared with other countries in the EU, especially those with strong Christian Democratic traditions, Clegg (2005) concludes that while the UK has achieved more radical change in social policy than many of its European counterparts, it lacks the institutional anchors to sustain that change in the long term. He argues that the guiding principle of subsidiarity, largely absent from UK political life, led to a different set of policy goals in continental Europe than the UK: 'The goal of Christian Democratic social policy was thus more to reinforce the capacity of social actors to regulate society than it was to protect individuals against social risks *per se*' (Clegg 2005: 236). He also suggests that the organisational expression of this goal in countries such as The Netherlands, Germany and, without the influence of Christian Democracy, France and Sweden, was to create social protection institutions in which 'normally antagonistic private actors' (employers and trade unions) came to share responsibility for the 'governance of public social policies' and form a devolved barrier between civil society and the state, 'moderating the political demands made on, or against, collective social provision' and controlling employers' hostility to social provision (Clegg 2005: 238). The key point for emphasis is that subsidiarity and social policy are institutionalised in continental Europe in ways that may make social change slower, but policy goals are more broadly consensual and accepted by the public because they are anchored in civil society rather than government.

By contrast, welfare provision in the UK remains a highly centralised instrument of government. Policy changes have never been grounded in or sponsored by institutions in civil society in the way they are in continental Europe. Despite the idealists shaping the post-war British welfare state, such as Titmuss, T.H. Marshall and even Beveridge, social policy has not focused on matters of vision and governance but has instead been about targeting particular benefits and services on clearly identified social problems in order to achieve policy goals established by government. And even today, when devolution of power has been generally accepted by all political interests, the British government has not been willing to release the large social security budgets to devolved Parliaments in Scotland and Wales, let alone non-governmental agencies. It would seem that New Labour and 'the third way' are not entirely committed to the 'Christian democratisation of social democracy'. Nevertheless, 'the third way' has been committed to redirecting responsibility for the delivery of social policy goals away from government while, it should be stressed, continuing to retain a centralised welfare system and, as Giddens (1999) observes, retaining 'the hand of active government protection'. The civil renewal strategy is not, therefore, only about redistributing responsibility, but is also about budgetary reform and creating new legal entities in a context in which there remains strong state steering power over civil society.

The real problem confronting a civil renewal strategy aimed at tackling the fragmentation of marginal communities, and the attendant anti-social behaviour that is a manifestation of a search for excitement in unexciting communities and sense of abandonment by a retreating welfare state, is, as Clegg (2005) has observed, how to consolidate a consensus about policy goals in a system that lacks anchors in civil society. Or, as William Robson (1976) observed, a welfare society is 'what people do, feel and think about matters which bear on the general welfare' and that is different from the idea of a welfare state in which policies are driven downwards by political and partisan interests: a strategy that dictates to people that they 'must be active citizens'. The question is how to manage the 'yawning gulf' Robson alludes to and how to sustain change once it has been created. The 'third way' is seeking answers to this question by releasing the pent-up energy that has, supposedly, been trapped in communities since the welfare state project assumed total responsibility for social integration and social needs in the early twentieth century. The civil renewal strategy has become part of a wider effort to combat social exclusion. However, the involvement of the Home Office and Justice Ministries in Scotland, as key drivers of the strategy, has, as I have argued in Chapter 5, resulted in the boundary between family policy and criminal justice policy becoming blurred, especially for families living in peripheral housing estates and poor, inner-city areas. For example, programmes such as *Sure Start*, which are aimed at providing social, health and educational support for the under fives in deprived areas, and mentoring schemes, such as *Mentor Plus* (Shiner *et al.* 2004), providing social and educational guidance to teenage children with the aim of diverting them from deviant activity, are primarily aimed at the anti-social behaviour problem and have drawn in the voluntary sector of care to provide key workers for these services as part of a community-building approach. We could say that these schemes are benign examples of social steering by encouraging people living in disadvantaged areas of British society to change in order to improve their lives, sometimes by becoming actively involved in service delivery and informal tutelage of young people in their local communities. However, these types of initiatives also have a strong social control dimension which taints the civil renewal strategy. Anti-social families and their declining regard for 'respect' in society have been identified as the key factors undermining community and family life. The focus on strong communities has too often slipped into a strategy of crime prevention, emphasising community safety rather than community development, as the criminal justice arms of government have taken the lead in driving policy (Blunkett 2003a; b; Home Office 2003b).

However, the central problem is that 60 years of state welfare, including 25 years of creeping marketisation in the field of social policy, has inevitably destroyed the sense of mutualism and social solidarity that existed prior to the establishment of the welfare state project in the period after 1945. It is amoral familism rather than social and community solidarity that has resulted from the last 25 years of welfare state reform: the widespread abandonment of collectivism and the continuing stress on individual and family responsibilities and obligations encourage an inward-looking and selfish attitude to the well-being of those needing public welfare (see Rodger 2003a). To repeat an observation made in Chapter 2, in the affluent and consumerist societies of Western Europe it is post-emotionalism that is dominant: caring about others is intellectualised by those distanced by affluence from direct experience of social deprivation, while those at the bottom of the social hierarchy inevitably focus on the well-being of themselves and their immediate family before those with whom they share neighbourhood and community. The problem is that insufficient numbers of the middle classes want to volunteer and embrace civic activism, and those living in disadvantaged communities continue to expect services to be delivered by the state. And this is the primary reason why welfare and criminal justice are increasingly being seen as necessarily related and why strategies such as civil renewal, community safety and the 'partnership culture' have emerged. Institutionalised forms of social solidarity secured through the Keynesian welfare state have largely collapsed, and there is a search for an alternative mechanism, controlled and coordinated by government, to ensure that society continues to remain orderly while also being compatible with a 'hollowed-out' state system. This is the main reason why the New Labour government is now having to pursue a strategy of civil renewal to encourage active citizenship and strengthen civic engagement in communities: social, human and cultural capital are weak throughout society but particularly in poor, inner-city communities and peripheral housing estates where expectations are highest about welfare support.

Civil renewal and inauthenticity

The irony of the current situation is that in order to enliven the voluntary sector and strengthen communities to combat incivility, the New Labour government is having systematically to build 'community capacity', or build functional performance at devolved levels, because the welfare state project over the past 50 years has steadily weakened associational forms of democracy at local level by the centralisation of power.

Crawford (2001) characterises the New Labour 'third way' in this area in terms of being 'joined-up but fragmented'. The policy strategy of encouraging greater levels of voluntary sector involvement in community safety, for example, has led to multiple agency partnerships that have succeeded in fragmenting efforts to develop a coherent civil renewal strategy: the 'initiative-itis' which has created drug action teams, YOTs, child protection committees, Sure Start, crime-reduction initiatives, and a host of other voluntary-based agencies have fragmented policing and effective control, and this, in turn has probably meant that central government control is strengthened rather than devolved, as suggested by 'third-way' theory. The three strands of the strategy, aimed at building community efficacy, establishing partnership working, founded on joined-up policy stakeholders and networks, and establishing a more accountable and effective system of public fund management, have probably led to a greater emphasis on managerialism at the expense of communitarianism and partnership working.

A number of commentators (see Lewis 1999; 2005; Dahrendorf 2001) have suggested that the New Labour government's conception of partnership remains grounded in a theory of government rather than of civil society: a theory of civil society would acknowledge that in complex social systems government steering power over social policy is always imprecise and that effective governance today is about autonomous self-governing networks of actors and institutions that work with but are also independent of government and the state (see Stoker 1998). The concern that many have with the civil renewal initiative is, for example, that the 'partnership culture' ushered in by the compact with the voluntary sector, may *appear* significantly different from the 'contract culture' that it has displaced, but in reality it simply tightens the control and steering capacity of the government over the voluntary sector while simultaneously distancing government from direct accountability for the delivery and failures of policy. The compact appears to have resulted in an increase in the flow of funding to some significant big players in the voluntary sector, but it fails to address issues relating to the independence and autonomy of those organisations. Indeed, under the guise of the 'professionalisation' of voluntary sector organisations, and the prescribing of strict new management and accountancy rules as a condition for participation in the compact, government control over those organisations receiving funding has inevitably strengthened (see Lewis 1999; 2005). As suggested earlier, the concept that best describes this phenomenon is 'inauthenticity': confronted by the difficulties of the political administration of complex social and political systems, governments tend to conceal their manipulative and controlling activities by devoting considerable resources to appearing to be responsive to community and individuals. There is little evidence that the voluntary sector in the UK is actively engaged with government in shaping social policy or is genuinely embedded in policy networks. Indeed, research has indicated that awareness of the government's compact with the voluntary sector is low among voluntary organisations (Hayton, Gray and Stirling 2004). Phillips (2002) has drawn attention to the implications of these wider political processes for crime-prevention partnerships. The statutory agencies, primarily the police and local authorities, given legal obligations to plan, coordinate and deliver initiatives in crime-prevention and community safety have dominated the partnerships. The extent to which there is authentic community participation in the process of building community efficacy is questionable. The nature of the strategy is in reality one which has stimulated division rather than solidarity and is obfuscatory rather than illuminating about community involvement in crime prevention.

Community safety and established–outsiders relations

The argument of this book rejects the overly sanguine, often patronising and potentially divisive thrust of the civil renewal strategy. The core social problem that is being addressed by the civil renewal strategy is the fragmentation occurring in communities blighted by industrial decline. Jock Young's colourful description of the present-day social malaise as *social bulimia* encapsulates the key idea: those who were once integrated into society through a Keynesian welfare state and corporatist relations between capital and labour are now being 'puked up' into the margins of society, without employment, skills and incentives in the declining regions, towns and communities of post-industrial society (see Young 1999). The orientation of welfare policy is to manage the incentives of problem populations more explicitly than was the practice at the height of the Keynesian welfare state. At community level, the policy emphasis is on 'activeness' and 'civic engagement', and not compensation for the vagaries of post-industrialism.

The de-civilising tendencies evident in post-industrial societies can be observed in the relationship between the 'contended society' of a property-owning, employed majority, the origins of which were described many years ago by Galbraith (1992), and a significant minority of those living in marginal communities who are without work and credentials, and are dependent on a range of means-tested welfare benefits that most Western governments are predisposed to adjust downwards to coerce compliance with the new orthodoxy of 'active citizenship'. De-civilisng processes as a form of degenerate modernity have become a reality in pockets of our cities and towns where post-industrialism, a failing education system, and poor work have created cultures, lifestyles and social behaviour which are antithetical to the active and disciplined ways of life required of modern consumer society. These deviant lifestyles are being addressed by a new hybridised form of criminalised social policy, variously referred to as community safety, social crime prevention, or restorative justice, but which is mainly concerned to repackage traditional strategies for community development through civil renewal. This is the space where the task of compensating poor people for their lives is offered in 'opportunities' to learn, to be engaged in public projects, and to develop a sense of pride in their local communities and neighbourhoods rather than receive social benefits and social services. Unemployment, immigration, and unstable populations characterise those local communities targeted by the strategy. Civil renewal is primarily a way of approaching the multiple social problems in poor areas and addressing the established–outsiders conflicts which lie at their core.

The theoretical construct of the established–outsiders relationship, described by Elias and Scotson (1965) in their research on a Leicestershire village between 1958 and 1960, gets to the heart of the problem with current civil renewal and community safety strategies. The original research was based on a master's degree project undertaken by Scotson. It was conventionally designed to describe and explain why juvenile delinquency occurred disproportionately in one neighbourhood of the village. However, under Elias' guidance,

163

it gave way to a study of the uneasy relationship between the 'established' residents of the village and the newly arrived 'incomers' taking residence in the new housing estate. On closer inspection of their data, it became clear that a broader sociological phenomenon was revealing itself, and one that was consistent with Elias' broader theoretical and historical conceptualisation of the civilising process. The phenomenon that underpinned this social and cultural division is best described by Elias' concept of functional democratisation, which I described in Chapter 2. To repeat briefly here, as advanced industrial societies have developed, the distinctions between the social classes have diminished, and networks of interdependence, pulling people from different strata together throughout society, have become denser. The incorporation of all social groups into mainstream society is founded on their functional contribution to a complex social and economic division of labour. The habits and practices of elites have permeated those of the lower classes as a by-product of increased interactions and interdependence in the functional division of labour: as functional democratisation occurs, contrasts between social groups have lessened. The long-run developmental movement has been towards the greater control of aggression, increased sensitivity to others, and the development of a growing sense of shame and guilt about all manner of habits and practices relating to personal and sexual conduct. Where this process remains incomplete, or sizeable minorities of people are socially and spatially excluded from full membership of society, the progress of functional democratisation is stalled. In the context of late-1950s Leicestershire, the feature that was used to distinguish the 'established from the outsiders' was the display of the less socially restrained and often deviant behaviour of the latter and the perception that the 'outsiders' were defined by their incivilities and marginal contribution to community life. The absence of routine and frequent social interaction across class and spatial boundaries between the diverse social groupings in the study also meant that limited knowledge and understanding of alternative life experiences and pathways led to partial and distorted views of those living on the housing estate by those residents of in the old village centre.

What was being described in Elias' book *The Established and the Outsiders* is the reversing of the civilising process in isolated pockets of society. The phenomenon of de-civilisation can take root in those areas of the social structure where interdependence and social solidarity break down. In those circumstances where marginality, social exclusion, racism or sectarianism emerges, the sense of empathy for the other and the mutual restraint on behaviour which is built by frequent social interaction are absent. This tendency should be understood as a structural property of social systems where social polarisation and inequality are present or deepening, and not as a property of pathological individuals.

In the broader context of the Elias and Scotson study of a thriving Midlands town where unemployment was low and the Keynesian welfare state ensured that the vagaries of negative social evaluation were not underpinned by real material disadvantages, the labelling of the outsiders was merely vacuous name calling, because, in reality, there was no significant difference found between the majority of the outsiders and the established groups with respect to social and behavioural values, and attitudes to work and the maintenance of property. However, today, the contribution to society and the economy of those who live visibly in spatially distinct enclaves of disadvantage in post-employment communities is negligible and, as argued in Chapter 3, the marginality of many is carried in their lifestyle and culture, which signals adaptation to a social and life situation without expectation of material improvement. In other words, anti-social behaviour is at its worst where functional democratisation is at its weakest. And the civil renewal strategy manifesting itself as community safety and social crime prevention is attempting to mobilise communities and neighbourhoods against those deemed to be outsiders by their anti-social and criminal behaviour and often their stylistic choices. In essence, it has become less about socially integrating those who live at the margins of society and more about guarding the boundaries between the established and the outsiders.

Interdependence is weakened by the forces of postmodernity. In a discussion comparing points of similarity and difference between Zygmunt Bauman and Norbert Elias, Dennis Smith (2001) identifies Bauman as the main theorist of de-civilising processes, attributing to him the view that 'postmodernity is decivilised modernity' (Smith 2001: 127). To place this theoretical discussion in a more mundane context, what is being suggested here is that the socio-economic background shaping community safety strategies is the fragmentation and tearing of the webs of interdependence in postmodern society by industrial decline and globalisation, and so creating divisions between established and outsider groups at community, national and international level. In place of the 'tension-filled mutual engagement between established and outsider groups within a dense web of interdependence under the aegis of a stable power monopoly' (Smith 2001: 127), as characteristic of the civilising process, we have a situation where the

165

state wants to give away powers and governments prefer the idea of civil society as the place where social problems are addressed; where the market principle seems to rule and individuals are increasingly encouraged to think of themselves and their immediate family rather than community and society. This leads to a 'decline in the public' (see Marquand 2004) and a degeneration of the other-regarding social values and civic culture being sought by the civil renewal strategy. A danger of this situation is that, in the absence of state-sponsored mechanisms that will maximise participation in debate and reflection on policy matters, and so activate a process of building a civic culture, 'populism' rather than reason will shape both policy and the relationships between increasingly divided people. Marquand (2004) describes this in terms of the pre-eminence attributed to the popular will and to ordinary opinions over those of experts and elites, an observation which features prominently in Garland's (2001) analysis of contemporary society, particularly with respect to the politicisation of criminal justice issues and the decline of criminological expertise. What becomes accepted is what is popularly believed and accepted. Herein lies the danger in the appeal to community in a context of de-civilising tendencies: the views of the established can become hostile and aggressive towards outsider groups. The immigrant, the NEET and the chav are visible targets, easily designated as 'outsiders' and consequently readily available to be accused of being the source of community disharmony. Community solidarity becomes the cohesion of the most articulate members against the inarticulate and the most visibly deviant.

Community safety and the appeal to community

Community safety and civil renewal are closely related and as strategies rest upon a major paradox: they seek to build social capital and trust in local communities often by adopting solutions that at best undermine social capital and at worst actually weaken social capital and trust. For example, Prior (2005) has drawn attention to the irreconcilable aims of attempting to build social capital and trust in communities beleaguered by anti-social behaviour by arousing a sense of suspicion, often placing neighbour against neighbour. The feelings of insecurity which that engenders encourages the anticipatory social reaction to people and groups *thought* to pose a threat rather than reacting only to those that *are* posing a threat. We live in a risk society and communities are being mobilised to anticipate threats and label and classify those that do not conform to what is typical, routine and predictable. Many communities are relying on wardens, CCTV and neighbourhood policing to convey the idea that surveillance will ensure that neighbourhoods remain orderly and peaceful. This results in 'thin trust' because it is insubstantial, not grounded in improved social relations *between* people living in a community and almost totally reliant on a combination of technology and sources of professional authority external to the locality (see Crawford 2000). As an approach to building community efficacy, it is flawed because it contradicts the basic premise of community safety policies that strong, interdependent communities act as a defence against incivility and criminality.

The complexity of the very concept of 'trust' is revealed by the community safety movement. Trust in abstract systems, expertise and technology is often accepted as somehow more reliable than having trust in people. In order for people to be constructed as being trustworthy, they must be classified and constructed into what Crawford (2000) has referred to as 'environments of trust'. Contractual communities are formed by first classifying those that are not trustworthy and therefore to be excluded. A great deal of crime-prevention effort is, therefore, built not on bringing people together as the civil renewal strategy intends, but dividing the populations in communities between 'established' and 'outsider groups'. The restorative justice movement discussed in Chapter 6 will continue to be a major challenge unless more effort is made to integrate those people in communities that are consigned to the margins. However, focusing on surveillance and suspicion, and creating established and outsider groups as a basis for 'defending' a community against deviance and crime is the wrong place to start.

In order to address these contradictions and tensions, a distinction has been drawn between situational crime prevention and social crime prevention. The civil renewal strategy is bound up with both approaches and therein lies one of its major drawbacks. Situational crime prevention attempts to remove the opportunities for criminality and anti-social behaviour largely by ignoring issues concerning behavioural dispositions and concentrating on routine activities: designing crime out of communities, disrupting areas where youths gather, and relying on the wardens and CCTV to diminish the rewards of criminality and spoil the fun of anti-social behaviour. In contrast, social crime prevention addresses the underlying social causes of anti-social behaviour and criminality and should seriously attempt to understand the dispositions stimulating deviance. However, the complex and difficult area of building social capital and trust between people living in a community is not tackled by a focus solely on criminality and incivility. The emphasis on aligning social policy with criminal justice distracts policymaking from the wider issues that must be acknowledged if a civilised society is to be constructed: there must be appreciation of the sociological impact of economic and social structures on social behaviour. The underlying structural forces destroying social interdependence in marginal communities remains a huge issue that policymakers avoid by opting to confront the shallow behavioural manifestation of their influence in the guise of dealing with 'realities'. A low-tax economy and a minimal state, dictated by a neo-liberal policy agenda, has consequences for social disorder in those parts of the social hierarchy that cannot cope with the extreme meritocratic ethos that such a policy strategy brings in its wake. That 'reality' has to be confronted. The work of Wancquant on the American ghetto discussed in Chapter 2 points to the ultimate consequence of postmodern society's refusal to contemplate the big structural impact of racist segregation combined with low taxation and a weak social state: the established and outsider groups become polarised and underpinned by real material and racist inequalities, and penal policy quickly replaces social policy when governments seek a solution to the criminality and violence that results.

Concluding observations

The appeal to community in dealing with anti-social behaviour and dysfunctional families has, in some areas, encouraged prejudice and intolerance rather than community efficacy or social capital (Crawford 1999). Rather than social solidarity emerging through sustained voluntary sector engagement in community development and education, the criminal justice legislation has, it seems, encouraged the over-reliance on and overuse of civil law by the police and local authorities, primarily through the ASBO obsession, rather than facilitate the cultivation of authentic community interests to deal with the problems of incivility. Additionally, the threat of withholding welfare support from families deemed to be anti-social, which has become an orthodoxy in contemporary welfare thinking as evidenced by the euphemistically labelled strategy to 'create independence at the heart of the welfare state', indicates a subtle change in the stance of the welfare state from its traditional role of social steering towards a more explicit stress on social control (see Rodger 2003b; 2006; Purnell 2008). The continued attenuation of the social state, focused on national society and national government, will exacerbate tendencies to de-civilisation in the postmodern era. The most fundamental premise of Elias' theory, and the theoretical thesis he builds around the civilising process, is that a strong monopoly state power which exercises its authority on a national scale must be maintained to ensure order and maximise solidarity and social interdependence across all social divisions.

The key issue to emphasise is that the problems of social exclusion and disadvantage cannot easily be devolved to community and voluntary action: subsidiarity as a principle, and civil renewal as a strategy, must be founded on the related idea of 'functional performance'. And it is evident that many post-employment communities cannot cope with the reduced welfare support and raised government expectations of activeness that have accompanied the civil renewal strategy. Communities that are conflictual and divided, as many are in the peripheral housing estates and poor, inner-city areas, cannot take effective responsibility for building human and cultural capital (Wagner 2004). The balance is inevitably tipped towards the need for greater rather than less state intervention. However, the problem is that the form that intervention is taking is weighted towards forms of coercive law rather than social policy. The announcement by Prime Minister Tony Blair on 2 September 2005 that he was establishing a 'Respect Task Force' was accompanied by an admission that parenting orders will soon be issued by a wider range of interests (see Jamieson 2005). Schools and social workers are expected to apply for parenting orders, and they will be allowed to do this prior to children actually offending if they are considered to be 'at risk'. Family behaviour considered inappropriate by key interests within a neighbourhood or community could also lead to actions which have the issuing of parenting contracts as their primary objective, resulting in compulsory attendance at parenting classes. The danger is that responsibility for community development and family support, in some circumstances, may be likened to a process that amounts to aiding and abetting by a distant unit of government. In place of 'real' government action to develop communities materially, we are likely to observe a 'strategy' directed remotely that disingenuously implies that the management of social change and community development has little to do with government. The strategy for civil renewal seems to be focused on individuals and their attitudes to volunteering and responsibility for active citizenship. However, despite the emphasis on civic activeness and greater involvement of the voluntary sector in community efficacy building, there remains a major issue to be addressed about how such a strategy can be effective in the absence of work for people and resources to refurbish declining neighbourhoods, especially in areas blemished by youth gangs and violence. Civic renewal can work only if a society and a community have first been civilised.

There is confusion regarding the very idea of 'respect' driving the New Labour criminal justice policy: it appears to be a quality that has to be expressed only by individuals living in poor communities. There is also a duty on governments to create the conditions first that will allow people to feel at ease with their neighbours and their community. Respect implies recognising in people that they should be accorded a degree of dignity and support from the wider collectivity in which they live: the notion that certain 'kinds of people' lack respect and that they somehow live in but are not of our society is not a sustainable view in an increasingly global and interdependent world. The policy dilemma confronting contemporary governments attempting to deal with community fragmentation is that civil renewal may be an inappropriate strategy for neighbourhoods and localities where fear and insecurity are rife. As Jamieson (2005) has argued, the 'respect' agenda has encouraged 'authoritarian penal populism', while it 'encourages intolerance and hostility, but also serves to mask the often complex and diverse needs underlying *parenting deficits* and *anti-social and criminal behaviour*' (p. 189). The next chapter addresses this issue and the fear of crime and anti-social behaviour that blemishes some communities. We also need to begin to think about the deep-seated sense of insecurity that pervades some areas of society today and consider the question, posed by Loader and Walker (2007), of how to 'civilise security'.

Chapter 8

Fear of the uncivil and the criminal

> Fearful citizens tend to be inattentive to, unconcerned about, even enthusiasts for, the erosion of basic freedoms. They often lack openness or sympathy towards others, especially those they apprehend as posing a danger to them. They privilege the known over the unknown, us over them, here over there. They often retreat from public life, seeking refuge in private security 'solutions' while at the same time screaming anxiously and angrily from the sidelines for the firm hand of authority – for tough 'security' measures against crime, or disorder, or terror .... Fear, in all these ways, is the breeding ground, as well as the stock-in-trade, of authoritarian, uncivil government. (Loader and Walker 2007: 8)

The words of Loader and Walker encapsulate the central problem facing governments and civil renewal strategies. Many poor communities are being undermined by fear and by a sense of insecurity. They are willing to trade human rights for an assurance from government that society will be protected from the violent criminality that is *perceived* to be everywhere. The stress on the word 'perceived' is crucial here because it is now well understood that there is not a necessary relationship between fear and direct experience of a threat (see Davies, Francis and Jupp 2003; Jackson 2004). Indeed, the key research from victimology point clearly to the fact that those who are most afraid of crime and anti-social behaviour are those who are least likely to be victims (see Hale 1996). The reason for this is that the elderly, women and young children are those groups who tend to live more privatised and, in the case of children, more supervised, lives. It is because of this mismatch between perception and experience that the focus of this chapter will be on the *social construction* of fear of crime and social disorder. It will begin by examining the notion of security before considering some recent research that is helpful in understanding some of the paradoxes found by victim research.

The broad socio-economic background informing this analysis can be restated again briefly to provide a context for the discussion of fear and insecurity in many marginal communities today. The loosening of the webs of interdependence caused by the individualising effects of market society has been exacerbated by the structural unemployment and de-industrialisation experienced in many regions of Western Europe and North America in the past 30 years. The compensatory forms of social and economic intervention that were a feature of the Keynesian welfare state in the period between 1945 and the mid-1970s, and I include the 'war on poverty' welfare surge in America between the 1960s and 1970s, have given way to a society that is polarising in terms of both the wealth and the cultural experience of its citizens. The sense of security and order that was a feature of the old welfare settlement has gone with the onset of welfare retrenchment.

What appears to be happening in the poor and fragmenting communities of late modernity is that some residents withdraw in partial 'retreatist' mode and adopt strategies for action which suit their material and social situation (Merton 1938). The 'cultural toolkit' they have developed in response to their anomic situation includes a closing down of their behavioural if not their spatial universe (see Young 2007: 17–40 on the cross-boundary activities of working people in late modernity). A key feature of this anomic situation is that it is often accompanied by a lack of empathy for outsiders. Young males in the peripheral housing estates, in particular, become very territorially defensive and are as active in the processes of what Young (2007) calls 'othering' as the policymakers, the politicians and the middle classes living some distance away. The young soldiers of the community public sphere scan the boundaries of their territory for intruders such as the police, who might be intent on disrupting informal economic activity, or 'others' from a nearby estate intent on inflicting physical violence on the local gang or racket. These tendencies to 'othering' are manifested by all social groups whether resident in the ghetto or the suburbs of the contended society. Such amoral familist and post-emotional attitudes are rooted in a rejection of solidarism. It is these forces that provide the context for de-civilised tendencies to incubate. Where there is a lack of knowledge and understanding of others, there is always fear and prejudice. Lying at the heart of this process is fear of the uncivil and the anti-social, which often is disproportionate to the threats that people actually face. In such circumstances, 'fearful citizens' lose interest in due process, social justice and human rights – they just want security and order restored by any means available. This, of course, worries the middle classes, who want to maintain a balance between the maintenance of their security and the broader maintenance of human freedoms in an open-market society.

Civilising security

The primary aim of the analysis advanced by Loader and Walker (2007) is to identify the ingredients that will convert the issue of security from something that people see as a threat to freedom into something that is perceived as being essentially good for society. The premise of their argument is that security is a 'thick public good'. It is something that we all want and must have, but it should not be something that is won for the benefit of few in the community at the expense of others. Security makes society possible, and for that reason it should be built collectively and in the common interest. A strong theme emerging from their analysis is, however, that current political efforts to place security issues at the heart of a strategy to maintain a well-ordered society are contradictory; attempting 'to quench the unquenchable' demand for security is not leading to a society at peace with itself but instead to one that is riddled with fear and suspicion. In such a situation, we have seen the private security industry grow and a relentless obsession about crime and anti-social behaviour dominate the social welfare agenda. This has diverted social policy away from its primary task of securing the material well-being of the disadvantaged in society to focus increasingly on the management of deviance in its harmless as well as disturbing forms.

   The problem that Loader and Walker rightly identify is that this emerging orthodoxy that views present-day society in terms of threats and disorder has spawned a counter-view grounded in what they call the liberty lobby. This view tends to reduce all discussion of security and disorder to a question of human freedoms and human rights, and typically slants debate about security to a discussion of the anti-democratic propensities of those who support a strong law-and-order strategy. The liberty view tends to understand all policing and security matters in militaristic terms and effectively ignores the complexities involved in maintaining social order in a post-industrial society. If both the security-obsessed view and the liberty-obsessed view are found wanting by Loader and Walker, so, too, is the human-crisis view that issues of security should be 'decoupled' from the problem of law and order and recoupled to the big human and social issues that confront modern market societies: the problems of homelessness, extreme poverty and social exclusion (they also rightly refer to ecological disaster, but considering that mammoth issue here would divert attention from the main theme of the book). However, these large social issues get to the heart of the challenge posed by fear and insecurity. The paradox is that as Western societies have become more affluent they have also generally become more unequal and socially and culturally polarised. Indeed, addressing the human crisis of poverty and social exclusion may well be a precondition for a successful solution of the problem of finding civil security.

The answer to the problem of civilised security provided by Loader and Walker is to seek it in political and legal institutions that will make contemporary forms of associational democracy possible. This seems to amount to the state institutionalising a Habermasian public sphere founded on authentic public conversation about security needs in a community (see Habermas 1979). While this is a laudable objective, it is the decline of the public sphere and, in Habermas' terms, its 'distorted forms' that make this project largely beside the point because of where we are today. What emerges from their analysis is that attention should be paid to the mechanisms in society which distort perceptions of security and incivility.

Mass media and perception of threats

One of the intriguing issues surrounding fear and insecurity in society today is that knowledge of those who are 'not like us' is often not obtained by direct experience or social interaction but is instead mediated through the popular press, television, the Internet and even cinema. It is the absence of the sense of social interdependence in contemporary Western societies that breeds distrust and wariness of strangers. When those strangers are described by the mediated narratives that saturate our homes through the daily absorption of television and newspapers as being in some indefinable way threatening because of their culture, their age or their style, then it is unsurprising that many people acquire a sense of insecurity.

However, it is not only the lurid and prurient reporting of the tabloid press that shapes conceptions of criminality and creates a sense of fear in the population. An additional source of information about crime and anti-social behaviour, and perhaps a neglected aspect, is criminal justice policy itself. Legislation, reinforced by social policy initiatives targeted at problem behaviour and problem populations, has the effect of making some types of behaviour and populations visible and therefore liable to be feared, especially when harnessed to the objectives of the criminal justice agenda and publicised by prominent politicians and opinion formers (see Estrada 2004). It also furnishes the population with a ready-made partisan vocabulary to describe and evaluate particular events, styles and behaviours. This process relates to what I referred to in Chapter 4 as the construction of a 'regulatory community'. In that context, I drew attention to the analysis advanced by Carr, Cowan and Hunter (2007) about the process by which the governance of anti-social behaviour in the private, rented-housing sector was made more effective. That task was accomplished by isolating and classifying a problem population in such a way that rendered it visible for legislative intervention. The conversion of a private trouble into a public issue, to draw on C. Wright Mills' (1959) well-known conceptual phrase, was facilitated by the formulation and presentation of policy and legislation which marked out in governance terms what had to be changed. The classic example of the construction of a problem population is the way in which the underclass discourse was connected to the thesis on 'broken windows' to create a solution for a problem that was subsequently constructed, namely, that profligate welfare spending should be reduced in favour of hard law and order strategies in poor neighbourhoods to discourage the formation of single-female-headed households, which, the argument suggested, were related to badly supervised, anti-social children and high crime rates. This popular discourse travelled from neo-liberal American think tank to popular parlance in America and Europe, aided and abetted by both broadsheet and tabloid press. The problem group, which in this case was the fatherless family, was isolated to enable legislative instruments to control its deviance, which in America were the Clinton welfare reforms of 1996 and in the UK the creation of the Child Support Agency, and these instruments are fast becoming the anti-social behaviour legislation (see Jones and Newburn 2007). This process *signalled* to the public at large that popular opinions and attitudes antithetical to fatherless, lone-parent families were justified. The legislation was possible because of the success of partisan political interests in creating a policy agenda around fear and suspicion, which signalled to the population what they ought to be concerned about while also suggesting particular policy solutions, or *control signals,* that would address their fears in policy terms. It is to the signal-crime perspective that we should turn in search of a clearer understanding of these processes.

Signal crimes and fear

Innes and Fielding (2002) and Innes (2004a; 2004b) have developed a number of related concepts which provide us with a very useful way of thinking about how a 'climate of unsafety' is created, and partly relieved, in society. Their particular focus is on the issue of *risk perception*, and their premise is that the awareness of risk is inherently subjective and always a social construction. Central to this type of perspective is the importance of understanding the situational context that frames a problem or behaviour as presenting threat or risk, or, indeed, of being indicative of social disorder. The clearest statement on the concept of signal crimes comes from Innes (2004a; 2004b), who makes a distinction between micro- and macrolevels of analysis: signal crimes relate to a process in which the public problem of crime is imbued with personal meaning at a microlevel. This is different from the more widely known and used term, *moral panic*, which relates to the process whereby private troubles are given a societal dimension through the actions of the mass media and the voices of those opinion formers deemed to be authoritative and credible by the mass media. I will deal with this issue separately below. For example, Innes and Fielding's (2002) key distinction between *situated* signals and *disembedded* signals assists us to make sense of how conceptions of criminality and fear are generated at different levels of society. The former clearly relates to the ways and means by which fear is generated through direct experience and observation in the local community and neighbourhood, while the latter relates to the reality that much of what we know about crime for most people is influenced by the mass media, particularly television and mass circulation newspapers. Indeed, what is popularly understood about politics and policy is also mediated through television and the popular press. I will look at each level of analysis in turn.

Situated signal crimes

The notion of signal crimes has the greatest utility for understanding fear and insecurity at the level of the community, especially the subjectivities of those who are surrounded by what is perceived as social disorder. Innes argues that to understand the fear of crime it is important that we understand the ways and means in which people construct understanding of risk situations. The theoretical foundations of this perspective lie in a Goffmanesque reading of labelling theory. In particular, Innes refers to Goffman's notion of the 'veneer of normalcy' as a taken-for-granted feature of everyday and routine social interaction. Initially, acts of deviance and incivility may stand out against the background of what is normal in a neighbourhood, signalling to the local population that the area may be in decline. And, of course, once crime and incivility become a routine aspect of a neighbourhood, and people just expect and accept it, then that air of resignation may quicken the decline of a community, stimulating an exodus by those residents with the means to escape. Applied to the 'broken-windows thesis', we can readily understand why people might consider a neighbourhood with an abundance of dilapidated houses and graffiti-strewn walls to be menacing and full of risk. Similarly, some youth styles, body demeanours and types of crime, specifically predatory street crime and violence, act as signal threats and signal crimes, pointing towards a larger problem of community degeneration in the mind of the onlooker. Risk is announced to observers by such signals not because of a direct experience of a threat but because of the perceived potential risk which is feared.

A neglected aspect of this analysis, but one which Innes and Fielding (2002) draw attention to through the signal crimes perspective, is that social disorder and anti-social behaviour are not something that arises in communities because they are being attacked by 'outsiders' or by those who exist outside the framework of normal, sociable living. Many in policy and politics have a tendency to view community disorder in terms of orderly and disorderly segments of the population. This isolates groups within a community and identifies them as worthy of being feared, it creates scapegoats and targets for criminal justice intervention, and it reduces the problem to one of individual deviance and behaviour that can be corrected by appropriate punishments. Instead there is evidence, and here Innes and Fielding (2002) cite Girling, Loader and Sparks (2000) and Jock Young (1999), that many of the poorer and disadvantaged communities are literally 'imploding': it is the local youths who destroy the built fabric of their own neighbourhoods; who cause alarm by congregating in large numbers in streets adjacent to local shops and services; and who appear to have acquired the attitudinal posture of disrespect and aggression. There is a structural element to this problem in that unemployment, de-industrialisation and welfare retrenchment create a vacuum of resources in some communities, making them dull and difficult to escape from because of the absence of reliable and affordable transport (see Cahill 1994 on the significance of transport and consumption for understanding social exclusion). In such circumstances, some young people drift into anti-social behaviour through their need to express what Matza and Sykes (1961) have called *subterranean values* (the search for excitement and fun in a social environment that often is unexciting). The search for kicks which emerges from this situation, and which often is a mode of survival in a degenerating community, paradoxically also hastens that decline and signals to the residents that they are living on the margins of mainstream economic and social activity. It is precisely this that suggests that a de-civilising process may be at work because the networks linking some communities to the rhythms of life in the worlds of work and consumption are absent.

The relationship between social policy and crime control is clearly evident at the level of the community in the reaction to what Innes (2004b) and Innes and Fielding (2002) have called control signals. What is of particular interest here is not only the way in which popular perceptions of a community or neighbourhood can be shaped by signal crimes and signal disorder, but also how particular policy interventions can act as signs that something is being done to address a social problem. Fear of crime, and perceptions of social order or social decline, can be influenced by the way in which policy affects the 'situational' or neighbourhood level.

Bottoms and Wilson (2004; 2005) have provided an excellent piece of research exploring the issues surrounding community efficacy and civil renewal, as well as the utility of the signal-crimes perspective. Interestingly, it also points to the equally important concept of the control signal emanating from policy impact and service provision. The research was carried out in two high-crime areas of Sheffield, with each study area divided into what the research calls Inner A and B and Outer A and B. One area is described as an inner-city area on the edge of the city centre; the other area is three miles from the city centre and consists of two former council estates. Each area appeared to have a better and worse district with respect to crime rates and perceived neighbourhood problems, while also displaying some variation in terms of meeting the criteria of being effective communities as designated by the civil renewal strategy. A key finding of this work is that what happens in 'public space' is crucial for determining levels of security and fear. In ways echoing Loader and Walker, the conclusions arrived at by Bottoms and Wilson (2005) clearly identify the presence of safe streets and safe public spaces as the foundation for civil security: 'Safe public spaces ... [are] a central prerequisite for a secure daily life' (p. 14). Indeed, the research tends to reveal that many responses suggest that while burglary remains a very threatening and distasteful crime, it is less significant in shaping people's perception of security and feelings of fear than events in public spaces. As a more hidden crime, burglary did not seem to elicit the same level of anxiety in respondents as issues such as 'youths hanging around', drug dealing, criminal damage and assault; these caused most fear and anxiety, and, it should be added, anger (see Hale 1996; Ditton, Bannister, Gilchrist and Farrell 1999). However, the most interesting finding suggested by the research, and which is used to explain some of the variation between areas with respect to popular perceptions of decline and levels of fear and anxiety about crime rates, is the notion of *control signal*. For example, the research was stimulated to enquire into this phenomenon partly on the basis of research in the USA by Taub, Taylor and Dunham (1984), which concentrated on the issue of safety in public spaces.

> As well as investing heavily in the urban infrastructure, and (since it is the area where the University of Chicago is located) urging faculty members to live in the area, these planners introduced some initiatives that directly addressed safety in public space issues – such as free buses and free emergency telephones ... the whole package of measures ... sent a strong 'control signal'; for while crimes such as burglary remained high ... the area was nevertheless perceived as safe. (Bottoms and Wilson 2005: 14)

Similarly, the research reports on a before-and-after scenario for the area: the area described as 'Inner' changed from being perceived as a place where residents were 'fearful' and 'intimidated' to one which improved immeasurably through urban regeneration funding that led to improved street lighting, the removal of void properties, the clearing up of litter, and the establishment of a dedicated community policing unit. Additional measures such as drug action to eliminate street dealing and the installation of a network of CCTV cameras further signalled the view that the area was being improved and incivility and criminality were being addressed and controlled. These developments represented for many residents a successful campaign for change that in turn reinforced their sense of empowerment, confirming that their complaints to their local councillors and local authorities had been effective. There seemed to be a relationship between the establishment of appropriate control signals and the community efficacy to act to maintain informal social control in the area (see Innes 2004a; 2004b). Where these developments had not occurred, there were higher rates of anti-social behaviour. Where there was a perception that the local services were poor or had declined, there was also a view that residents were not listened to, that the area was in decline, and that other areas appeared to be benefiting unfairly by comparison: not all areas in the Sheffield study shared in the same service initiatives (see Bottoms and Wilson 2004).

Walklate (1998) has focused a useful piece of research on how people's perception of fear of crime is influenced by their relationship to their community. Her research in Salford was based on comparing two areas, which in this case had similar unemployment rates and youth unemployment rates but differing patterns of housing tenure. Specifically, one area had a stable resident population and the other accommodated a more transient population. The interesting observation to emerge from Walklate's research is that we need to understand the local reactions to changing patterns of social disorder rather than assume that all communities respond to criminality, anti-social behaviour and fear of crime in the same way (see Jackson 2004 on this theme). The two communities which she describes appeared to differ in the degree to which local people felt a sense of attachment to and security in their neighbourhood. Perceptions of change were based on whether residents perceived their area as being populated by 'local' people who could be 'trusted', or as full of 'strangers' who had moved into the area for one reason or another and were threatening because they were different. While the area referred to as Oldtown may have had levels of criminality that more affluent and middle-class communities would find intolerable, nevertheless there appeared to be a sense of security for those who had lived and grown up with the 'local villains'. The importance of local belonginess was a key factor generating trust and a sense of protection. Walklate reports a frequently expressed view that she describes as a 'neighbourhood dogma' that 'people round here don't rob off their own'. A quasi-political network generated by local organised crime provided a measure of protection for the community.

> So whilst people living in this area are intimidated by the presence of the criminal gang and its activities, they also believe that that same presence affords them a level of protection from criminal victimisation not provided by official agencies .... [As a] resultant effect ... the fear of crime is one that does not resonate with their expressed feelings about crime in their area ... these views leak an image of a highly organised community well defended from outsiders and outsiders' view of the area as problematic. (Walklate 1998: 559)

By contrast, the area she describes as Bankhill is perceived by residents as 'going down hill'. A strong sense of loss of community and declining levels of trust are reported because of factors such as rapid social change, a housing market that has facilitated an influx of newcomers with problems, and, interestingly, a lack of confidence in the local authorities, who are perceived as doing little to arrest the community's decline. An absence of control signals therefore leads to a view of local amenities as failing the residents. These concerns were compounded by the instability of a population of 'strangers'. Fear and mistrust of neighbours and strangers seemed to colour popular observations on the community. Walklate describes a community in which people think and talk in terms of fear, mainly fear of young people. One resident likens life in Bankhill to living in the midst of terrorism – like Northern Ireland at the height of the troubles. People are frightened in Bankhill by the localness of criminality rather than protected by it as they are in Oldtown. However, this is qualified in Walklate's discussion of trust: the trust found in Oldtown is a negative phenomenon that is actually built on fear – the fear of public shaming if a local 'grasses' on 'local villains'. Elements of this perspective on fear of crime can be found in Jackson's analysis of the 'expressive' component involved in community reactions (Jackson 2004). In particular, he points to the significance of local socio-cultural influences shaping 'expressive' fears, which he differentiates from experientially based fears. His analysis points to the importance of building in to our understanding of the fear of crime an appreciation of the shared social meanings in a community. This 'expressive' dimension is evident in the differences found by Walklate between communities in Salford. While the control signals were absent in Bankhill, and led to a sense of deterioration and fear, in Oldtown the control signals were commanded by local people, even if they were underwritten by elements of criminality.

We should recognise that fear and uncivil security are also a product of the failure of the state and local authorities to control and pacify an area and a neighbourhood for the benefit of all. What Walklate provides is a glimpse of the reason why many communities, whether apparently orderly or disorderly, are best described in terms of the theory of de-civilisation. Organised crime may establish social order in the absence of effective policing and the social state, but the predictability of routine social interactions is compromised; it is the 'codes of the street' commanded by the informal control by 'villains' that ensures compliance with the situational norms of the neighbourhood and that is volatile and always liable to degenerate into violence should it be violated. Bursik and Grasmik (1993), for example, have explicitly related the levels of social disorganisation, or social disorder, in a community to the perception that the local social structure is weak. The absence of informal social and intercommunity networks is viewed by local people as a sign that their neighbourhood is stigmatised and in decline, with all that implies about the absence of shared social norms of behaviour and a decline in the levels of predictability of violence and criminality. This is a condition which is caused by the failure of the state's integrative policies: wherever social exclusion is present, the processes of de-civilisation are also likely to be found. While a community remains marginal to the rhythms and disciplines associated with full participation in the activities of mainstream society, then the lack of predictability of events and people will inevitably generate feelings of fear, anxiety and anger. Those fears and anxieties are also vulnerable to exploitation by local, regional and sometimes national media pursuing social and criminal justice agendas disembedded from the social and economic situation in the local area. Often such media campaigns succeed only in creating moral panics.

Disembedded signal crimes

The classic study of the moral panic surrounding an apparent increase in street crime in the late 1970s by Stuart Hall and his colleagues (Hall, Critcher, Jefferson, Clarke and Roberts 1978) provides an excellent model of precisely how conceptions of criminality and public order are constructed by the mass media. Their study developed a model of the media in action that illustrated how the process of determining what was 'newsworthy' was selected and, in particular, how the pressures of news production can lead to distorted and partial accounts of reality. My interest here is not in the specific social history of 'mugging' – Hall *et al.*'s *Policing the Crisis* can be consulted for the detailed analysis of that phenomenon – but in the linked processes that are a routine part of news production. This process can be represented here as a series of bullet points. The popular or tabloid press are often regarded as the stalking horses of the news-production process, allowed to pursue the salacious and more extreme stories, which the quality newspapers track and use only at that point when the broader political, public or legal ramifications are made evident by the popular reactions and debate surrounding the issue. The model is something like the following:

- Journalists seek out what is unusual and extraordinary, or what they perceive as 'newsworthy'; this is frequently defined in terms of crime, violence, public disorder or sexuality.

- The pressures of news production require readily available sources of authority for comment who are able to delineate the parameters of the public debate by selecting the terrain on which public discussion will be organised. There is a stock of key personnel, specialists and voices, normally drawn from a limited range of institutional locations, that constitute a 'hierarchy of credibility' and define the issues at the heart of the story – the primary definers (as Hall *et al.* refer to them) have agenda-setting power. In the case of issues of law and order, the voice of the local and national politicians, senior policemen and women, senior social workers and selected academics will collectively determine *what has to be known* and *what should be done*. The voices of the street and the local community will join the discussion on terms decided by the mass media and the primary definers.

- The media work to construct 'an angle' around the theme or event to be reported which has two elements: (1) the determination by the newspaper or television production team of how their assumed audience might prefer to receive information about the story; and (2) the conversion of the issue into a language which the assumed audience will understand – coding the elements of a story into the rhetoric, common stock of knowledge and prejudices of its assumed audience.

- The public idiom creates for the media an external reference which they claim legitimises speaking out on behalf of their assumed audience; this provides the media thereafter with the authority to claim to 'speak for the public' – 'our readers demand answers', 'the public seek assurances'.

- The study by Hall *et al.* (1978) argues that the media take the public language and returns it to the public inflected with dominant and consensual connotations.

- The media sensitise the public to look for particular events, activities and practices. The media create an atmosphere in which people develop an *anticipatory* reaction to further evidence that the phenomenon being reported will recur, and provide the public with a vocabulary which can be used tendentiously to describe and evaluate events in ways consistent with the views and perspectives popularised by the media.

- The media have the power to construct understandings of events in terms which might suggest a wider malaise in society. The mass media provide a forum in which *particular* voices can be heard and *particular* views publicised – recent cases of involving the murder of young boys such as Damilola Taylor, James Bulger and Rhys Jones are presented as signalling a deeper problem in present-day society and often requiring harder and more punitive measures to resolve. Fear in the community is exacerbated by the 'thin edge of the edge' analyses.

- The identification of social targets and problem populations marked out by their style, their residence and often their ethnicity often follows.

The research on crime reporting and fear of crime has done a great deal to illuminate the processes contributing to the 'climate of insecurity' in society today.

Williams and Dickenson (1993), for example, have reviewed key research on the relationship between fear of crime and newspaper reporting and offered their own analysis of British newspapers, specifically their coverage of crime events and their style of reporting. What is revealed by this research is that newspapers, and the journalists assembling crime stories, create an impression of crime and disorder by the editorial choices they make about what is newsworthy and the amount of space specifically devoted to the most violent and sexually disturbing crimes. However, the readers are also active participants in a process of validating the value of this type of crime reporting by seeking out stories and styles of reporting that satisfy their interests and confirm their prejudices and fears about crime: readers are drawn to a particular newspaper because they are attracted to its message, editorial style and its coverage. With respect to the role of editing and presentation style, research also points to the significance of headline construction and the use of photo journalism to convey a story (see Williams and Dickinson 1993). Serial learning theory suggests that the presentation of a news item and its location within the newspaper, or indeed its position within a news programme on television, generates a sense of significance to those receiving its message. The central purpose of this type of research is, of course, to point up a correlation between the readership of particular types of newspaper and public perceptions of law and disorder and the fear of crime. The conclusion drawn from a great deal of research on crime reporting and fear of crime, while acknowledging that relationships between key variables relating to readership, class and media style are never clear-cut, is that, in general, those readers expressing the highest levels of anxiety and fear about crime also tend to read those newspapers that devote most space to feeding the prurient public interest in crime. Newspapers also construct news by the way they select what will and will not be reported as well as by the style in which they report crime and anti-social behaviour, as the model from Hall *et al.* suggests. The tabloid press tend to be the most sensationalist in their style of reporting and in the prominence they give to the violent, the sexual and the anti-social deviant. The social location of the reader emerges as an important issue, because the highest levels of fear are found in those areas where crime and anti-social behaviour are most frequently observed and where the largest tabloid readership can be found.

The relationship between fear of crime and the media should be extended to consider the impact of crime reporting on the levels and quality of interdependence within a community. For example, Salmi, Solej and Kivivouri (2007) draw attention to the impact of crime news media on weakening trust. The focus of this research is particularly important for an understanding of the media's role in exacerbating tendencies to what they call 'dangerisation', or de-civilising processes, in the marginal communities, especially the role played by the media in creating a 'climate of insecurity' that undermines trust and social capital. Salmi *et al.* (2007) distinguish between *particularised trust*, which is based on direct knowledge and experience of people through engaging in a relationship with them, and *generalised trust*, which, they concede, is more complicated but is grounded in knowledge derived from sources other than direct knowledge and contact. In a world flooded by mass media of all sorts, the latter is clearly a source of major significance, especially in some circumstances which might undermine generalised trust. They also suggest that it might be based on a moral trust acquired through socialisation, which, I think, could be reformulated to address the informal processes of the street, which I discuss separately below.

In many poorer communities, such as those described by Walklate (1998), it is possible to see how a common history and growing up together, irrespective of the deviant activities engaged in by some members of a community, can lead to particularised trust and an absence of 'fear'. What was missing in the studies described above was a sense of generalised trust. Wariness of strangers in communities where there is a tradition of violence and gangs, for example, is a protective mechanism. In contexts where social bonding does not emerge organically from the community itself, informal security is displaced by sources of surveillance and authority external to a community through, for example, CCTV, community wardens and policing. Such control signals replace 'thick trust' between people with 'thin trust' in abstract systems. In a sense, the clamour by politicians, the media, and the local community itself for evidence of 'something being done' about incivility ironically tends to weaken generalised trust by campaigning for the abstract systems of surveillance that contribute little to embedding security in relationships between people. This typically alerts the media to the presence of a social malaise. It is the weakening of generalised reciprocity, or *reciprocal trust*, in marginal communities that has been associated with the problem of anti-social behaviour and which the civil renewal strategy was designed to address. A prominent feature of this development is, as the research by Walklate (1998) shows, the decline in the trust of strangers. The openness to people who are not local and who might establish a connection between one neighbourhood and another has been replaced by fear and territoriality as a filtering mechanism to identify who is and is not a threat. This has also had consequences for trust in neighbours and those who live in the same community (see Walklate 1998). In a social environment of mistrust, no one can be relied upon. These conceptual distinctions drive the Finnish research of Salmi *et al.* (2007) on whether the mass media today portray a 'mean world' contributing to our fears, anxiety and distrust, not only of strangers but also those who may be our immediate neighbours in our communities.

Table 8.1 summarises the levels of influence surrounding the fear of crime and disorder and the role performed by the mass media, politicians and policy in shaping public conceptions and agendas. It is clear that fear and insecurity are created and reinforced at a

Table 8.1 Fear of crime

Determinants of fear of crime	Causal link
Degree of social interdependence	Weak connections between people within and between communities that are socially, economically and spatially different will create a lack of mutual empathy: particularised trust emerges in contexts of 'dangerisation' as a coping mechanism in situations where generalised trust is absent. The social ambience surrounding issues of threat, fear and disorder will be greatest in areas disconnected from the rhythms of mainstream society. Links networking a community to mainstream society lessen suspicion and fear.
Patterns of reporting of crime and antisocial behaviour	The typical level of coverage of antisocial behaviour by tabloid newspapers is disproportionate to its incidence. It is also typically reported in a less analytic and more sensationalist way. Tabloid coverage tends to portray a view of society as more disorderly and threatening than it actually is, and amplifies processes of 'dangerisation'.
Focus of political debate	Politicians and their think tanks have an agenda-setting power to determine what is and is not a problem requiring policy intervention and what the individual *ought to feel*. They form a *hierarchy of credibility* routinely supporting and reproducing partisan views of criminal justice issues that are voter-oriented and aided and abetted by the mass media.
Social and criminal justice policy	The legislative output from political deliberation frames the ways in which the problem of crime and antisocial behaviour has to be dealt with. The strategic policy 'constructs' a regulatory community and identifies measures through which a problem must be approached – 'broken-windows' thesis; the underclass and fatherless families thesis leads to zero tolerance and withdrawal of welfare. This signals crime and disorder as a social problem to be feared.
Social location of perceiver	The onlooker who has indirect experience of crime and disorder, and who receives information mediated by mass press, TV and political debate, will typically express lower levels of fear but higher levels of anger at what is perceived as policy failure. Levels of fear locally are determined by control signals (picking up on service provision) as well as signal threats (reaction to events and symbols).

number of levels, and sometimes by the unintended consequences of interventions into the public debate about law and order by well-intentioned opinion formers. By raising the profile of the issue of anti-social behaviour, politicians such as Frank Field (2002; 2003; 2004; 2005) and, more significantly, Tony Blair – who, when prime minister, launched his 'respect' agenda (Home Office 2005) – have succeeded in alerting the world of media to a newsworthy public policy issue. The mass circulation newspapers amplify the theme of incivility, collating and forming opinion about its nature and the most effective ways to tackle it, but in doing so they always risk generating anxiety in some communities through the effect of what Stanley Cohen (1972) and Stuart Hall and his colleagues (Hall *et al.* 1978) have called *anticipatory sensitisation*. Collectively as a society, we are so focused on the problem of incivility and social disorder today that we see it everywhere, and often we are overly sensitive to the signal threats and signal crimes that the media sometimes enthusiastically draw to our attention. I am suggesting here that where there has been a break in the links of interdependence between communities and social groups, ignorance of 'others' heightens receptivity to negative views based on partial, media-generated accounts.

Streetwise behaviour as inverted fear

The mass media research reported above can be said to be at least implicated in the process of what Salmi *et al.* (2007) have called the 'dangerisation' of present-day society. It is also implicated indirectly in loosening the social bonds which bind people together and, ironically, contributing to the problem of de-civilisation. The phenomenon they refer to as particularised trust is difficult to attain, but it is very important if it can be acquired because it provides an intangible form of social capital in situations where relationships are characterised by suspicion and fear. Particularised trust can be understood as emerging as a defence mechanism in de-civilised conditions against processes of 'dangerisation', driving people to seek security in gangs and subcultures as a way of coping with fear. Following the dictum that the 'best form of defence is attack', young males and established community residents, such as those described by Walklate (1998) in Oldtown, seek membership of the informal networks that will afford protection for the local community in both its legitimate and illegitimate activities. Comfortable living outside such local networks becomes more precarious and no doubt leads to vulnerability to the charge of being a 'grass', or to becoming a victim of what sometimes must appear to be an internecine war between 'respectable' and 'deviant' factions in some communities. Signalling that one is a person to be 'trusted' and is 'streetwise' in a disorderly community is a form of inverted fear.

A frequently overlooked issue surrounding discussion of fear of crime and anti-social behaviour is that the world does not divide neatly into those who are law-abiding, and are therefore assumed to be burdened with the fear of the deviant minority, and those presented as the deviants, who are typically presented as being 'fearless', brazen and lacking in moral scruples. Criminality as an enterprise is full of dangers and risks, and engaging in anti-social behaviour is not necessarily prompted by an absence of conscience or a disregard for others. It is often a by-product of a strategy of survival in the sense that to remain aloof from the incivility and criminality of peers can present significant risks to the non-participant because it might suggest that one is not to be trusted. It follows that many of the behavioural manifestations of incivility that lead to such public outrage are in some circumstances motivated by a need to seek peer approval and to symbolise that one can be relied on. The acceptance of a vocabulary of motives rationalising behavioural excesses, and the acquisition of a language and body capital of the street, signal conformity to the unwritten rules of a peer group or gang, as the classical criminology textbooks describe at length (see Newburn 2007: 186–207).

Fear of 'not belonging', or being viewed as a stranger in a socially disorganised environment, can, therefore, drive some people towards criminality and incivility as a way of protecting themselves and their family. Having to live in inner-city areas and peripheral housing estates where levels of perceived incivility are high, closes down options for the young person. It also makes survival in some particularly poor and disorganised communities less secure unless the 'codes of the street' are learnt and the natural fear of having to negotiate a social environment saturated with threats and threatening people is conquered. The ethnographic descriptions of streetwise behaviour by Elijah Anderson (1990; 2000) and Christopher Mullins (2006) are good places to start the search for an understanding of what I am calling *inverted fear*. In particular, Anderson's description of the 'codes of the street' in the urban ghettos of Philadelphia, and Mullins' research on the masculinities of the street in St. Louis, Missouri, tell a story of young men adopting styles of behaviour or learning what I referred to in Chapter 3 as a 'cultural toolkit' that is more defensive than predatory. It is about the presentation of self and of 'fitting in' rather than engaging in intimidation for its own sake.

I have already alluded to a key distinction made by Anderson between 'street families' and 'decent' families' in Chapter 5. The outlaw culture followed by the 'street families' is not described in terms of a lack of social and moral integrity but as the product of a complex process of adaptation to the economic, racist and criminal realities of life in the ghetto. To belong to a 'street family' is to encounter risk and danger on a routine, daily basis. The incivility and aggression that grow from embracing this style of living are a mode of survival, and not a product of deviant value orientations, or at least not just deviant value orientations. To survive as a 'decent family' in such communities also requires adaptations to the local habitat: maintaining connection with street realities while retaining a pragmatic distance. Indeed, Anderson (2000) talks about 'switching codes' and the pressures on the 'decent' kids to negotiate the street while maintaining their sense of personal worth. He talks about the 'decent kids' getting 'cool with the people who dominate the public spaces', and in order to find a place in the community, 'they must let others know how tough they are, how hard they are to roll on, how much mess they will take' (p. 99). The streets are where identities are forged and everyone in that community, 'decent' or 'street', must join in the same game.

> Life under the code might be considered a kind of game played by rules that are partly specified but partly emergent. The young person is encouraged to be familiar with the rules of the game and even use them as a metaphor for life – or else feel left out, become marginalised, and, ultimately risk being rolled on. So the young person is inclined to enact his own particular role, to show his familiarity with the game, and more specifically his street knowledge, so as to gain points with others. (Anderson 2000: 100)

In his earlier study of street life, Anderson (1990) talked about the hegemony of public spaces and the Goffman-like processes involved in the presentation of self as a mechanism to ensure a position within the local community. Blackness, maleness, and youngness had to be carried in accordance with the appropriate style and bearing in order to signal that a person had a legitimate right to be there, to be recognised and to be feared. Only after accomplishing the presentation of self effectively could safety and security be ensured. And, of course, the presentation of style and body capital had to be harnessed to the protocols of eye contact and the ability to make instantaneous judgements about strangers on the street. Young people, men and women (see Ness 2004), work hard at acquiring the 'master status' of being hard and displaying the right kind of masculinity and, as Ness has shown, the right kind of femininity with a strange combination of sexual allure and a capacity to fight.

Mullins (2006) deepens our understanding of the 'masculinities of the street' and reinforces the insights which Anderson makes. His research found men who were 'highly concerned with projecting images of toughness, independence, self-sufficiency and potential violence (p. 49). The principles that he found to guide street life are *trust nobody*, *be independent*, and work to *avoid being regarded as a 'punk'* – someone who fails to live up to the demands of street masculinity. Punks are there to be intimidated and bullied. They are viewed as being 'failed men' and worthy of being harassed and abused. And by way of underscoring the fear that drives this street masculinity and style, Mullins colourfully lets his subjects talk about the importance of reputation; of flossing (conspicuously displaying wealth and style) and dealing with the challenges to a person's masculinity whenever and wherever they arise by violently confronting those who offer slights or who 'talk them down'. As one of his chapter headings suggests, the street code is summed up by the principle of 'every motherfucker gonna try to punk you'. The fear and humiliation of being 'punked' drives even the conformist kids to ensure that they are not found wanting by the 'code of the street'.

Even though the analysis described here by Anderson and by Mullins is of urban America, it could be applied equally well to the streets of most European cities. The same pressures to survive economically and physically in communities ravaged by post-welfare policies, and in a rampant, hidden economy lubricated by illicit drugs and prostitution, ensure that the protocols of street life are largely shaped by the ability of the individual to understand how to negotiate the threats and opportunities of living in marginal communities. The racism, poverty and impact of global markets have had a fairly standardising impact on the inner cities and peripheral housing estates.

Social policy and the problem of security

What kind of social policy should be designed to address these realities? The problem of the inner cities and peripheral housing estates, in particular, is that the 'cultural toolkits' assembled by young residents are not geared to facilitate their placement in the world of disciplined work. They live in and negotiate a local community environment dominated by illicit trades, which for some will provide entry into and tutelage in activities that may be episodic and do not build up a pension, but in the short-to-medium term are probably more financially lucrative than shelf stacking, waiting on tables, or fetching and carrying in a factory. Informal working and dealing replace the mainstream economy, and the drugs trade is the main activity at the centre of the 'irregular economy'. The local working-class dealers are the foot soldiers of a global market system that reproduces in its hierarchical and reward structures all the worst excesses of the main economy (see Ruggiero and Vass 1992; Ruggiero and South 1997). Indeed, the drugs issue is symptomatic of the tensions and contradictions of social policy more generally and represents the extreme example of the criminalising of social policy. Access to testing and treatment services is invariably through the criminal justice system after an offence has been committed. This is a strategy that is led by criminal justice professionals, who are predisposed to view drug dealing and drug use in the local neighbourhoods as the problem rather than a symptom of a more complex and difficult, underlying malaise of unmet social need. The complexities of the different audiences and statuses involved in the drugs trade have meant that developing effective drug policies has been characterised by a great deal of public health and criminal justice activity that has largely missed its targets. Young children who are inquisitive about drugs, young people who have experimented with drugs, young people who are on the verge of addiction, and those who are confirmed addicts all represent different policy audiences with quite different, if related, social and human needs. Similarly, those who have drifted into delinquent and anti-social behaviour for fun and those who have demonstrated a clear commitment to criminality are not necessarily the same people, although the relationship between these categories of activity may be open and synergetic.

Withdrawing welfare benefits, withdrawing and rationing social services, and responding to the problems of the inner cities with an intemperate criminal justice strategy rather than social policy is not self-evidently the most productive way to tackle the problems of incivility and the social disorganisation of the declining post-industrial areas. A community development strategy that focused on the cultural dimension of anti-social behaviour, together with educational policies (interpreted in the broadest sense), may have more success in integrating young people into the mainstream avenues of employment and society. For example, the 'war on poverty' in the Kennedy and Johnson era of 1960s USA concentrated a great deal of money and effort into a community action strategy. In that context, it was largely driven by the USA reluctance to build on the welfare principles first introduced by Roosevelt, although it did introduce the USA approximation of the European welfare systems by expanding benefits such as the Old Age, Survivors and Disability Insurance, Aid to American Families with Dependent Children, and Medicaid. However, for the inner-city ghettos of Los Angeles, Chicago and the eastern states, the focus was primarily on community action programmes aimed at combating the delinquency and violence that were a reaction to a racist and exclusionary economic and social system. It was a strategy that at its best aimed at empowering poor people by providing them with services, legal information and social support to realise their rights. In their classic study of public welfare in the USA, Piven and Cloward (1974) provide a useful social history of that period in US welfare. They point to the impact of the Juvenile Delinquency and Youth Offenses Control Act, the Economic Opportunity Act, and the Demonstration Cities and Metropolitan Development Act on the urban ghettos: legislation pushed through by the federal government, despite reactionary opposition from the political Right, focused on the poor and blighted ghettos disfiguring the major cities. There was a recognition of the need for collective action and state support for the poor if the problems of crime and violence were to be addressed. The peculiarities of US welfare need not detain us any further; suffice it to say that the retrenchment and resistance to welfare programmes in the USA, as elsewhere, from the mid-1970s onwards have culminated in the destruction of the welfare initiatives of the 1960s through two pieces of antiwelfare legislation that signalled a paradigm shift in thinking about criminality and social obligation from *social causes* to *pathological behaviour*: the Reagan Omnibus Budget Reconciliation Act 1981 and the Clinton Personal Responsibility and Work Opportunity Act 1996. The descriptions and analyses of the USA ghetto discussed in this book by Wacquant and Anderson, among others, testify to the consequences of the USA return to its natural antiwelfare posture. That short-sighted, post-emotional reaction to social disorder has led to extremely high levels of crime and violence, and has reinforced social divisions in an already hierarchical and divided society. The same processes are evident throughout Europe.

To end this chapter where I began is to return to the issue of security, and the search for the ingredients that will contribute to civil security in a society of risk and vulnerability. There should be an acknowledgement that a great deal of delinquency, crime and violence is born out of fear and a desire to develop strategies for living that will protect the person on the streets and in the communities where the problems of security are at their worst. As Loader and Walker (2007) recognise, the state has a pre-eminent responsibility to organise and oversee the processes that will lead to civil security, and that means that the warring communities must be pacified, not simply by coercion but also by community development actions.

Concluding observations

This chapter has addressed an issue that lies at the heart of criminal justice but is largely ignored by social policy – fear of crime and anxiety about life in poor communities. The pursuit of a form of state-sponsored security that limits the excesses and abuses of the state, the police and the security industry is a laudable objective, but it cannot be pursued without addressing the reasons why some communities experience social disorder and de-civilisation while others experience relative peace and quiet yet complain about incivility and disorder. Security is a 'thick public good', but unfortunately many citizens do not experience it. The reasons for this lie in the wider forces shaping policy agendas and policy strategies. Perceptions of social disorder are shaped by signal crimes and signal threats, and are partially alleviated by the presence of signal controls, the services and personnel that convey to the public that something, irrespective of effectiveness, is being done to address a publicly identified social problem. The mass media are particularly influential in shaping public conceptions of social problems, often distorting their true levels and nature. The social ambience created by both the policy agenda and the media reporting of that agenda contributes to the fear of the uncivil and the criminal. The reaction to that process is to create situational anxiety in the poor inner cities and housing estates about how best to survive socially, culturally, economically and, ultimately, physically in communities where there are threats and threatening people. The acquisition of a 'cultural toolkit' that is grounded in learning the 'codes of the street' requires a social policy response focused on community action and development rather than single-mindedly on social control and criminal justice. The concluding chapter will consider these issues further.

Chapter 9

Conclusions: criminology and social policy

To understand the purpose of the welfare state in terms of a grand humanitarian project to eradicate poverty, and improve the health and well-being of all in a welfare society, is to misinterpret the history of the Western welfare ideal. To repeat an observation made in Chapter 1, the welfare state in the twentieth century should be described more accurately as a *worker-benefit state* (see Atherton 2002). As an institution, the welfare state pays little attention to the nature of work, or whether it is arduous, boring or dangerous; the only concern is that it is through industriousness that eligibility to receive social services and welfare benefits is demonstrated. Given that this fundamental principle underpins the welfare state, the system has primarily been geared to the management of incentives to ensure that as many people as possible contribute to the costs and benefits of social welfare through their taxes and social insurance payments.

It is certainly true that such an interpretation of the welfare state has been challenged, first by the liberal reformers of the early twentieth century and then by welfare theorists such as T. H. Marshall (1992) and Richard Titmuss (see Alcock, Glennerster, Oakley and Sinfield 2001), all of whom presented the welfare movement as part of the modernist drive for social justice and equality. The observations by Viet-Wilson (2000) on the nature of the contemporary welfare state represent the kernel of the welfare ideal advanced by Titmuss and Marshall when he argues that the label 'welfare state' should be applied only to systems that are redistributive from rich to poor, and provide for the needs of the poor and those at the bottom of the social hierarchy regardless of desert. However, the period between

1945 and 1973 was probably the height of what has been variously called the Fordist welfare state or the Keynesian welfare state, and that was also the only time when there was a significant measure of universalism in the system geared to the pursuit of social justice and social equality. That is not the situation today. The welfare state has mutated into what Featherstone (2006) has accurately described as the *social investment state*, in which everyone, but especially our children, is regarded primarily as a resource for the future creation of wealth and productivity. Central to this endeavour are hard work and education to ensure that Britain plc can compete effectively in the global market. Today, there is little talk of social justice and equality as principles essential for the maintenance of social order. As Levitas (2005) has argued, social integration in the Western welfare systems is conceived of entirely in terms of work, and this is often a narrow conception of work in the marketplace which excludes all the informal labour activity dealing with children and the elderly that bolsters a failing welfare state. The pursuit of equality has been replaced by the maintenance of equity, and the idea of social justice has been collapsed into the meritocratic sounding notion of 'equal opportunities', which, as most students of criminology know from the work of Merton (1938; 1957) and Runciman (1966), tends to generate a sense of relative deprivation, social division and anomie rather than social harmony. The policy developments that most accurately signify the purpose and character of the welfare state today all relate to the 'modernisation' or cutting back of benefits: strategies aimed at getting lone mothers to work, or efforts to reduce the numbers of those claiming incapacity benefit. When claimants resist efforts to place them in work, the welfare system typically resorts to coercive inducements in the form of benefit reduction or withdrawal to make them do what the state desires them to do. It is at this stage that what was once social welfare can be transformed into something that looks very much like criminal justice policy, as, for example, in the policy change announced in November 2007 relating to teenagers with the NEET classification attaching to them, who may find themselves on the pathway to a fine and a criminal record should they refuse to attend school or a take up a training opportunity.

This becomes an issue when the worlds of work and non-work clash in what Daniel Bell has called the 'cultural contradictions of capitalism'. It is not only that the capitalist market creates desirable products and services for purchase, and so inflames the 'thing addiction' that drives the consumer society and the greed and motivation to obtain those products by any means possible, but also that the axial principles which underpin this system are internally contradictory because consumption encourages hedonism and undermines the work ethic, something that Matza and Sykes (1961) capture well with their concept of *subterranean values*. This contradiction has become a chronic condition in some areas of post-industrial society. Bell is worth quoting at length on this theme.

> What I find striking today is the radical disjunction between the social structure (the techno-economic order) and the culture. The former is ruled by an economic principle defined in terms of efficiency and functional rationality, the organisation of production through the ordering of things, including men as things. The latter is prodigal, promiscuous, dominated by an anti-rational, anti-intellectual temper in which the self is taken as the touchstone of cultural judgements, and the effect on the self is the measure of the aesthetic worth of experience. The character structure inherited from the nineteenth century, with its emphasis on self-discipline, delayed gratification, and restraint, is still relevant to the demands of the techno-economic structure; but it clashes sharply with the culture, where bourgeois values have been completely rejected – in part, paradoxically, because of the workings of the capitalist economic system itself. (Bell 1979: 37)

More recently, Jock Young (2007) has examined similar terrain in terms of 'the vertigo of late modernity': 'a sense of insecurity of insubstantiality, and of uncertainty, a whiff of chaos and a fear of falling' (p. 14). The giddiness and unsteadiness he describes is the malaise of modernity. It is caused by an attitude to work which is, at best, instrumental in pursuit of resources to enjoy the cornucopia of leisure choices available, but, at worst, is defined by an absence of commitment to anything much beyond the self, and for the young delinquents roaming the streets, the primary objective is pursuit of status and celebrity through anti-social and sometimes vicious acts of violence. These are themes I described in Chapter 3 (see Hall and Winlow 2005). One way of interpreting Young's observations in current times is to focus attention on what Habermas (1975) has called a 'motivation crisis': or the difficulty of integrating people into society by requiring them to undertake boring, low-waged labour in a post-welfare society. The *legitimation crisis* that Habermas (1975) described as a potential crisis in the 1970s focused attention on the 're-politicisation' of the relations of production' and the pressing need for governments to justify the private accumulation of wealth in a society in which fair exchange in the market had lost its 'natural' appearance, or as Thomas McCarthy describes it, the problem of 'how to distribute the social product inequitably and yet legitimately' (McCarthy 1978: 368). As the neo-liberal obsession with markets and personal freedom has attained the status of a global orthodoxy, the problem of integrating and motivating those losing out is becoming more difficult. Habermas originally suggested that what had to be accomplished to deal with this dilemma was a 'high output-low input' citizenry combined with reform of the welfare system to ensure what he called 'familial-vocational privatism': this amounts to what I have called *amoral familism* and post-emotionalism (Rodger 2000), and what Habermas has presented as the contemporary concentration on consumption, leisure and career at the expense of a politically engaged consciousness. In terms of Habermas' scheme, we do not have a legitimation crisis today because those integrated into the world of work and consumption are content to subscribe to an economic system that is delivering low inflation and rising living standards for their families, although the potential for a negative reaction against the neo-liberal orthodoxies of present-day society remains subdued only to the extent that the public sphere is, in Habermasian language, de-politicised. What this means is that the impact of a disembedded market system has lifted the principles of the free market to the status of a 'natural force' beyond the capacity of politicians, or, indeed, economists, to change. Civil privatism is therefore the natural condition of the late modern polity. While the potential legitimation crisis identified by Habermas, in which the rationality of the market and the state's competence to manage it stimulate a negative reaction from the citizenry, is some way off, the socially polarising impact of the neo-liberal market in a post-industrial society is generating a form of unrest at the level of what Taylor, Walton and Young (1973) a few years ago called 'pre-political oppositional action'. We can understand this in more mundane terms as anti-social behaviour. What we certainly do have is a *motivation crisis* for sizeable numbers of citizens who are excluded from the full fruits of the consumer society by their economic marginalisation and are loath to take up the low-waged drudgery that is a feature of work in postmodern conditions. Many try to resist being coaxed and coerced into poor jobs by the threat of withdrawal of benefits and the euphemistically called 'support' provided by the job centre. However, dealing with the motivation crisis that exists at the edge of the welfare system is fast becoming the normal face of the welfare state. With the possible exception of Scandinavia, most other Western countries have been engaged in a process of squeezing the remnants of universalism from their welfare systems while reinforcing traditional concerns about 'managing incentives' to work. It is the principle of the 'something for something' exchange that has become embedded in their benefit systems and has led to the abandonment of any pretence that social welfare is part of a modernist and humanitarian project aimed at social equality and social justice. Meanwhile conditionality and the withdrawal of welfare benefits have been harnessed to the world of criminal justice to reinforce the project of building a disciplined society suitable for the economic and political conditions of the postmodern era. It is sometimes known as the 'respect' agenda, and this is the context in which the process of criminalising social policy is taking place.

Social policy or moral regulation?

Anti-social behaviour and petty criminality can be one manifestation of the motivation crisis in present-day Western societies. In addressing the challenge of disorderly behaviour in the wake of welfare state retrenchment, those in policy circles have increasingly adopted the language of 'moral regulation' and moved away, both linguistically and in terms of policy, from concerns about the structural causes of inequality. Redistributive social policies are now no longer seriously considered by modern politicians of the centre Left or middle ground. Elsewhere I have distinguished between a number of what I will call 'spheres of activity' (Table 9.1) to highlight the focus of policy and politics on this issue (see Rodger 2003b).

I suggest that the changing focus of social policy has been away from attempting to effect change by targeting welfare benefits and services on the *private sphere* and towards targeting criminal justice strategies on the *personal sphere*. The public sphere of dominant opinion, which in the past has supported social policies that seek to steer social behaviour towards ends considered desirable by the state, such as family policies aimed at improving the health, education and well-being of children, has today become preoccupied with matters of 'moral regulation' and requires policies that target social discipline rather than social justice. This is accomplished by a redirected social sphere in which policy is preoccupied with dysfunctional families (Sure Start) and the juvenile justice system is preoccupied with NEET status and anti-social behaviour among teenagers. There are

Table 9.1 Dimensions of social intervention

The state sphere	The source of legislative controls which underpin laws governing welfare benefits, social service regulations and child and youth policy. It consists of the institutional infrastructure of central and local government that organises the social sphere – welfare state retrenchment has led to the removal of vestiges of universalism, with the exception of child benefit.
The social sphere	The source of all those activities concerned with counselling, advocacy and negotiation practised by credentialed welfare state professionals. It is the domain of the social worker, the voluntary worker, health visitor and community mental health practitioner – these practitioners mediate between the state and the private sphere as employees or contracted workers of the state increasingly targeting antisocial behaviour from children to adults.
The public sphere	This is the arena of public opinion formation and the shaping of public debate about policy and politics. It is dominated in present-day society by the electronic media and mass circulation publications, shaping public conceptions of policy and social problems. It defines the forms social intervention should take. It is largely de-politicised and reduces politics to electoral and policy spin.
The private sphere	This is the domain of the family and familial relationships. It is the place where children reside, are socialised and placed into society. It is the focus of welfare services and benefits aimed at supporting the reproductive costs of raising the next generation – the target for family policies and family services. It is also, increasingly, the target for those who seek to define and isolate the dysfunctional family.
The personal sphere	This relates to activities concerned with personal identity formation; with the presentation of self and the fulfilment of personal narratives as people attempt to participate in and reconcile the tensions of living in a complex consumer market society and culture. This is the sphere of the 'antisocial' understood in the broadest sense of being selfish, amoral and personal rather than other-regarding.

two main drivers of this changing emphasis in the world of welfare. First, the retreat from the Keynesian idea of a welfare state in favour of a residual model means that the pursuit of social justice goals has been largely abandoned in favour of a view of welfare as a matter of individual responsibility and willingness to embrace the opportunities generated by the market system. Secondly, because the state sphere cannot easily influence what takes place in the personal sphere by using social policy as an instrument of inducement, politicians and policy planners have a tendency to convert social issues into moral issues and use the criminal justice system to manage and control the residual problem populations unreceptive to the 'respect agenda'. However, as Bell (1979) and Habermas (1975) have recognised, this is not an easy task for governments to achieve. The preferred solution to the dilemma of how to control personal behaviour in a liberal society has been the creation of a sphere of activity, here called the social sphere, to employ a range of techniques of intervention to manage problem populations in the language of *social therapism* or *social education*. This strategy has been augmented in present-day Britain by an expanded voluntary sector under the guise of a strategy for civil renewal. When discipline breaks down, social order is maintained by the selective use of civil law, but the sting in the tail appears to be the retention of the criminal law as a back-up to deal with policy failures: people who will not submit to the disciplines of living orderly lives in a market society. It is the criminal law platform underpinning many apparent social policy initiatives that has led to the current concern about criminalising social policy.

Welfare and institutional anomie

The real concern today is, as Susze Ferge (1999) asks, 'and what if the state fades away?' The tendency towards a de-civilising process has been reinforced by the disembedded nature of the market system, which subordinates the institutions of civil society to its logic, forcing them to accommodate to the demands of work and the market first (Messner and Rosenfeld 2001). Get what you can by any means possible becomes a principle followed by *all* in our materialist and consumer society, but it is a particularly negative guide for living for those who find themselves without the means to participate fully in the consumer culture. And the tendency is reinforced by the actions of modern governments when economy and society relationships are coordinated as if the nation state had become a large limited liability company in which everything must be subordinated to the goal of global economic competitiveness. That has invariably meant welfare state retrenchment and the harnessing of social policy to the criminal justice system to deal with the behavioural fallout resulting from the anomic ethic generated by market society. Where key social institutions such as the family or the voluntary sector fail to control anti-social behaviour appropriately, Western governments have typically replaced social policy with enforcement policies to ensure that deviant behaviour is not allowed to undermine productivity or disfigure the presentation of image in the global marketplace: the judicious use of ASBOs and dispersal orders can do wonders to clear a tourist attraction in London or Edinburgh of rowdy teenage skateboarders, beggars or tramps.

However, the decline in institutionalised solidarity, which has followed the devolving of responsibility for welfare and crime prevention to the market and the local community, can be interpreted as the state partially reneging on its historical purpose of adjudicating and pacifying society. Without an effective central political authority to ensure that a social order is founded on the solidaristic functioning of interdependent interests and, in the Western liberal democratic tradition, is a society founded on principles of social justice, the civilising process may be undermined. The state's welfare obligations have historically been directed at making decisions about who gets what and who loses out in the ebb and flow of managing a complex, postmodern society. In order to fulfil that key responsibility, political authority must be legitimate, and, of course, it must be sovereign over the market. That is highly problematic in today's globalised world. Loader and Walker (2007) are correct when they argue that civilised security is a 'thick public good'. Without agreement about how social order is to be maintained, society becomes fragmented and permeated with social divisions. But a society that collapses all matters of disorder to the failings of individuals without also considering the failings of government and the unforgiving nature of global economic forces is liable to make a principle out of frustration in attempting to build an orderly society on a foundation of anti-social behaviour orders.

Thomas Hobbes has been described as the first postmodern political theorist by Noel O'Sullivan (1993), because he understood the essential nature and importance of the existence of a central political authority. He also understood the necessity of combining a strong central authority with a vibrant structure of civil associations that recognised the importance of the state's legitimate control over a whole territory, geographical and institutional. The fading of the state in keys areas of social politics today is creating a form of legitimation crisis manifesting itself as a motivation crisis among a sizeable minority of the population who are effectively refusing to participate in the world of poor work in a low-waged economy. The problem confronting Western governments today is what kind of social and public policy mix is appropriate to deal with this reality.

Social policy and criminal justice: finding the balance

In thinking about what kind of social policy is best suited to tackle the dilemmas and problems of the twenty-first century, I am drawn to the field of drug policy. I am mindful that the conclusion to a book is not the appropriate place to open up discussion of a new subject. That is not my intention, and we should look at the history and changing patterns of drug policy as an exemplar of what is happening more broadly in social and criminal justice policy. In many respects, it is a template for the criminal justice/social policy tension which has been discussed throughout this book. First, the problems relating to illicit drugs can be viewed from a variety of perspectives and viewed through a variety of policy lenses, some of which are drawn from the field of criminal justice while others are clearly concerned with health and social policy at both an individual and societal level. The virtue of examining drug policy lies in the fact that it illustrates the boundary problems that lie at the heart of the debate about criminalising social policy very clearly.

Incivility has gone through a process of moving from behaviour that was regarded as a normal part of growing up to become the focus of major legislation and policy activity as part of a criminalisation process. Similarly, the history of drugs policy tells a story of a changing policy posture by British governments, from seeing self-medication with addictive drugs as a 'normal' part of domestic life in the nineteenth century, through to a medicalised view adopted in the interwar years of the twentieth century, culminating in criminalisation in the 1960s and a contemporary stance that is confused and complex. Drugs policy is valuable for my purposes because it is in search of a point of equilibrium between punitive criminalising tendencies and health and social intervention strategies. The criminalising approach in drugs strategy has coincided with a rapid increase in addiction and drug-related crime. This has led to the exploration of a return to a medico-centred approach (see

Stimson and Metrebian 2003). The medico-centric approach to illicit drugs was known as the British system because it differed from the USA criminalisation approach established by the 1914 Harrison Act, which first taxed addictive drugs and then criminalised them. The British system treated drug use as a 'manifestation of a morbid state', and not a form of 'vicious indulgence', as it was referred to by the Rolleston Committee in 1926 (see Barton 2003). The abandonment of the medico-centric approach from the 1960s onwards was the result of a succession of moral panics that were not dissimilar to the current outspoken reaction to anti-social behaviour today and that culminated in the adoption of a criminalisation stance. Today that harsh criminal justice approach is competing with a variety of alternative policy models, as Table 9.2 below indicates, but the boundaries between them are porous and remain largely shaped by a policy agenda drawn from the world of criminal justice. Drug-related health care is accessed through the criminal justice system, and the anti-social behaviour legislation accentuates the criminality of illicit drug use rather than its antecedents in socially disadvantaged living conditions. Indeed, the disproportionate focus of drug strategies in poor neighbourhoods on enforcement sometimes clashes with the media indulgence of celebrity drug use, which tends to be more tolerated and seen, at worst, as a by-product of living a self-indulgent life that can be easily resolved by periodic visits to private clinics. There is no easy access to medical support for the street addict, unless it is through a court order, and drug treatments remain well down the priorities of the NHS.

The emphasis in youth policy for anti-social behaviour can be said to have led to a similar growth in the very phenomenon that is being targeted. Both the anti-social behaviour strategy and that for illicit drug use, like the relationship between social policy and criminal justice more generally, reveal a broken-backed approach in which the wider structural and global forces shaping the societal level problems are acknowledged but not allowed to interfere with the pursuit of individualistic and behavioural policies. Changing social conduct and manners is perceived as an easier policy target than addressing the intractable issues relating to the political economy of drugs and crime. It is in fact just as difficult to effect change in behaviour through criminalising strategies as to address the issues surrounding Third World debt and poppy production, but, irrespective of their ineffectiveness, politically it appears that 'tough' approaches at least resonate with public opinion and are more likely to win votes. While efforts continue to address the global supply and distribution of illicit

Table 9.2 Drug policy – competing models

Policy model	Policy focus
Public health	• Harm reduction to drug user • Control of the spread of HIV/hepatitis through needle-exchange schemes • Public health education campaigns aimed at teenagers and guidance intervention in schools • Stress on the health rather than legal dimension of decriminalisation arguments
Medico-centric	• Licensed GPs and treatment centres allowing supervised prescription of illegal drugs • Advocacy of access to drug treatment centres primarily through the NHS rather than criminal justice system • Supportive of prescription of heroin on the NHS rather than limiting intervention to methadone-maintenance programmes
Antisocial behaviour	• Focus on crime prevention partnerships and community safety strategies as a mechanism to tackle drug-related street crime • Closing 'crack houses' by antisocial behaviour legislation • Increase in community and neighbourhood strategies to combat street-level dealing
Criminalisation	• Asset freezing of convicted drug suppliers • Downplaying criminal penalties against drug possession and use, while targeting distribution and supply • Developing international cooperation between police forces to target drug production and distribution
Political economy	• G8 countries and IMF write-off Third World debt • Third World aid and development funding to subsidise cash crops and target peasant production of raw material for Western drugs

drugs, for most people such efforts belong to a different universe of meaning and one that is largely ignored in favour of pursuing the anti-social wheeling and dealing on the city streets. Meanwhile any talk of social causation and drug misuse is dismissed as apologetic avoidance of personal responsibility.

It is the management of control signals that politicians are primarily concerned with, and the launch of the Children's Plan by Ed Balls, Secretary of State for Children, Schools and Families, on the 11 December 2007, appears to mark a slight change of emphasis by New Labour away from enforcement to a more explicit concern with the life chances of Britain's children (Department for Children, Schools and Families 2007). The Children's Plan is pre-eminently a control signal aiming to convey an active policy strategy. The news headlines were very much in terms of fewer ASBOs and more 'play strategies'. The ambitious agenda announced by Balls is a 10-year programme designed to tackle the disadvantages and social problems surrounding children's lives in twenty-first century Britain. However, in the published document, Chapter 5 on keeping teenagers in education until they are 18, and Chapter 6, enigmatically headed 'On the Right Track', contain elements of a social policy strategy aimed at managing youth deviance: reference is made to a Youth Task Force, Acceptable Behaviour Contracts, a Youth Alcohol Action Plan, and a Youth Crime Action Plan. The intention is clearly to redress the balance between criminal justice and social policy rather than change direction. Social policy will, if anything, be even more aligned to the objectives of preventing young people's criminality and anti-social behaviour. The very fact that a department exists with responsibilities straddling the fields of children, education and youth policy will ensure that this alignment is made even more secure in the future. However, if such a strategy is embedded in a broader approach that seriously addresses the material, educational and cultural needs of Britain's children, and acknowledges the responsibility of governments to maintain a civilised level of welfare support as part of that agenda, then a better balance may be struck between social policy and criminal justice policy. The creation of the hybrid department and the plan itself are testimony to the need for a more appropriate balance and, perhaps, a belated recognition that we do indeed need *more* social policy and *fewer* ASBOs in the sense of actions that are not singularly focused on work and social discipline but address the social and cultural dimensions of life chances.

In the context of present-day economic uncertainty and community dislocation in our major cities, there may need to be a broad recognition that taxes and redistributive policies must be readmitted to the public debate. The decline of the welfare state must be arrested, and we must authentically attempt to address the problems of the inner cities and peripheral housing estates with dedicated resources. A community action strategy that is based on civil security for those young people who populate the streets and the gangs would seem to be essential. And it should be grounded more broadly in meeting the real material needs of communities than implied by past civil renewal strategies, which often appear more about governments inveigling the voluntary sector to deliver policy and winning votes from the established by isolating and punishing the outsiders. The real policy problem today is not how to manage the risk posed by the unruly and the marginalised but how to reintegrate them in a way that reduces the threats and dangers they are perceived to pose. The welfare state, despite its disciplinary purpose and orientation, especially today, is essential to re-establish the conditions for the civilising process to flourish. When there is broader understanding that collectivism and social solidarity are not antithetical to individual freedom but, as Elias understood, are a precondition for it because interdependence is enhanced, the relationship between de-civilising processes and anti-social behaviour will be broken.

References

Adams, M. (2006) 'Hybridizing Habitus and Reflexivity: Towards an Understanding of Contemporary Identity?', *Sociology*, 40 (3): 511–28.

Addley, E. and Travis, A. (2006) 'Record Number in Jails Raises Fear of Violence', *Guardian*, 31 August.

Alcock, P., Glennerster, H., Oakley, A. and Sinfield, A. (2001) *Welfare and Wellbeing: Richard Titmuss's Contribution to Social Policy*. Bristol: Policy Press.

Anderson, E. (1990) *Streetwise: Race, Class, and Change in an Urban Community*. London: University of Chicago Press.

Anderson, E. (1999) *The Code of the Street: Decency, Violence and the Moral Life of the Street*. New York: Norton.

Arthur, R. (2005) 'Punishing Parents for the Crimes of Their Children', *Howard Journal*, 44 (3): 233–53

Arts, W. and Gelissen, J. (2001) 'Welfare States, Solidarity and Justice Principles: Does the Type Really Matter?', *Acta Sociologica*, 44: 283–99.

Ashford, D. (1986) *The Emergence of the Welfare State*. Oxford: Blackwell.

Ashworth, A. (2004) 'Social Control and Anti-Social Behaviour: The Subversion of Human Rights', *Law Quarterly Review*, 120 (April): 263–91.

Atherton, C. (2002) 'Welfare States: A Response to John Viet-Wilson', *Social Policy and Administration*, 36 (3): 306–11.

Audit Commission (1996) *Misspent Youth: Young People and Crime*. London: Audit Commission.

Ball, C. (2000) 'The Youth Justice and Criminal Evidence Act 1999: Part 1. A Significant Move Towards Restorative Justice, or a Recipe for Unintended Consequences?' *Criminal Law Review* (April): 211–22.

Bannister, J., Hill, M. and Scott, S. (2007) 'More Sinned Against Than Sinbin? The Forgetfulness of Critical Social Policy?', *Critical Social Policy*, 27 (4): 557–60.

Barton, A. (2003) *Illicit Drugs: Use and Control.* London: Routledge.

Bauman, Z. (1988) *Modernity and the Holocaust.* Cambridge: Polity.

Baumrind, D. (1991) 'The Influence of Parental Style on Adolescent Competence and Substance Use', *Journal of Early Adolescence,* 11 (1): 56–95.

Baumrind, D. (1967) 'Child Care Practices Anteceding Three Patterns of Preschool Behaviour', *Genetic Psychology Monographs,* 75 (1): 43–88.

Baumrind, D. (1966) 'Effects of Authoritative Parental Control on Child Behaviour', *Child Development,* 37 (4): 887–907.

Beck, U. and Beck-Gernsheim, E. (2002) *Individualization.* London: Sage.

Bell, D. (1979) *The Cultural Contradictions of Capitalism.* London: Heinemann.

Bendix, R. (1952) 'Compliant Behaviour and Individual Personality', *American Journal of Sociology,* 58: 292–303.

Bendix, R. (1969) *Nation Building and Citizenship.* New York: Anchor.

Bernburg, J. (2002) 'Anomie, Social Change and Crime: A Theoretical Examination of Institutional-Anomie Theory', *British Journal of Criminology,* 42, 729–42.

Bernstein, B. (1973) *Class, Codes and Control.* St Albans: Paladin.

Biggart, A., Deacon, K., Dobbie, F., Furlong, A., Given, L. and Hinds, K. (2004) *Findings from the Scottish School Leavers Survey: 17 in 2003.* Research Findings 4, December, Scottish Executive Education Department.

Blanden, J., Gregg, P. and Machin, S. (2005) *Intergenerational Mobility in Europe.* London: Sutton Trust and LSE Centre for Economic Performance.

Blunkett, D. (2003b) 'Civil Renewal: a new agenda', The CSV Edith Kahn Memorial Lecture, 11 June, London: Home Office and CSV.

Blunkett, D. (2003b) 'Active Citizens, Strong Communities: Progressing Civil Renewal', Scarman Lecture, 11 December, London: Home Office.

Bonoli, G., George, V. and Taylor-Gooby, P. (2000) *European Welfare Futures.* Cambridge: Polity.

Bottoms, A. and Wilson, A. (2004) 'Attitudes to Punishment in Two High Crime Communities', in A. Bottoms, S. Rex and G. Robinson (eds) *Alternatives to Prison: Options for an Insecure Society.* Cullompton: Willan.

Bottoms, A. and Wilson, A. (2005) *Report on Sheffield University Civil Renewal Research.* University of Sheffield.

Bourdieu, P. (1977) *Outline of a Theory of Practice.* Cambridge: Cambridge University Press.

Boutellier, H. (2001) 'The Convergence of Social Policy and Criminal Justice', *European Journal on Criminal Policy and Research,* 9 (4): 361–80.

Bowditch, G. (2006) 'The Enforcers', *Sunday Times,* 25 June.

Bowling, B. (1999) 'The Rise and Fall of New York Murder: Zero Tolerance or Crack's Decline?', *British Journal of Criminology,* 39 (4): 531–54

Braithwaite, J. (1989) *Crime, Shame and Reintegration.* Cambridge: Cambridge University Press.

Braithwaite, J. (2000) 'The New Regulatory State and the Transformation of Criminology', *British Journal of Criminology,* 40: 222–38.

Bratton, W. and Dennis, N. (1997) *Zero Tolerance: Policing a Free Society.* London: Institute of Economic Affairs.

Brown, A. (2004) 'Anti-Social Behaviour, Crime Control and Social Control', *Howard Journal*, 43 (2): 203–11.

Brown, G. (2000) 'Civic Society in Modern Britain', 17th Arnold Goodman Charity Lecture, London: Smith Institute.

Bryman, A. (1999) 'The Disneyisation of Society', *Sociological Review*, 47 (1): 25–47.

Burke, R. and Morrill, R. (2002) 'Anti-Social Behaviour Orders: An Infringement of the Human Rights Act 1998?', *Nottingham Law Journal*, 11 (2): 1–16.

Burnett, R. and Appleton, C. (2004) 'Joined-Up Services to Tackle Youth Crime: A Case Study in England', *British Journal of Criminology*, 44 (1): 34–54.

Burney, E. (2005) *Making People Behave: Anti-Social Behaviour, Politics and Policy.* Cullompton: Willan.

Bursik, R. and Grasmick, H. (1993) 'Economic Deprivation and Neighbourhood Crime Rates 1960–1980', *Law and Society Review*, 27 (2): 265–83.

Cahill, M. (1994) *The New Social Policy.* Oxford: Blackwell.

Carr, H., Cowan, D. and Hunter, C. (2007) 'Policing the Housing Crisis', *Critical Social Policy*, 27 (1): 100–7.

Cernkovich, S. and Giordano, P. (1987) 'Family Relationships and Delinquency', *Criminology*, 25 (2): 295–321.

Chamlin, M. and Cochran, J. (1995) 'Assessing Messner and Rosenfeld's "Institutional Anomie Theory: A Partial Test"', *Criminology*, 33, 3: 411–29.

Churchill, H. (2007) 'Children's Services in 2006', in K. Clarke, T. Maltby and P. Kennett (eds) *Social Policy Review 19.* Bristol: Policy Press.

Clegg, D. (2005) 'A Rootless Third Way: A Continental European Perspective on New Labour's Welfare State, Revisited', in M. Powell, L. Bauld and K. Clarke (eds) *Social Policy Review 17.* Bristol: Policy Press.

Cloward, R. and Ohlin, L. (1960) *Delinquency and Opportunity: A Theory of Delinquent Gangs.* London: Routledge.

Cohen, A. (1955) *Delinquent Boys: The Culture of the Gang.* New York: Free Press.

Cohen, S. (1972) *Folk Devils and Moral Panics.* London: Paladin.

Cohen, S. (1985) *Visions of Social Control.* Oxford: Polity.

Cook, D. (2006) *Criminal and Social Justice.* London: Sage.

Cook, F. and Barrett, E. (1992) *Support for the American Welfare State: The Views of Congress and the Public.* New York: Columbia University Press.

Connell, R. (1987) *Gender and Power.* Cambridge: Polity Press.

Cowan, D., Pantazis, C. and Gilroy, R. (2001) 'Social Housing as Crime Control: An Examination of the Role of Housing Management in Policing Sex Offenders', *Social and Legal Studies*, 10 (4): 435–57.

Craib, I. (1992) *Anthony Giddens.* London: Routledge.

Crawford, A. (1998) *Crime Prevention and Community Safety: Politics, Policies and Practices*, Harlow: Longman.

Crawford, A. (1999a) *The Local Governance of Crime: Appeals to Community and Partnerships*. Oxford: Oxford University Press.

Crawford, A. (1999b) 'Questioning Appeals to Community Within Crime Prevention and Control', *European Journal on Criminal Policy and Research*, 7: 509–30.

Crawford, A. (2000) 'Situational Crime Prevention and Urban Governance', in A. Von Hirsch, D. Garland, and A. Wakefield (2000) *Ethical and Social Perspectives on Situational Crime Prevention*. Oxford: Hart.

Crawford, A. (2001) 'Joined-Up but Fragmented: Contradiction, Ambiguity and Ambivalence at the Heart of New Labour's Third Way', in R. Matthews and J. Pitts (eds) *Crime, Disorder and Community Safety*. London: Routledge.

Crawford, A. (2002) 'The Growth of Crime Prevention in France as Contrasted with the English Experience: Some Thoughts on the Politics of Insecurity', in G. Hughes, E. McLaughlin and J. Muncie (eds) *Crime Prevention and Community Safety: New Directions*. London: Sage.

Crawford, A. (2003) 'Contractual Governance of Deviant Behaviour', *Journal of Law and Society*, 30 (4): 479–505.

Crawford, A. and Newburn, T. (2003) *Youth Offending and Restorative Justice: Implementing Reform in Youth Justice*. Cullompton: Willan.

Dahrendorf, R. (2001) 'Challenges to the Voluntary Sector', Arnold Goodman Charity Lecture, 17 July, www.cafonline.org/goodman/go_lect01.cfm.

Damer, S. (1976) 'The Sociology of a Dreadful Enclosure', in P. Wiles (ed.) *The Sociology of Crime and Delinquency in Britain: Volume II. The New Criminologies*. London: Martin Robertson.

Davies, P., Francis, P. and Jupp, V. (2003) *Victimisation: Theory, Research and Policy*. Basingstoke: Palgrave Macmillan.

Deacon, A. (2004) 'Justifying Conditionality: The Case of Anti-social Tenants', *Housing Studies*, 19 (6): 911–26.

De Castella, T. (2004) 'Peace Process: Manchester Has Just, Very Quietly, Opened the Doors to England's First Unit for Housing Neighbours from Hell', *Guardian (Society)*, 18 February.

Dennis, N. (1993) *Rising Crime and the Dismembered Family*. London: Institute of Economic Affairs.

Dennis, N. and Erdos, G. (1992) *Families Without Fatherhood*. London: Institute of Economic Affairs.

Department for Children, Schools and Families (2007) *The Children's Plan: Building Brighter Futures*. London: HMSO, Cm7280.

De Smith, S. (1973) *Judicial Review of Administrative Action*. London: Stevens.

De Swaan, A. (1988) *In Care of the State*. Oxford: Polity.

DfES (2005) *14–19 Education and Skills*. London: HMSO.

DfES (2000) *Youth Cohort Study: Education and Employment of 16–18 Year-Olds in England and the Factors Associated with Non-participation. Statistical Bulletin*, May, London.

Dignan, J. (1999) 'The Crime and Disorder Act and the Prospects for Restorative Justice', *Criminal Law Review*, 48–61.

Dignan, J. (2005) *Understanding Victims and Restorative Justice*. Maidenhead: Open University Press.

Dillane, J., Hill, M., Bannister, J. and Scott, S. (2001) *Evaluation of the Dundee Families Project, Final Report*. University of Glasgow, Centre for the Child and Society and Department of Urban Studies.

Ditton, J., Bannister, J., Gilchrist, E. and Farall, S. (1999) 'Afraid or Angry? Recalibrating the 'Fear of Crime'', *International Review of Victimology*, 6 (2): 83–99.

Donald, A. (2007) 'The Offender and Victim Are Often the Same Person', *Herald (Society)*, 20 November.

Donzelot, J. (1979) *The Policing of Families*. London: Hutchinson.

Drapela, L. (2006) 'Investigating the Effects of Family, and School Domains on Postdropout Drug Use', *Youth and Society*, 37 (3): 316–47.

Duncan, C. (1999) *Worlds Apart: Why Poverty Persists in Rural America*, New Haven, CT Yale University Press.

Durkheim, E. (1952) *Suicide*. London: Routledge & Kegan Paul.

Durkheim, E. (1964) *The Division of Labour in Society*. New York: Free Press.

Eeklaar, J. and MacLean, M. (2004) 'Marriage and the Moral Basis of Personal Relationships', *Journal of Law and Society*, 31 (4): 510–38.

Eitzen, S. and Baca Zinn, M. (2000) 'The Missing Safety Net and Families: A Progressive Critique of the New Welfare Legislation', *Journal of Sociology and Social Welfare*, 27 (1): 53–72.

Elias, N. (1978) *The Civilising Process: Volume 1. The History of Manners*. Oxford: Blackwell.

Elias, N. (1982) *State Formation and Civilisation*. Oxford: Blackwell.

Elias, N. (1997) 'The Civilising of Parents', in J. Goudsblom and S. Mennell (eds) *The Norbert Elias Reader*. Oxford: Blackwell.

Elias, N. (2000) *The Civilising Process: Sociogenetic and Psychogenetic Investigations*. Oxford: Blackwell.

Elias, N. and Scotson, J. (1965) *The Established and the Outsiders*. London: Frank Cass.

Elias, N. and Dunning, E. (1986) *Quest for Excitement: Sport and Leisure in the Civilising Process*. Oxford: Blackwell.

Esping-Andersen, G. (1990) *The Three Worlds of Welfare Capitalism*. Cambridge: Polity.

Estrada, F. (2004) 'The Transformation of the Politics of Crime in High Crime Societies', *European Journal of Criminology*, 1 (4): 419–43.

Etzioni, A. (1968) *The Active Society*. New York: Free Press.

Fabian Society (2006) *Narrowing the Gap.* London: Fabian Commission on Life Chances and Child Poverty.

Farrington, D (1995) 'The Development of Offending and Antisocial Behaviour from Childhood: Key Findings from the Cambridge Study in Delinquent Development', *Journal of Child Psychology and Psychiatry,* 360 (6): 929–64.

Farrington, D. (2002) 'Understanding and Preventing Youth Crime', in J. Muncie, G. Hughes and E. McLaughlin (eds) *Youth Justice: Critical Readings.* London: Sage.

Farrington, D. (2007) 'Childhood Risk Factors and Risk-Focused Prevention', in M. Maguire, R. Morgan and R. Reiner (eds) *The Oxford Handbook of Criminology,* 4th edn. Oxford: Oxford University Press.

Featherstone, B. (2006) 'Rethinking Family Support in the Current Policy Context', *British Journal of Social Work,* 36: 5–19.

Felson, M. (1994) *Crime and Everyday Life.* Thousand Oaks, CA: Pine Forge Press.

Ferge, S. (1997) 'The Changed Welfare Paradigm: The Individualisation of the Social', *Social Policy and Administration,* 31 (1): 20–44.

Ferge, Z. (1999) 'And What If the State Fades Away? The Civilising Process and the State', in S. Svalfors and P. Taylor-Gooby (eds) *The End of the Welfare State?,* London: Routledge.

Field, F. (2002) 'How to Tame the Barbarians', *Sunday Times,* 16 June.

Field, F. (2003) *Neighbours from Hell: The Politics of Behaviour.* London: Politico's.

Field, F. (2004) 'Give Mothers a Real Option to Stay at Home With Young Children', *Eleanor Rathbone Lecture,* 9 December [www.frankfield.co.uk/MainPress_rathbone.htm].

Field, F. (2005) 'You Can't Shame Yobs, But You Can Let Their Victims Drag Them to Court', *Sunday Times,* 6 March.

Fionda, J. (1999) 'New Labour, Old Hat: Youth Justice and the Crime and Disorder Act 1998' *Criminal Law Review,* January: 36–47.

Fletcher, J. (1995) 'Towards a Theory of Decivilising Processes' *Amsterdam Sociologisch Tijdschrift,* 22 (2): 283–96.

Fletcher, J. (1997) *Violence and Civilisation: An Introduction to the Work of Norbert Elias,* Cambridge: Polity.

Flint, J. (ed.) (2006a) *Housing, Urban Governance and Anti-Social Behaviour.* Bristol: Policy Press.

Flint, J. (2006b) 'Maintaining an Arm's Length? Housing, Community Governance and the Management of 'Problematic' Populations', *Housing Studies,* 21 (2): 171–86.

Frank, A. (1969) *Capitalism and Underdevelopment in Latin America.* New York: Monthly Review Press.

Freud, S. (1994) *Civilization and Its Discontents.* New York: Dover.

Galbraith, J.K. (1992) 'Culture of Contentment', *New Statesman and Society,* 8 May: 14–16.

Garland, D. (1985) *Punishment and Welfare*. Aldershot: Gower.

Garland, D. (2000) 'The Culture of High Crime Societies', *British Journal of Criminology*, 40: 347–75.

Garland, D. (2001) *The Culture of Control*. Oxford: Oxford University Press.

Garrett, P. (2007) ' "Sinbin" Solutions: The Pioneer Projects for "Problem Families" and the Forgetfulness of Social Policy Research', *Critical Social Policy*, 27 (2): 203–30.

Giddens, A. (1999) 'The Role of the Voluntary Sector in the Third Way', Arnold Goodman Charity Lecture, 15 June www.cafonline.org/goodman/go_speech99.cfm.

Giddens, A. (1973) *The Class Structure of the Advanced Societies*. London: Hutchinson.

Giddens, A. (1991) *Modernity and Self-Identity: Self and Society in the Late Modern Age*. Cambridge: Polity.

Giddens, A. (1992) *The Transformation of Intimacy: Sexuality, Love and Eroticism in modern societies*. Cambridge: Polity.

Giddens, A. (1998) *The Third Way: The Renewal of Social Democracy*. Cambridge: Polity.

Gilbert, N. (1999) 'The Size and Influence of the Underclass: An Exaggerated View', *Society*, 37 (1): 42–43.

Gillies, V. (2005) 'Raising the "Meritocracy": Parenting and the Individualization of Class', *Sociology*, 39 (5): 835–53.

Gilling, D. (2001) 'Community Safety and Social Policy', *European Journal on Criminal Policy and Research*, 9: 381–400.

Gilling, D. and Barton, A. (1997) 'Crime Prevention and Community Safety: A New Home for Social Policy', *Critical Social Policy*, 17 (3): 63–83.

Girling, E., Loader, I. and Sparks, R. (2000) *Crime and Social Change in Middle England*. London: Routledge.

Gleuck, S. and Gleuck, E. (1950) *Unravelling Juvenile Delinquency*. Cambridge, MA: Harvard University Press.

Goldson, B. and Jamieson, J. (2002) 'Youth Crime, the "Parenting Deficit" and State Intervention: A Contextual Critique', *Youth Justice*, 2 (2): 82–99.

Gove, W. and Crutchfield, R. (1982) 'The Family and Juvenile Delinquency', *Sociological Quarterly*, 23: 301–19.

Guthrie, T. (2005) *Antisocial Behaviour Legislation*. Edinburgh: W. Green.

Haas, H., Farrington, D., Killias, M. and Sattar, G. (2004) 'The Impact of Different Family Configurations on Delinquency', *British Journal of Criminology*, 44: 520–32.

Habermas, J. (1975) *Legitimation Crisis*. London: Heinemann.

Habermas, J. (1979) *The Structural Transformation of the Public Sphere*. Cambridge: Polity.

Hakkert, A. (1998) 'No More Excuses: A New Approach to Tackling Youth Crime in England and Wales', *European Journal on Criminal Policy and Research*, 6: 279–91.

215

Hale, C. (1996) 'Fear of Crime: A Review of Literature', *International Review of Victimology*, 4: 79–105.

Hall, S. and Winlow, S. (2005) 'Anti-Nirvana: Crime, Culture and Instrumentalism in the Age of Insecurity', *Crime, Media, Culture*, 1 (1): 31–48.

Hall, S., Critcher, C., Jefferson, T., Clarke, J. and Roberts, B. (1978) *Policing the Crisis*. Basingstoke: Macmillan.

Harris, J. (1992) 'Political Thought and the Welfare State 1870–1940: An Intellectual Framework for British Social Policy', *Past and Present*, 135: 116–41.

Hayton, K., Gray, L. and Stirling, K. (2005) 'Monitoring and Evaluation of the Scottish Compact Baseline Results 2004', Scottish Executive, *Social Justice Research Programme, Research Findings no. 17* www.scotland.gov.uk/ socialresearch.

Hayward, K. and Yar, M. (2006) 'The "Chav" Phenomenon: Consumption, Media and the Construction of a New Underclass', *Crime, Media, Culture*, 2 (1): 9–28.

Hill, D. (1992) 'The American Philosophy of Welfare: Citizenship and the "politics of conduct" ', *Social Policy and Administration*, 26 (2): 117–28.

Hill, M., Walker, M., Moodie, K., Wallace, B., Bannister, J., Khan, F., McIvor, G. and Kendrick, A. (2005) *Fast Track Children's Hearings Pilot: Final Report of the Evaluation of the Pilot*. Edinburgh: Scottish Executive.

Hill, M., Walker, M., Moodie, K., Wallace, B., Bannister, J., Khan, F., McIvor, G. and Kendrick, A. (2007) 'More Haste, Less Speed? An Evaluation of Fast Track Policies to Tackle Persistent Youth Offending in Scotland', *Youth Justice*, 7 (2): 121–38.

Hillyard, P., Sim, J., Tombs, J. and Whyte, D. (2004) 'Leaving a "Stain upon the Silence": Contemporary Criminology and the Politics of Dissent', *British Journal of Criminology*, 44: 369–90.

Hirschi, T. (1969) *Causes of Delinquency*. Berkeley, CA: University of California Press.

HM Treasury (2002) *The Role of the Voluntary and Community Sector in Service Delivery: A Cross Cutting Review*. London: HMSO.

Hochschild, A. (1979) 'Emotion Work, Feeling Rules and Social Structure', *American Journal of Sociology*, 85 (3): 551–75.

Hochschild, A. (2003) *The Managed Heart: Commercialisation of Human Feeling*. Berkeley, CA: University of California Press.

Home Office (1998) *Compact on Relations Between Government and the Voluntary and Community Sector*, Cm 4100. London: HMSO.

Home Office (2003a) *World Prison Population List* (4th edn), Findings 188. London: HMSO.

Home Office (2003b) *Building Civil Renewal: A Review of Government Support for Community Capacity Building and Proposals for Change*. London: HMSO.

Home Office (2007) *Cutting Crime: A New Partnership 2008–2011*. London: HMSO.

Hudson, B. (1996) *Understanding Justice*. Buckingham: Open University Press.

Hughes, G. (2007) *The Politics of Crime and Community*. Basingstoke: Palgrave.

Innes, M. (2004a) 'Signal Crimes and Signal Disorders: Notes on Deviance as Communicative Action', *British Journal of Sociology*, 55 (3): 335–55.

Innes, M. (2004b) 'Reinventing Tradition? Reassurance, Neighbourhood Security and Policing', *Criminal Justice*, 4 (2): 151–71.

Innes, M. and Fielding, N. (2002) 'From Community to Communicative Policing: Signal Crimes and the Problem of Public Reassurance', *Sociological Research Online*, 7 (2), www.socreonline.org.uk/7/2/innes.html.

Jackson, J. (2004) 'Experience and Expression: Social and Cultural Significance in the Fear of Crime', *British Journal of Criminology*, 44: 946–66.

Jamieson, L. (1998) *Intimacy: Personal Relationships in Modern Society*. Cambridge: Polity.

Jamieson, J. (2005) 'New Labour, Youth Justice and the Question of "Respect" ', *Youth Justice*, 5 (3): 180–93.

Jessop, B. (1999) 'The Changing Governance of Welfare: Recent Trends in Its Primary Functions, Scale and Modes of Coordination', *Social Policy and Administration*, 33 (4): 348–59.

Jessop, B. (2002) *The Future of the Capitalist State*. Oxford: Polity.

Jochun, V., Pratten, B. and Wilding, K. (2005) *Civil Renewal and Active Citizenship: A Guide to the Debate*. London: National Council for Voluntary Organisations.

Johnson, N. (2004) 'The Human Rights Act 1998: A Bridge Between Citizenship and Justice?', *Social Policy and Society*, 3 (2): 113–22.

Johnstone, G. (2002) *Restorative Justice*. Cullompton: Willan.

Joliffe, D. and Farrington, D. (2004) 'Empathy and Offending: A Systematic Review and Meta-Analysis', *Aggression and Violent Behaviour*, 9: 441–76.

Jones, T. and Newburn, T. (2007) *Policy Transfer and Criminal Justice: Exploring US Influence over British Crime Control Policy*. Maidenhead: Open University Press.

Juby, H. and Farrington, D. (2001) 'Disentangling the Link Between Disrupted Families and Delinquency', *British Journal of Criminology*, 41: 22–40.

Kilbrandon Report (1995) *Children and Young Persons, Scotland*. Edinburgh: HMSO. Available online at www.scotland.gov.uk/publications/2003/10/18259/26874.

Kim, S. and Pridemore, W. (2005) 'Social Change, Institutional Anomie and Serious Property Crime in Transitional Russia', *British Journal of Criminology*, 45: 81–97.

Knepper, P. (2007) *Criminology and Social Policy*. London: Sage.

Kolvin, I., Miller, F., Fleeting, M. and Kolvin, P. (1988) 'Social and Parenting Factors Affecting Criminal-Offence Rates: Findings from the Newcastle Thousand Family Study (1947–1980)', *British Journal of Psychiatry*, 152: 80–90.

Kolvin, I., Miller, F. Scott, D. and Gatzanis, S. (1990) *Continuities in Deprivation: the Newcastle 1000 Family Study.* Aldershot: Avebury.

Lampl, P. (2007) 'Kicking Away the Social Ladder', *Sunday Times,* 24 June.

Larzelere, R. and Patterson, G. (1990) 'Parental Management: Mediator of the Effect of Socioeconomic Status on Early Delinquency', *Criminology,* 28 (2): 301–23.

Laub, J. and Sampson, R. (1988) 'Unravelling Families and Delinquency: A Re-analysis of the Gleucks' Data', *Criminology,* 26 (3): 355–79.

Laub, J. and Sampson, R. (1991) 'The Sutherland-Gleuck Debate: On the Sociology of Criminological Knowledge', *American Journal of Sociology,* 96 (6): 1402–40.

Laub, J. and Sampson, R. (2003) *Shared Beginnings, Divergent Lives: Delinquent Boys to Age 70.* London: Harvard University Press.

Lawler, S. (2005) 'Class, Culture and Identity', *Sociology,* 39 (5): 797–806.

Lea, J. (2002) *Crime and Modernity.* London: Sage.

Levitas, R. (2005) *The Inclusive Society? Social Exclusion and New Labour.* Basingstoke: Palgrave/Macmillan.

Lewis, J. (1999) 'Reviewing the Relationship Between the Voluntary Sector and the State in Britain in the 1990s', *Voluntas,* 10 (3): 255–70.

Lewis, J. (2001) *The End of Marriage? Individualism and Intimate Relations.* Cheltenham: Edward Elgar.

Lewis, J. (2005) 'New Labour's Approach to the Voluntary Sector: Independence and the Meaning of Partnership', *Social Policy and Society,* 4 (2): 121–32.

Lewis, J., Clark, D. and Morgan, D. (1992) *Whom God Hath Joined Together.* London: Routledge.

Liebow, E. (1967) *Tally's Corner: A Study of Negro Street Corner Men.* Boston: Little, Brown.

Loader, I. and Walker, N. (2007) *Civilizing Security.* Cambridge: Cambridge University Press.

Macaskill, M. (2008) 'How the Nation Is on a Knife Edge', *Sunday Times,* 9 March.

Margo, J. (2007) 'Gordon's Plan to Keep the Kids Under Control', *Sunday Times,* 8 July.

Marquand, D. (2004) *Decline of the Public.* Cambridge: Polity

Marshall, T. (1992) *Citizenship and Social Class.* London: Pluto.

Marsland, D. (1996) *Welfare or Welfare State?* Basingstoke: Palgrave/Macmillan.

Martin, F. and Murray, K. (eds) (1976) *Children's Hearings.* Edinburgh: Scottish Academic Press.

Matza, D. (1969) *Becoming Deviant.* New York: Prentice-Hall.

Matza, D. and Sykes, G. (1961) 'Juvenile Delinquency and Subterranean Values', *American Sociological Review,* 26: 712–19.

McAra, L. (2006) 'Welfare in Crisis? Key Developments in Scottish Youth Justice', in J. Muncie and B. Goldson (eds) *Comparative Youth Justice.* London: Sage.

McAra, L. and McVie, S. (2007) *Criminal Justice Transitions.* Edinburgh: Number 14, Edinburgh Study of Youth Transitions and Crime.

McCarthy, T. (1978) *The Critical Theory of Jürgen Habermas,* London: Hutchinson.

McCord, J. (1979) 'Some Child-Rearing Antecedents of Criminal Behaviour in Adult Men', *Journal of Personality and Social Psychology,* 37: 1477–87.

McCord, J. (1991) 'Family Relationships, Juvenile Delinquency and Adult Criminality', *Criminology,* 29 (3): 397–417.

McDiarmid, C. (2005) 'Welfare, Offending and the Scottish Children's Hearing System', *Journal of Social Welfare and Family Law,* 27 (1): 31–42.

McIvor, G. (2004) 'Reparative and Restorative Approaches', in A. Bottoms, S. Rex and G. Robinson (eds) *Alternatives to Prison: Options for an Insecure Society.* Cullompton: Willan.

Mennell, S. (1990) 'Decivilising Processes: Theoretical Significance and Some Lines of Research', *International Sociology,* 5 (2): 205–23.

Mennell, S. (1998) *Norbert Elias: An Introduction.* Dublin: University College Dublin Press.

Mennell, S. (2006) 'Civilising Processes', *Theory, Culture and Society: Problematising Global Knowledge, special issue* 23 (2–3): 429–30.

Merton, R. (1938) 'Social Structure and Anomie', *American Sociological Review,* 3: 672–82.

Merton, R. (1957) *Social Theory and Social Structure.* New York: Free Press.

Messner, S. (1988) 'Merton's "Social Structure and Anomie": The Road Not Taken', *Deviant Behaviour,* 9: 33–53.

Messner, S. and Rosenfeld, R. (2001) *Crime and the American Dream.* Belmont, CA: Wadsworth.

Mestrovic, S. (1997) *Postemotional Society.* London: Sage.

Miller, W. (1958) 'Lower-Class Culture as a Generating Milieu of Gang Delinquency', *Journal of Social Issues,* 15: 5–19.

Mills, C.W. (1959) *The Sociological Imagination.* Oxford: Oxford University Press.

Mooney, J. (2003) 'It's the Family, Stupid: Continuities and Reinterpretations of the Dysfunctional Family as the Cause of Crime in Three Political Periods', in R. Matthews and J. Young (eds) *The New Politics of Crime and Punishment.* Cullompton: Willan.

Moore, B. (1967) *Social Origins of Dictatorship and Democracy.* London: Penguin.

Moore, S. and Statham, E. (2006) 'Can Intergenerational Practice Offer a Way of Limiting Anti-Social Behaviour and Fear of Crime?', *Howard Journal,* 45 (5): 468–84.

Mount, F. (2004) *Mind the Gap: The New Class Divide in Britain.* London: Short Books.

Moynihan, D. (1993) 'Defining Deviance Down', *American Scholar,* Winter (see www.2sunysuffolk.edu/formans/DefiningDeviancey.htm).

Mullins, C. (2006) *Holding the Square: Masculinities, Streetlife and Violence.* Cullompton: Willan.

Muncie, J. (2004) *Youth and Crime,* 2nd edn. London: Sage.

Muncie, J. and Hughes, G. (2002) 'Modes of Youth Governance: Political Rationalities, Criminalisation and Resistance', in J. Muncie, G. Hughes and E. McLaughlin (eds) *Youth Justice: Critical Readings.* London: Sage.

Murray, C. (1994) *The Underclass: The Crisis Deepens.* London: Institute of Economic Affairs.

Murray, C. (1997) *Does Prison Work?,* London: Institute of Economic Affairs.

Murray, C. (1999) 'And Now for the Bad News (the Underclass)', *Society,* 37 (1): 13–16.

Murray, G. (1976) 'Juvenile Justice Reform', in F. Martin and K. Murray (eds) *Children's Hearings.* Edinburgh: Scottish Academic Press.

Nayak, A. (2006) 'Displaced Masculinities: Chavs, Youth and Class in the Post-industrial City', *Sociology,* 40 (5): 813–31.

Ness, C. (2004) 'Why Girls Fight: Female Youth Violence in the Inner City', *Annals of the American Academy of Political and Social Science,* 595: 32–48.

Newburn, T. (2007) *Criminology.* Cullompton: Willan.

Nixon, J. (2007) 'Deconstructing "Problem" Researchers and "Problem Families": A Rejoinder to Garrett', *Critical Social Policy,* 27 (4): 546–64.

Nixon, J., Hunter, C., Parr, S., Myers, S., Whittle, S. and Sanderson, D. (2006) *ASB Intensive Family Support Projects: An Evaluation of 6 Pioneering Projects.* London: Department for Communities and Local Government.

ODPM (2005a) *Citizen Engagement and Public Services: Why Neighbourhoods Matter.* London: HMSO.

ODPM (2005b) *Sustainable Communities: People, Places and Prosperity*, London: HMSO.

O'Sullivan, N. (1993) 'Political Integration, the Limited State and the Philosophy of Postmodernism', *Political Studies,* 41: 21–42.

Parton, N. (1985) *The Politics of Child Abuse.* Basingstoke: Macmillan.

Phillips, C. (2002) 'From Voluntary to Statutory Status: Reflecting on the Experience of Three Partnerships Established under the Crime and Disorder Act 1998', in G. Hughes, E. McGlaughlin and J. Muncie (eds) *Crime Prevention and Community Safety: New Directions.* London: Sage.

Piacentini, L. and Walters, R. (2006) 'The Politicisation of Youth Crime in Scotland and the Rise of the "Burberry Court"', *Youth Justice,* 6 (1): 43–59.

Pierson, C. (1991) *Beyond the Welfare State,* Oxford: Polity.

Pitts, J. (2001) *The New Politics of Youth Crime: Discipline or Solidarity?* Basingstoke: Palgrave.

Piven, F. and Cloward, R. (1974) *Regulating the Poor: The Functions of Public Welfare.* London: Tavistock.

Polyani, K. (1957) *The Great Transformation: The Political and Economic Origins of Our Time.* Boston: Beacon.

Pratt, J. (1989) 'Corporatism: The Third Model of Juvenile Justice', *British Journal of Criminology,* 29 (3): 236–54.

Pratt, J. (1998) 'Towards the "Decivilising" of Punishment?', *Social and Legal Studies,* 7 (4): 487–515.

Pratt, J. (2002) *Punishment and Civilisation.* London: Sage.

Pratt, J. (2005) 'Elias, Punishment and Decivilisation', in J. Pratt, D. Brown, M. Brown, S. Hallsworth and W. Morrison (eds) *The New Punitiveness: Trends, Theories, and Perspectives.* Cullompton: Willan.

Presdee, M. (2000) *Cultural Criminology and the Carnival of Crime.* London: Routledge.

Prior, D. (2005) 'Civil Renewal and Community Safety: Virtuous Policy Spiral or Dynamic of Exclusion?', *Social Policy and Society,* 4 (4): 357–68.

Purnell, J. (2008) 'Independence at the Heart of the Welfare State', speech on 20 February by the Secretary of State for Work and Pensions to the Social Market Foundation: Department for Work and Pensions.

Reckless, W. (1967) *The Crime Problem,* 4th edn, New York: Meredith.

Reinke, H. (2005) 'Robert Heindl's *Berusverbrecher*: Police Perceptions of Crime and Criminals and Structures of Crimes Control in Germany during the First Half of the Twentieth Century', in A. Srebnick and R. Levy (eds) *Crime and Culture: An Historical Perspective.* Aldershot: Ashgate.

Riesman, D. (1969) *The Lonely Crowd.* London: Yale University Press.

Ritzer, G. (1992) *The McDonaldisation of Society.* London: Sage.

Robson, W. (1976) *Welfare State and Welfare Society.* London: Allen and Unwin.

Roche, K., Ensminger, M., Ialongo, N., Poduska, J. and Kellam, S (2006) 'Early Entries into Adult Roles: Associations with Aggressive Behaviour from Early Adolescence into Young Adulthood', *Youth and Society,* 38 (2): 236–61.

Rock, P. (ed.) (1988) *A History of British Criminology.* Oxford: Clarendon Press.

Rodger, J. (1996) *Family Life and Social Control: A Sociological Perspective,* Basingstoke: Palgrave/Macmillan.

Rodger, J. (2000) *From a Welfare State to a Welfare Society: The Changing Context of Social Policy in a Postmodern Era.* Basingstoke: Palgrave/Macmillan.

Rodger, J. (2003a) 'Social Solidarity, Welfare and Post-Emotionalism', *Journal of Social Policy,* 32 (3): 403–21.

Rodger, J. (2003b) 'Family Life, Moral Regulation and the State: Social Steering and the Personal Sphere', in S. Cunningham-Burley and L. Jamieson (eds) *Families and the State: Changing Relationships,* London: Palgrave/Macmillan.

Rodger, J. (2006) 'Antisocial Families and Withholding Welfare Support', *Critical Social Policy*, 26 (1): 121–43.

Rose, N. (1996) 'The Death of the Social? Re-figuring the Territory of Government', *Economy and Society*, 25: 327–56.

Rosenfeld, R. and Messner, S. (1997) 'Markets, Morality and an Institutional-Anomie Theory of Crime' in N. Passos and R. Agnew (eds) *The Future of Anomie Theory*, Boston, MA: Northeastern University Press.

Ruggiero, V. and Vass, A. (1992) 'Heroin Use and the Formal Economy', *British Journal of Sociology*, 32 3: 273–91.

Ruggiero, V. and South, N. (1997) 'The Late-Modern City as a Bazaar: Drug Markets, Illegal Enterprise and the "Barricades", *British Journal of Sociology*, 48 (1): 54–70.

Runciman, W. (1966) *Relative Deprivation and Social Justice.* London: Routledge and Kegan Paul.

Salmi, V., Smolej, M. and Kivivuori, J. (2007) 'Crime Victimisation, Exposure to Crime News and Social Trust Among Adolescents', *Young*, 15 (3): 255–72.

Sampson, R. and Groves, W. (1989) 'Community Structure and Crime: Testing Social-Disorganisation Theory', *American Journal of Sociology*, 94 (4): 774–802.

Sampson, R. and Laub, J. (1992) 'Crime and Deviance in the Life Course', *American Review of Sociology*, 18: 63–84.

Sampson, R. and Laub, J. (1999) Crime and Deviance over the Life Course: The Salience of Adult Social Bonds', in F. Scarpitti and A. Nielson (eds) *Crime and Criminals.* Los Angeles: Roxbury.

Savolainen, J. (2000) 'Inequality, Welfare State and Homicide: Further Support for the Institutional Anomie Theory', *Criminology*, 38 (4): 1021–38.

Schwartz, B. (1999) 'Capitalism, the Market, the "Underclass" and the Future', *Society*, 37 (1): 33–43.

Scott, S. (2006) 'Tackling Anti-Social Behaviour: An Evaluation of the Dundee Families Project', in J. Flint (ed.) *Housing, Urban Governance and Anti-Social Behaviour*, Bristol: Policy Press.

Scottish Executive (2002) *The Scottish Compact: Annual Review of the Implementation of the Scottish Compact 2000–01.* Edinburgh: HMSO.

Scottish Executive (2003) *Putting Our Communities First: A Strategy for Tackling Anti-Social Behaviour.* Edinburgh: HMSO.

Scottish Executive (2004) *Getting It Right for Every Child.* Edinburgh: HMSO.

Sefton, T. and Sutherland, H. (2005) 'Inequality and Poverty Under New Labour', in J. Hills and K. Stewart (eds) *A More Equal Society?* Bristol: Policy Press.

Sennett, R. (2003) *Respect: The Formation of Character in an Age of Inequality.* London: Penguin.

Sennett, R. and Cobb, J. (1973) *The Hidden Injuries of Class.* New York: Vintage.

Shaw, C. and McKay, H. (1969) *Juvenile Delinquency and Urban Areas,* 2nd edn, Chicago: University of Chicago Press.

Shiner, M. Young, T. Newburn, T. and Groben, S. (2004) *Mentoring Disaffected Young People: An Evaluation of Mentoring Plus.* York: Joseph Rowntree Foundation.

Silver, H. (1994) 'Social Exclusion and Social Solidarity: Three Paradigms', *International Labour Review,* 133 (5–6): 531–78.

Silver, H. (1996) 'Culture, Politics and National Discourses of the New Urban Poverty', in E. Mingione (ed.) *Urban Poverty and the Underclass,* Oxford: Blackwell.

Simon, J. (1997) 'Governing Through Crime', in L. Friedman and G. Fisher (eds) *The Crime Conundrum.* Boulder, CO: Westview Press.

Simon, J. (2007) *Governing Through Crime: How the War on Crime Transformed American Democracy and Created a Culture of Fear.* Oxford: Oxford University Press.

Simons, R., Simons, L. and Wallace, L. (2004) *Families, Delinquency and Crime: Linking Society's Most Basic Institution to Antisocial Behaviour.* Los Angeles: Roxbury.

Smith, D. (2001) *Norbert Elias and Modern Social Theory.* London: Sage.

Smith, D.J. (2005) 'The Effectiveness of the Juvenile Justice System', *Criminal Justice,* 5 (2): 181–95.

Smith, R. (2003) *Youth Justice: Ideas, Policy and Practice.* Cullompton: Willan.

Smith, R. (2005) 'Welfare Versus Justice – Again!', *Youth Justice,* 5 (3): 3–16.

Smout, T. (1987) *A Century of the Scottish People 1830–1950.* London: Fontana.

Social Policy Justice Group (2006) *Fractured Families.* London: Conservative Party.

Spear, R. (2001) 'United Kingdom: A Wide Range of Social Enterprises', in C. Borzaga and J. Defourny (eds) *The Emergence of Social Enterprise.* London: Routledge.

Squires, P. (1990) *Anti-Social Policy.* Brighton. Harvester Wheatsheaf.

Squires, P. and Stephen, D. (2005) *Rougher Justice: Anti-Social Behaviour and Young People.* Cullompton: Willan.

Stearns, E. and Glennie, E. (2006) 'When and Why Dropouts Leave High School', *Youth and Society,* 38 (1): 29–57.

Stenson, K. (2001) 'The New Politics of Crime Control', in K. Stenson and R. Sullivan (eds) *Crime, Risk and Justice.* Cullompton: Willan.

Stewart, K. (2005) 'Towards an Equal Start? Addressing Childhood Poverty and Deprivation', in J. Hills and K. Stewart (eds) *A More Equal Society?* Bristol: Policy Press.

Stimson, G. and Metrebian, N. (2003) *Prescribing Heroin? What Is the Evidence.* York: Joseph Rowntree Foundation.

Stoker, G. (1998) 'Governance as Theory: Five Propositions', *International Social Science Journal,* 50: 17–28.

223

Such, E. and Walker, R. (2005) 'Young Citizens or Policy Objects? Children in the "Rights and Responsibilities" Debate', *Journal of Social Policy*, 34 (1): 39–57.

Sullivan, D., Tifft, L. and Cordella, P. (1998) 'The Phenomenon of Restorative Justice: Some Introductory Remarks', *Contemporary Justice Review*, 1 (1): 7–20.

Sutherland, E. and Cressey, D. (1966) *Principles of Criminology*, 7th edn. Philadelphia: J.P. Lippincott.

Swaaningen, R. (2002) 'Towards a Replacement Discourse on Community Safety: Lessons from The Netherlands', in G. Hughes, E. McLaughlin and J. Muncie (eds) *Crime Prevention and Community Safety: New Directions*. London: Sage.

Swidler, A. (1986) 'Culture in Action Symbols and Strategies', *American Sociological Review*, 51: 273–86.

Taub, R., Taylor, D. and Dunham, J. (1984) *Paths of Neighbourhood Change: Race and Crime in Urban America*. Chicago: University of Chicago Press.

Taylor, I. (1999) *Crime in Context*. Cambridge: Polity.

Taylor, I., Walton, P. and Young, J. (1973) *The New Criminology*. London: Routledge.

Thompson, E. (1971) 'The Moral Economy of the English Crowd in the Eighteenth Century', *Past and Present*, 50: 76–136.

Thompson, E. (1975) *Whigs and Hunters*. London: Allen and Unwin.

Unnever, J., Cullen, F. and Agnew, R. (2006) 'Why Is 'Bad' Parenting Criminogenic? Implications for Rival Theories', *Youth Violence and Juvenile Justice*, 4 (1): 3–33.

Utting, D., Bright, J. and Henricson, C. (1993) *Crime and the Family: Improving Child-Rearing and Preventing Delinquency*. London: Family Policy Studies Centre.

Valentine, C. (1968) *Culture and Poverty: Critique and Counter Proposals*. Chicago: University of Chicago Press.

Van Krieken, R. (2005) 'The "Best Interests of the Child" and Parental Separation: On the Civilising of Parents', *Modern Law Review*, 68 (1): 25–48.

Van Wel, F. (1992) 'A Century of Families under Supervision in The Netherlands', *British Journal of Social Work*, 22: 147–66.

Vaughan, B. (2000) 'The Civilizing Process and the Janus-Face of Modern Punishment', *Theoretical Criminology*, 4 (1): 71–91.

Viet-Wilson, J. (2000) 'States of Welfare: A Conceptual Challenge', *Social Policy and Administration*, 34 (1): 1–25.

Von Hirsch, A., Garland, D. and Wakefield, A. (2000) *Ethical and Social Perspectives on Situational Crime Prevention*. Oxford: Hart.

Wacquant, L. (1997) 'Elias in the Dark Ghetto', *Amsterdams Sociologisch Tijdschrift*, 24 (3–4): 340–48.

Wacquant, L. (2000) 'The New "Peculiar Institution": On the Prison as Surrogate Ghetto', *Theoretical Criminology*, 4 (3): 377–89.

Wacquant, L. (2001) 'The Penalisation of Poverty and the Rise of Neo-Liberalism', *European Journal on Criminal Policy and Research*, 9: 401–12.

Wacquant, L. (2005) 'The Great Penal Leap Backwards: Incarceration in America from Nixon to Clinton', in J. Pratt, D. Brown, M. Brown, S. Hallsworth and W. Morrison (eds) *The New Punitiveness: Trends, Theories, Perspectives*. Cullompton: Willan.

Wacquant, L. and Wilson, W. (1989) 'The Cost of Racial and Class Exclusion in the Inner City', *Annals of the American Academy of Political and Social Science*, 501: 8–25.

Wagner, A. (2004) 'Redefining Citizenship for the 21st Century: From the National Welfare State to the Global Compact', *International Journal of Social Welfare*, 13: 278–86.

Walklate, S. (1998) 'Crime and Community: Fear or Trust?', *British Journal of Sociology*, 49 (4): 550–69.

Walklate, S. (2007) *Understanding Criminology: Current Theoretical Debates*, 3rd edn. Buckingham: Open University Press.

Walters, R. and Woodward, R. (2007) 'Punishing Poor Parents: "Respect" Responsibility and Parenting Orders in Scotland', *Youth Justice*, 7 (1): 5–20.

Waterhouse, L. and McGhee, J. (2002) 'Children's Hearings in Scotland: Compulsion and Disadvantage', *Journal of Social Welfare and Family Law*, 24 (3): 279–96.

Waterhouse, L., McGhee, J., Whyte, J., Loucks, N., Kay, N. and Stewart, R. (2000) *The Evaluation of Children's Hearings in Scotland, Volume 3, Children in Focus*. Edinburgh: Scottish Executive Central Research Unit.

Waterhouse, L., McGhee, J. and Loucks, N. (2004) 'Distentangling Offenders and Non-Offenders in the Scottish Children's Hearings: A Clear Divide?', *Howard League*, 43 (2): 164–79.

Watson, D. (1976) 'The Underlying Principles: A Philosophical Comment', in F. Martin and K. Murray (eds) *Children's Hearings*. Edinburgh: Scottish Academic Press.

White, J., Moffitt, T., Earls, F., Robins, L. and Silva, P. (1990) 'How Early Can We Tell? Predictors of Childhood Conduct Disorder and Adolescent Delinquency', *Criminology*, 28 (4): 507–27.

Whyte, B. (2003) 'Young and Persistent: Recent Developments in Youth Justice Policy and Practice in Scotland', *Youth Justice*, 3: 74–85.

Whyte, W. (1955) *Street Corner Society*, 2nd edn. Chicago: University of Chicago Press.

Williams, P. and Dickenson, J. (1993) 'Fear of Crime: Read All About It? The Relationship Between Newspaper Crime Reporting and Fear of Crime', *British Journal of Criminology*, 33 (1): 33–56.

Wilson, H. (1987) 'Parental Supervision Re-Examined', *British Journal of Criminology*, 27 (3): 275–301.

Wilson, J.Q. (1975) *Thinking About Crime*. New York: Vintage.

Wilson, J.Q. and Hernstein, R. (1985) *Crime and Human Nature*. New York: Simon and Schuster.

Wilson, W. (1989) 'The Underclass: Issues, Perspectives and Public Policy', *Annals of the American Academy of Political and Social Science*, 501: 182–92.

Wincott, D. (2003) 'Slippery Concepts, Shifting Context: (National) States and Welfare in the Viet-Wilson/Atherton Debate', *Social Policy and Administration*, 37 (3): 305–15.

Winnett, R. (2005) 'Meet the 'NEETs': A New Underclass', *Sunday Times*, 27 March.

Wouters, C. (1987a) 'Formalisation and Informalisation: Changing Tension Balances in Civilising Processes', *Theory, Culture and Society*, 3: 1–19.

Wouters, C. (1987b) 'Developments in the Behavioural Codes Between the Sexes: The Formalisation of Informalisation in The Netherlands, 1930–85', *Theory, Culture and Society*, 4: 405–27.

Wouters, C. (1990) 'Social Stratification and Informalisation in Global Perspective', *Theory, Culture and Society*, 7: 69–90.

Wouters, C. (1999) 'Changing Patterns of Social Controls and Self-Controls: On the Rise of Crime Since the 1950s and the Sociogenesis of a Third Nature', *British Journal of Criminology*, 39 (3): 416–32.

Wouters, C. (2005) 'On the Sociogenesis of a "Third Nature" in the Civilizing of Emotions: Developments in Dealing with Strangers and "Strangeness" and with Feelings of Superiority and Inferiority', www.usyd.edu.au/su/social/elias/confpap/wouters1.html.

Wouters, C. (2007) *Informalization: Manners and Emotions Since 1890*. London: Sage.

Young, J. (1999) *The Exclusive Society: Social Exclusion, Crime and Difference in Late Modernity*. London: Sage.

Young, J. (2007) *The Vertigo of Late Modernity*. London: Sage.

Zehr, H. and Mika, H. (1998) 'Fundamental Concepts of Restorative Justice', *Contemporary Justice Review*, 1 (1): 47–55.

Index

Acceptable Behaviour Contracts 206
active citizenship 151, 153
Adams, M. 68–9
affective impulses 125–6
African American families 112
altruistic response xiii
amoral familism 42, 55, 77–8, 160, 198
Anderson, E. 113, 189–90
anomic strain 54
anomie theory 55, 61, 70, 100, 172, 201–3
anticipatory sensitisation 188
Anti-social Behaviour Act 2003
   children 127
   dysfunctional families 96
   housing benefits 92
   human rights 13
   natural justice 11–12
   Riyadh Guidelines 147
Anti-social Behaviour Act 2004 127
anti-social behaviour model 205t
anti-social behaviour orders (ASBOs) 13, 142
Anti-social Behaviour (Scotland) Act 2004 135, 142, 147
Anti-social Behaviour Units 94
anti-social children 16–18

anti-social tenants 7–9
antisubversion doctrine 13
Appleton, C. 85–6
Arnold Goodman Charity Lecture 150
Arthur, R. 128
Arts, W. 56–7
at arms' length 155
Atherton, C. 4–6
attendance orders 50
attitudes 37–43

bad parenting 99, 106, 108–9, 128
Ball, C. 131
Balls, Ed 148, 206
Bauman, Z. 165
Baumrind, D. 105
Beijing Rules 127, 146
Bell, D. 196–7, 201
Bendix, R. 23
benefits, withholding 86–90
Bernstein, B. 109
Biggart, A. 50
black ghettos 32–7
black street culture 52
Blair, Tony 72, 97, 169
Bloomsbury group 28
Blunkett, David 150, 152

boot camps 77
Bottoms, A. 178–9
Bourdieu, P. 67
Braithwaite, J. 131, 153
Brown, A. 8
Brown, Gordon 148, 149, 150, 151–4
Burke, R. 11, 12–13
Burnett, R. 85–6
Burney, E. 10
Bursik, R. 35–6, 181

Cambridge Institute of Criminology
    100
Cameron, David 73
capacity building 150
Carr, H. 93, 175
Casey, Louise 120
celebrity, pursuit of 62–3
centralisation 158
chavs 63–5
    as outsiders 166
    reflexivity 68–71
    value orientations 65–8
child poverty 16, 21, 115
child protection 115–18, 116t
Child Support Agency 175
child welfare
    see juvenile justice
Children Act 1989 127
Children Act 2004 146
Children Act (Scotland) 1995 127
children, anti-social 16–18
Children Services (Scotland) Bill 143
Children, Young People and Social
    Care Group 135
Children's Fund 115
Children's Hearing system 134–8
    anti-social behaviour control 141–3
    compulsion and disadvantage
        140–1
    corporatism 143
    debates about 18
    deprived and depraved 139–40
    effectiveness 146
    influence of 131

Children's Panels 135–6
Children's Plan 206
Christian Democratic traditions 153,
    157–8
citizen juries 149
citizenship as praxis 14
citizenship, teaching 88
civic activeness 149
'Civic Society in Modern Britain'
    150
civil contracts 88
civil law 9–16
civil property rights 83
civil renewal
    inauthentic politics 157–62
    overview 168–70
    strategies for 149–54
    third way 154–7
    voluntary sector compact 156–7
Civilisation and Its Discontents
    (Freud) 125
civilising process theory 22–30, 23t
    formalisation and informalisation
        26–30, 39
    functional democratisation and
        power 24–5, 29
    overview 95
Civitas 45
class 57–60
Clegg, D. 153, 157–8, 159
Cloward, R. 70, 193
code of the streets 113, 181, 189, 190
Cohen, A. 63, 66
Cohen, S. 4, 5, 45–6, 85, 188
commercial climate 29–30
commercial sector 154
Commission on Integration and
    Cohesion 45
communitarianism 129, 131, 153
community capacity 161
community policing 85
community reparation orders 8
community safety
    aim of 144
    appeal to the community 166–8

established-outsiders 162–6
    voluntary sector 156
compacts 156–7, 161–2
compensatory compulsory
    masculinity 111–12
compulsion and disadvantage 140–1
conditionality see also respect agenda
    effectiveness 192
    independence 168
    politics of 6, 9, 86–90
    social control management 19
Connexions Partnerships 49, 133
consumerism 54–6, 70
consumption patterns 60–1
contract culture 156
contractual governance 82–3
control signals 178–80, 206
corporatism 129–31, 143
Cowan, D. 7, 93, 175
Craib, I. 69
Crawford, A. 82–3, 161, 167
Cressey, D. 70
Crime and Disorder Act 1998
    bad parenting 96, 109, 127, 128
    development of 88–9
    restorative justice 144
Crime, Justice and Protecting the
    Public 128
crime-prevention partnerships 82,
    144
Criminal Justice Act 1991 128
criminal justice, balancing 203–7
criminalisation model 205t
criminalising social policy 2–4,
    18–19
criminology, social policy and 2–4
Cullen, F. 106
cultural toolkits 65–8, 123, 189
culture, coarsening of 52–7
culture of control 29
Cutting Crime: A New Partnership
    (Home Office) 156

dangerisation 188
de-civilisation 30–7

community safety 163–6
    hyperghettoes 32–7
    overview 95
    of parents 106–9
    in penal policy 43–5
de-differentiation process 84
de-pacification 34
de-professionalisation 85–6
de-proletarianisation 34–5
De Swaan, A. 24
Deacon, A. 6
decent families 113, 190
define deviancy down xii–xiii, 76
delinquency 101–6
Dennis, N. 100
Department for Children, Schools
    and Families 17, 151
Department for Education and Skills
    50
Department of Communities and
    Local Government 3, 151
Detention and Training Orders
    (DTOs) 132
developmental child psychology 105
Dickenson, J. 184
differential associations 70
Dignan, J. 144–5
Dillane, J. 120, 121
disciplinary policies 115–18, 116t
disembedded signal crimes 182–8
disembedding the economy 55–6
Disneyisation 40
distributive groupings 59
The Division of Labour in Society
    (Durkheim) 24
divorce, impact of 99–100
Donzelot, J. 56
Drapela, L. 50
drugs policy 203–7, 205t
drugs trade 34, 192
Duncan, C. 66
Dundee Family Project 118–23, 124
Dunning, E. 28
Durkheim, E. xiii, 24, 30, 55
dysfunctional families 16–18

economic informalisation 34
Eeklaar, J. 99
Elias, Norbert xviii, 22–5, 31, 46, 125–6, 163–6
emotions 37–43
empathy 104, 106–7
employment/unemployment
    class relationships 57–8
    de-industrialisation 34–5
    instrumentalism 61–5
    most agreeable work 77–8
enclosure 15
equal opportunities 196
Erdos, G. 100
Esping-Andersen, G. 54
The Established and the Outsiders (Elias) 164–5
established-outsiders 162–6
Estrada, F. 77
Etzioni, A. 81–2, 95
European Convention on Human Rights (ECHR) 12–13
everyday life, criminalisation of 3
expertise 166
extra-legal discourses 73

Fabian Society Commission 21
fading of the state 42
family policies 115–18 *see also* parenting
Farrington, D. 101, 103, 104–5
Fast Track Children's Hearings 138
fear of crime
    civilising security 173–4
    determinants 187t
    disembedded signal crimes 182–8
    mass media 174–6
    perception and experience 171–3, 174–6
    situated signal crimes 176–82
    social policy 191–4
    streetwise behaviour as inverted fear 188–91
Featherstone, B. 117–18, 196
feeling rules 41

Felson, M. 76
female violence 114
Ferge, S. 36–7, 56, 201
field concept 67–8
Field, Frank 15, 16, 65, 74, 87–90, 92
Fielding, N. 176–7
first-generation rights 12
Fletcher, J. 25, 31
Flint, J. 7–8, 9
Fordist welfare regime 80, 196
formalisation process 26–30
France 112–13
Freud, S. 125
functional democracy 24–5, 29, 164
Futurebuilders Investment Fund 150

Galbraith, J.K. 77–8, 95, 163
Garland, D.
    culture of control 29
    de-professionalisation 85–6
    expertise 166
    extra-legal discourses 73
    normal social facts xiii, 38, 75–6
    normality of crime 95
    prisons 5
    rehabilitation 45–6
Garrett, P. 121–2
gated communities 78
Gelisson, J. 56–7
gender 109–12
    in the dark ghetto 112–15
    masculinist family authority 109–12
    masculinities 64, 189, 191
generalised trust 185–6
Getting It Right for Every Child 138–9
ghettos 32–7, 112–15
Giddens, A.
    class relationships 57
    individualisation 58–9
    inertial drag 107–8
    influence of 150
    patterns of intimacy 98
    reflexivity 68, 69
    third way 155

Gillies, V. 59
Glennie, E. 50
globalisation 30–1, 155
Glueck, S. 101
governance 80–1
    as inauthentic politics 81–3
    joined-up policies 84–6
government climate 30
government through communities
    81
Grasmick, H. 35–6, 181
Groves, W. 36

Habermas, J. 33, 174, 197–8, 201
habitus 67–8
Hall, S. 61–2, 182, 188
Hayward, K. 63–4
hearsay evidence 11
Hernstein, R. 54
Himmler, Heinrich xiv–xv
Hirschi, T. 104
Hobbes, Thomas 202–3
Hochschild, A. 41
Housing Act 1996 7, 10
Housing Act 2004 92, 93
housing associations 156
Housing Benefit (Withholding
    Payment) Bill 87, 89, 90–2
housing management 7–9 see also
    Dundee Family Project
    human rights 10–11
    regulatory communities 93–4
    withholding benefits 87–8
Howarth, George 91
human rights
    civil law 10–14
    withholding benefits 90–1, 92
Human Rights Act 1998 12
humiliation 125–6

identity, reflexivity 68–71
imperialism 26–7
inauthentic politics 81–3, 157–62
incivility, criminalisation of 3
individualisation 56, 58–60

inequality gap management 21–2
informalisation 27–30, 74–8
Innes, M. 176–7
Institute of Economic Affairs 44–5
institutional-anomie theory 100
instrumentalism, culture and 61–5
integrative shaming 131
intensive family support 118–23, 124
Intensive Supervision and
    Surveillance Programme (ISSP)
    133
interests of the child 110–11, 135
intergenerational mobility 21
intervention dimensions 200t
intimacy, changing patterns of 98–9
inverted fear 188–91

Jamieson, J. 170
Jessop, B. 6, 80, 153
Jobcentre Plus 49
Johnson, N. 12
joined-up policies 3, 84–6, 131, 143
Joliffe, D. 104
Juby, H. 101
Justice Department 135
justice model 130
juvenile justice
    effectiveness 147–8
    history of 129–34
    punishing parents 128–9
    United Nations 127

Keynesian welfare state 6, 79, 80,
    95, 196
Kilbrandon Committee 134–5, 136–7,
    141
knowledge society 58
Kolvin, L. 100, 103
Kriminalpolizei xiv–xv

laager mentality 78
labelling theory 177
Laub, J. 103
Lawler, S. 59–60
Lea, J. 53, 58

Learning and Pupil Support
Schemes 133
legal policies 115–18, 116t
legitimation crisis 197–8
Levitas, R. 94, 99, 196
liberalism 38, 76
liberty lobby 173–4
life-course theories 101, 103
lifestyle changes 76
Loader, I. 171, 173, 194, 202

McAra, L. 142, 147
McCarthy, T. 198
McConnell, Jack 138
MacDonaldisation 40
McKay, H. 35
MacLean, M. 99
Major, John 43, 77
markets, privileging of 54
Marquand, D. 166
marriage, incentives for 97
Marshall, T.H. 24, 195
masculinist family authority 109–12
masculinities 64, 189, 191
master shifts 4–5
materialism 53–4, 61
Matza, D. 178, 197
media 182–8
medico-centred model 203–4, 205t
Mennell, S. 22, 24
Mentor Plus 159
Merton, R. 54, 76, 196
Messner, S. 55, 62, 113, 123
Mestrovic, S. 40
Miller, W.B. 67, 113
Mills, C. Wright 41
Minister for Children and Early
Years 135
Minister for Community Safety 142
Minister for Education and Lifelong
Learning 135
Minister for Schools and Skills 135
Minister for the Department for
Children, Schools and Families 148
modernist impulse 5–6

modernity, vertigo of 197
Mooney, J. 16
moral economy 14–16, 58
moral panic 176, 204
moral regulation 199–201
moral underclass discourse 94
Morrill, R. 11, 12–13
motivation crisis 197–9
Mount, Ferdinand 21
Moynihan, Daniel Patrick xiv
Moynihan, D.P. xii–xiii
Mullins, C. 110, 113–14, 189, 191
Murray, C. 51, 52, 100

National Council for Voluntary
Organisations 156–7
natural justice 9–16
Nayak, A. 64
NEETs
creation of 48–51
as outsiders 166
reflexivity 68–71
value orientations 65–8
Neighbourhood Policing Programme
156
neo-liberalism 168, 198
Ness, C. 114
net widening 8, 14, 85
Netherlands 118–19
new politics of welfare 79–86
new regulatory state 153
Newcastle study 100
Nixon, J. 121
normalising response xiii
normality of crime xiii, 38, 74–8, 95

Office of the Deputy Prime Minister
(ODPM) 3
Ohlin, L. 70
opportunistic response xiii
Organisation for Economic
Cooperation and Development
(OECD) 41
organised crime 181
O'Sullivan, N. 202

Pantazis, C. 7
parenting
    and criminality 100–6
    de-civilisation of parents 106–9
    divorce, impact of 99–100
    family policy 115–18
    gender in the dark ghetto 112–15
    masculine styles 109–12
    overview 123–4
    personal relationships 98–100
    psychological determinants 104–6
    punishing parents 128–9, 136–7
    quality of 103
    social determinants 102–4
    styles 105–6
parenting orders 18, 128, 142, 169
parenting programmes 17
particularised trust 185, 188
partnership working 129–34, 144,
    156–7, 161–2
pay-gap 21
penal policy 43–6
performance management 131
permissive society 27
personal relationships 98–100
personal sphere 199–201
Phillips, C. 162
Piacentini, L. 136
Pitts, J. 131
Piven, F. 193
Policing the Crisis (Hall) 183
political economy model 205t
Polyani, K. 55
Poor Law tradition 5
post-emotionalism 38–43, 77–8, 160,
    198
post-war era 74–5
power 25, 169
Pratt, J. 38, 46, 130, 145–6
Prior, D. 166
prison populations, rise in 43–4
prison works 45, 130
private landlords 93
private sphere 199–201
professional paradigms 85–6

professional witnesses 11
psychic integration conflict 74, 75
psychogenesis 22–3
psychological determinants 104–6
public health model 205t
punishment, de-civilisation of 45–6

Reckless, W. 105
redistributive discourse 94
referral orders 132
reflexivity 68–71
regulatory communities 93–4, 95,
    175
Reinke, H. xiv–xv
reintegration 144
repressed emotions 26
respect agenda 16–17, 29, 72–3,
    117–18, 170
Respect Task Force 169
respect tsar 120
Respect Unit 148, 151
responsibilisation strategy 8, 68,
    128–9, 149–50
restorative justice 11–12, 131, 133,
    143–6
retribution 134
Riesman, D. 23–4
risk perception 176
Riyadh Guidelines 127, 146
Robson, W. 152–3, 159
Roche, K. 50
Rose, N. 56, 81
Rosenfeld, R. 55, 62, 113, 123
Runciman, W. 196

safe public spaces 178–9
Salmi, V. 185, 186, 188
Salmond, Alex 49
Sampson, R. 36, 103
school drop outs 50
school-leaving age 49–50
Schumpeterian workfare state 6, 79,
    80
Schwartz, B. 53–5, 61, 70
Scotland see also Children's Hearing

system
  punishing parents 128–9, 136–7
  restorative justice 143–4
  voluntary sector 157
Scotson, J. 163
Scott, S. 121
second-generation rights 12
security, civilising 173–4, 191–4
selection theories 101
service users 131
shame 125–6, 131
Shaw, C. 35
Sheriff's Courts 136
signal crimes
  disembedded signal crimes 182–8
  situated signal crimes 176–82
Simon, J. 3, 17, 29, 57, 75, 77
sin bins 91, 118
single parent families 109–12, 175–6
situated signal crimes 176–82
situational crime prevention 167
Smith, D. 133, 147, 165
Smith, R. 130, 132
social bulimia 162–3
social capital 166–8
social citizenship 32
social control theories 2, 105–6, 109, 111
social crime prevention 167
social determinants 102–4
social disorganisation theory 35–6
social ecology 87
social education 201
social enquiry reports 130
Social Exclusion Unit 94
social government 81
social inclusion 93–4
social integrationist discourse 94, 196
social investment state 18–19, 69, 115, 117–18, 196
social learning theories 105–6, 109, 111
social policy, balancing 203–7
social policy, criminology and 2–4

social sphere 199–201
social steering 1–2, 79–80
social therapism 201
Social Work (Scotland) Act 1968 138
sociogenesis 22–3
Solej, M. 185
spheres of activity 200t
Squires, P. 5
stakeholder society 7
standard of proof 11, 13–14
standing commissions 149
state formation 22–3
state sphere 199–201
statism 83
Stearns, E. 50
street culture 113–14
street families 113, 189–90
streetwise behaviour, as inverted fear 188–91
style 60–1, 63–5
subsidiarity 158, 169
subterranean values 178, 197
Such, E. 17, 117
Suicide (Durkheim) 24
Sunday Times xiv
Sure Start 115, 133, 159
Sutherland, E. 70, 101
Swidler, A. 66
Sykes, G. 178, 197
synthetic traditions 40

taste 60–1, 63–5
Taub, R. 179
taxation 78, 168
Taylor, D. 179
Taylor, I. 198
Thatcherism 6, 7, 75
thing addiction 54, 70, 196
third way 154–7
Thompson, E.P. 15
Titmuss, R. 195
traditionalism, destruction of 68
trauma theories 101
Treasury 150
trust 166–8, 180–1, 185–6, 188

UNCR (United Nations Convention on the Rights of the Child (UNCR)) 127, 146
underclass 51, 52–7 *see also* chavs; NEETs
Unnever, J. 106, 108–9, 111
Unravelling Juvenile Delinquency (Glueck) 101
urban renewal programmes 7
USA
  Clinton reforms 175
  coarsening of culture 52–3
  consumerism 55–6
  drugs policy 204
  governed through crime 3
  hyperghettoes 32–7, 112
  penal policy 44
  Personal Responsibility and Work Opportunity Act 1996 90
  rural poverty 66
  war on poverty 192–3
  welfare legislation 52

value orientations 65–8
Van Krieken, R. 107, 108, 110–11
Van Wel, F. 118–19
Vaughan, B. 46
victims, villains and 138–9, 147
Viet-Wilson, J. 4, 79, 87, 195
vigilantism 145–6
voluntarism 68, 84
voluntary sector
  compact with government 156–7, 161–2
  confidence in 150–1
  inauthentic politics 161–2
  overview 168–70

Wancquant, L. 32–4, 43, 112
Walker, N. 171, 173, 194, 202
Walker, R. 17, 117
Walklate, S. 180, 186
Walters, R. 136
Walton, P. 198

Waterhouse, L. 139, 141
Watson, D. 134
welfare and discipline 4–6
welfare benefits
  see withholding benefits
welfare contracts 87–8
welfare model 129–30
welfare policies 115–18, 116t
welfare state
  role of 1–2, 79–80, 87
  terminology 4, 79, 195
welfare state/welfare society 152–3
what works 131
Whitelaw, Willie 77
Whyte, B. 138
Wicks, Malcolm 90
Williams, P. 184
Wilson, A. 178–9
Wilson, J.Q. 54
Winlow, S. 61–2
Winnett, R. 49
withholding benefits
  effectiveness 192
  human rights 12
  independence 168
  politics of 86–90, 196, 199
worker-benefit state 4, 195
Wouters, C. 26, 27–9, 74, 95

Yar, M. 63–4
Young, J. xvii, 39, 51, 62, 162–3, 197
Youth Alcohol Action Plan 206
Youth Crime Action Plan 206
Youth Justice and Criminal Evidence Act 1999 127, 132
Youth Justice Boards 147
Youth Offender Panel 132
Youth Offending Boards 17–18
youth offending teams 85
Youth Offending Teams (YOTs) 131, 132, 133
Youth Task Force 206

zero tolerance 45